"This book promotes biblical balance in every chapter. It offers an excellent, readable, orthodox, winsome presentation of Christianity. If even a quarter of our churches were living the kind of biblically balanced faith presented here, unbelievers would be knocking at our doors. A must-read."

Ronald J. Sider, professor of theology, Palmer Seminary at Eastern University, and author of *Rich Christians in an Age of Hunger*

"In our polarized world, and in an equally polarized church, Rich Nathan and Insoo Kim's book, *Both-And*, is a breath of fresh air. *Both-And* calls readers to embrace a powerful, compelling and holistic Christian faith. This is a hopeful, practical and inspiring look at what Christianity is meant to be."

Adam Hamilton, pastor and author of *Seeing Gray in a World of Black and White*

"Rich Nathan is one of the great communicators of his generation—and he is also a practitioner. The extraordinary development of the Vineyard church he leads in Columbus, Ohio, with its outreach programs to help the poorest and most marginalized in that city, is testament to his visionary leadership."

Nicky Gumbel, pastor and pioneer of the Alpha Course

"We live in a wounded day of cultural tension and polarity, which often bleeds into our faith communities. This book's call to 'both-and' thinking and living is a much-needed healing salve for the church."

James Choung, author of *True Story* and *Real Life*

"Our world is increasingly polarized, even among the followers of Jesus. Rich Nathan and Insoo Kim, using Scripture and illustrations from their own life and leadership, patiently explain a way forward through the tensions for believers who must live in this world. Read it a chapter at a time and reflect how your life and leadership can be more true to God's desires."

Dave Travis, CEO for Leadership Network and coauthor of *Beyond Megachurch Myths*

"Fearlessly, Rich Nathan and Insoo Kim speak truth to culture and church. Calling their readers to a mature and robust faith, they attack simplistic binary thinking such as 'healing vs. suffering,' 'love vs. holiness' and 'evangelism vs. social justice.' Rather than avoiding such theological tensions, they call us to embrace them. Why? Because it is at the nexus of these polarities that we best experience the grace and wisdom of God."

Alec Hill, president of InterVarsity Christian Fellowship/USA

"Rich Nathan has, by the grace of God, founded and fathered one of the most beautiful and fruitful churches I have ever had the privilege to experience. Consequently, whatever Rich has to say on church vision, practice and leadership are words of the righteous overflowing with wisdom (Proverbs 10:31), which is clearly what we have with his latest book, *Both-And*. Rich Nathan, with his gifted co-pastor Insoo Kim, boils down the kingdom principles which compass their church life and ministry: grounded in Sacred Scripture, dependent on the Holy Spirit and attuned to twenty-first-century culture. *Both-And* exposes some of the cul-de-sacs Christians have walked blindly into and recalibrates us to the pathways where Christ walks. The authors' thesis is that God's ways are seldom found by forcing a dogmatic either-or, far less in a compromised halfway house, but rather by a robust holding of polarities in creative tension. Irenic and pastoral, humble and wise, provocative and prophetic, *Both-And* is a vision for church that deserves the widest readership across the traditions. Everyone who cares about the church should read this brilliant book."

Simon Ponsonby, pastor and author of *Loving Mercy*

"Charles Simeon (the great eighteenth-century evangelical vicar of Holy Trinity, Cambridge, England), when addressing some of the more challenging dilemmas of the Christian faith, famously observed that 'the truth is not in the middle, and not in one extreme, but in both extremes.' Following in this tradition, with his rigorous mind and his intrepid spirit, Rich tackles some of the issues of our day, but never without bringing to bear the instincts of his pastoral heart. An absolute treasure of a book—a treat awaits you when you come to read it!"

John Mumford, national director, Vineyard UK

BOTH-AND

LIVING THE CHRIST-CENTERED LIFE
IN AN EITHER-OR WORLD

RICH NATHAN WITH INSOO KIM

IVP Books

An imprint of InterVarsity Press
Downers Grove, Illinois

InterVarsity Press
P.O. Box 1400, Downers Grove, IL 60515-1426
World Wide Web: www.ivpress.com
Email: email@ivpress.com

InterVarsity Press® is the book-publishing division of InterVarsity Christian Fellowship/USA®, a movement
of students and faculty active on campus at hundreds of universities, colleges and schools of nursing in the
United States of America, and a member movement of the International Fellowship of Evangelical Students.
For information about local and regional activities, write Public Relations Dept., InterVarsity Christian
Fellowship/USA, 6400 Schroeder Rd., P.O. Box 7895, Madison, WI 53707-7895, or visit the IVCF website
at www.intervarsity.org.

While all stories in this book are true, some names and identifying information in this book have been
changed to protect the privacy of the individuals involved.

Cover design: Adam Hines
Interior design: Beth Hagenberg

ISBN 978-0-8308-3766-3 (print)
ISBN 978-0-8308-9569-4 (digital)

Printed in the United States of America ∞

Library of Congress Cataloging-in-Publication Data
A catalog record for this book is available from the Library of Congress.

P	18	17	16	15	14	13	12	11	10	9	8	7	6	5	4	3	2	1
Y	28	27	26	25	24	23	22	21	20	19	18	17	16	15	14	13

I dedicate this book to all the amazing people
who call Vineyard Columbus their home!

You have bravely stepped onto the high wire, choosing to live in the
radical tension of Both-And faith. Doing life together with this
beloved community has truly been an incredible privilege.

Let us continue! Left foot. Right foot.

Contents

What Is Our Expectation?

What Is Our Calling?

Acknowledgments

In Romans 16, Paul goes to great lengths to mention by name all the people in Rome who made his ministry possible. As much as I would like to follow Paul's example, I simply cannot mention all the people who have played a significant role in making this book possible; there are too many. But I would like to acknowledge just a few individuals.

First of all, Insoo Kim has been a wonderful partner to work with in crafting and writing this manuscript. All the stories are from my (Rich's) experience and point of view.

Shelley McWherter, thank you for your amazing work to help put this book together. Your patience and generosity made the difficult process of writing easier. Thanks for twenty years of partnership in the gospel!

Joy Danison, thank you for your great feedback with the first draft of this book. Your thoughtful comments were invaluable.

Matt Shetler, this book has benefited greatly from your detailed research. Thank you for your support and encouragement throughout the whole process.

Adam Hines, thank you for designing such a beautiful cover for this book! Your creativity has been a huge blessing to us and our church.

And Insoo and I would also like to extend a special note of gratitude to Al Hsu, our editor at InterVarsity Press. Thank you for believing in this book and its message!

THE BOTH-AND CHRISTIAN

The world is becoming more polarized and less civil at the same time. That's a potent and dangerous combination! Whether in regard to politics, education or healthcare reform, people on opposite ends of the ideological spectrum are screaming louder and listening less, and the great divide between them widens and deepens with each passing day. Nobel Prize–winning economist and *New York Times* columnist Paul Krugman has made an astute observation about the current state of the United States: "The truth is that we are a deeply divided nation and are likely to remain one for a long time. By all means, let's listen to each other more carefully; but what we'll discover, I fear, is how far apart we are."[1]

It is too easy for us as Christians to hide in the safety of our church buildings and point fingers at people in the world for their great polarizations and incivility. It is painfully obvious that even within the church, however, a great chasm divides the followers of Jesus.

REDUCING THE GOSPEL, POLARIZING THE CHURCH

One of the great tragedies in the American church is the way that churches limit the message of Jesus according to their own particular versions of Christianity. For example, Roman Catholicism has been strong in maintaining church unity, fighting for orthodoxy in an increasingly secular world and creating innumerable charitable and educational institutions. It has been weaker in helping people discover a personal relationship with God. One woman I know was on a search for God for many years. She began reading Christian books and checking out videos on the life of Jesus from the library. She was looking for Jesus. She was also Roman Catholic. A church leader told her that her search was risky and that she simply needed to attend mass, participate in the sacraments and celebrate the holy days of obligation. But don't try to pursue a personal relationship with Christ, he essentially told her; "That's dangerous!"

Catholics certainly aren't the only ones guilty of limiting Jesus' message, however; we can see this reduction of the gospel at work in almost every brand of church. Fundamentalists have been great in focusing attention on the necessity of personal salvation and the truth of the Bible, but unfortunately they have historically reduced the message of Jesus to the saving of our souls for heaven. Although this is slowly changing, fundamentalist churches often don't have much in terms of social programs. They may have nothing to offer in terms of meeting basic human needs through career counseling, environmental care, engagement with the sciences, citizenship classes, medical clinics or economic development projects in Africa or Asia. "Why would you want to do that?" a fundamentalist might ask. "You are just rearranging the deck chairs on the Titanic. Don't you understand that this whole world is going down? Here you are wasting your time caring for people's material needs when it's all going to burn anyway. The only thing that matters is getting people into heaven!"

Mainline churches also contribute to the polarization by restricting the message of Jesus. Mainline churches have been strong regarding the Bible's teachings about caring for "the least of these" but weaker concerning the need for repentance and faith in Jesus alone in order to be saved. One friend told me about a mainline church that she used to attend. She was told in the membership class that the beauty of this particular denomination was that you could believe anything you wanted and still be a member of the church.

Like fundamentalists, conservative evangelicals have stressed the need for personal faith in Christ and the authority of Scripture. Unlike fundamentalists, they have been more engaged in the life of the mind and more willing to interact with modern science and scholarship. But conservative evangelical churches have often limited the teaching of Jesus by eliminating the supernatural elements of Jesus' ministry. Historically there has been almost no discussion of divine healing, the gifts of the Holy Spirit, deliverance or the demonic. Many conservative evangelicals have drunk so deeply from the well of the Enlightenment that they see no possibility of God communicating through dreams, visions or prophecy the way he did in biblical times. They see demons as holdovers from a medieval mindset and think that all psychological ailments must be treated entirely by material means, psychotropic drugs or counseling. The claim that someone living in America today is affected by a real demon would strike them as delusional.

Pentecostals and charismatics reminded the church that God was not *binatarian* (Father and Son) but *trinitarian*: Father, Son *and* Holy Spirit. Through teaching and experience, they have borne witness to the truth that without the gifts, power and guidance of the Holy Spirit, all Christian mission is merely human effort and will be in vain. Sadly, Pentecostals and charismatics have historically limited the message of Jesus by neglecting the life of the mind. In the past, many of these Pentecostal leaders were proud that they had never read any book other than the Bible. Historically, Pentecostals have held a very negative view of education. I can speak about this from my own experience.

When my wife, Marlene, and I were in college, we attended a little church led by a Pentecostal pastor. He was a very kind and godly man. But after I came to Christ, he took me aside and said, "Rich, why are you wasting your time going to college?" I was eighteen years old, and this older Christian man, whom I deeply respected, began pressuring me to quit college and to go to a Pentecostal Bible school. By God's grace,

I knew myself well enough even at age eighteen to know that following his counsel would be wrong for me. I wanted a strong liberal arts education, and I loved reading and learning. So I politely declined this pastor's counsel.

A couple of years later, when Marlene and I were preparing to marry, he counseled us to not use birth control but instead just to trust the Lord. After that meeting, I said to Marlene, "If we don't use birth control, I trust that the Lord will give us fourteen children!"

Maybe you can look back at your own Christian experience and see some area of life that your church disregarded and said, "Well, we don't talk about that subject here!" It's likely that if that particular subject came up in the congregation, it was raised in a negative and critical way.

Today the church in America is divided between those who limit the message of Jesus to the spiritual realm and those who limit his message to the material realm. The spiritual-realm-only folks believe that Christianity is simply about getting as many people as possible to invite Jesus into their hearts so that when they die, their souls will go to heaven. The spiritual-realm-only people also typically talk about private morality, giving priority to areas such as sex, marriage, divorce and perhaps appropriate gender roles. But the spiritual-realm-only people often say almost nothing about *public* morality: the rest of life that includes issues like education, poverty, immigration, racism, global hunger or war and peace. They assume that all those areas of life belong to politicians, TV pundits, economists and military leaders. For the spiritual-realm-only people, it is as if the Bible has nothing to say about anything other than personal morality. Their churches, their lives and their understandings of the Bible offer little wisdom about vast domains of life.

At the other end of the spectrum are the material-realm-only people. For them, the sole concerns of the Christian faith are issues such as the economy, minimum-wage legislation, big business and military expenditures. The material-realm-only people often have almost nothing to say about sexual holiness, the Holy Spirit, experiencing God's presence or—most importantly—the death of Christ that atones for our sins.

Indeed, some material-realm-only churches simply turn over the whole spiritual realm to other denominations. "If you want that sort of thing," they say, "you need to go to one of those emotional churches, or maybe an ethnic church. We're too sophisticated for the spiritual stuff."

THE CURE FOR A POLARIZED CHRISTIANITY

The gospel, according to the New Testament, is the wonderfully good news that the crucified and risen Jesus is Lord, that his life, death and resurrection began to transform the world and that this transformation can happen to us if we trust in and receive Jesus as our Lord and Savior. Almost as wonderful as this personal transformation is the gospel's declaration that those of us who receive Jesus get to partner with God in the great project of world transformation. Christ lived, died, rose again and gave us his Holy Spirit to transform the world. This process will not be completed before the Lord returns.

Our world-transforming message says, "The world is not the way it is supposed to be. Babies are not supposed to die in infancy. Thousands of children are not supposed to die every single day of hunger and preventable disease. Women should not be abused by their husbands. We were not made for chemotherapy. The world is not as it is supposed to be."

God began to change all of that in the coming of Christ, and he is at work transforming the world today. Some of us have reduced the world-transforming message of the gospel to a few spiritual laws primarily aimed at saving people from hell and getting them ready for heaven. At its worst, some people reduce the gospel to a kind of religious bingo game: if you pray the right prayer or sign the right form, you get to yell, "Bingo! I get to live in heaven forever."

According to this little, reduced gospel, it doesn't matter if you are bitterly unforgiving toward people who hurt you. It doesn't matter if you cling to your prejudices or racism. It doesn't matter if you harden your heart toward the poor, the hungry, immigrants, the unborn or their mothers. "Go ahead, get an abortion. Break your marital vows. Get divorced apart from biblical grounds. You can be radically disobe-

dient to Jesus and never allow him to interfere in your career or with
your money, your sex life, your relationships or your purchases. Go
your own way. Never walk in the steps of Jesus. As long as you pray the
sinners' prayer, you can yell, 'Bingo!' Live a hellish life right now and
live in heaven forever with Jesus." Is that really the gospel that Jesus
preached? "Don't follow me now, but live with me later. Be absolutely
loveless now and be embraced by the love of God later." Is that the
gospel of Jesus Christ?

The gospel—this world- and life-transforming good news that Jesus
died, rose, ascended and gave us his Spirit to transform us and the
world—has been reduced to nothing but a fire insurance policy that we
can buy in church or by watching Christian television. Once the insurance policy is in effect, you can go back to whatever you were doing
before—self-indulgent shopping, ugly unforgiveness, perverse pornography, horrific hatred. It doesn't matter what you do as long as your insurance policy is safely in your drawer—especially if you can remember
the date when you bought it. You are protected if and when your house
burns down. Live like hell now and receive heaven later.

The problem with this approach is that it is a gross perversion and a
disgraceful distortion of the life and message of Jesus. It reduces all that
Jesus did and said to something that doesn't radically and wonderfully
change our lives or the world.

One of the things I love about the person of Jesus is that no realm of
life is excluded from the kingdom that he inaugurated in his coming.
Jesus Christ redeems all of life. We can discover the enormous scope of
the message as we understand the meaning of various words in the
Bible. For example, the word *salvation* in the Bible does not mean,
"When I die, my soul goes to heaven." *Salvation* means the total transformation of human life. It means the forgiveness of sins, healing from
bodily sickness, release from debt, the mending of marriages and a
world safe for children. It means political liberation. Salvation involves
a reversal of all the evil consequences of sin and means the whole universe being set free. Salvation is both spiritual and material.

THE BOTH-AND BIBLE

From beginning to end, the Bible is a Both-And book. The God of the Bible is portrayed as the God of both creation *and* covenant. He cares about all the nations *and* he enters into a special relationship with his people. He is God over both the secular *and* the sacred, both the material realm *and* the spiritual realm.

There are two tablets of the Ten Commandments, not just one. The first four commandments concern our responsibility to God; the last six commandments are about our responsibility to other people. Both-And. Love God *and* love people.

The Old Testament prophets aimed at people's vertical sins (their violations of the first tablet of the commandments), and they aimed at horizontal sins (people's violations of the second tablet of the commandments).

During his ministry, Elijah had two great confrontations. One occurred on Mount Carmel and is recorded in 1 Kings 18, in which Elijah confronted the prophets of the fake god Baal. On Mount Carmel, Elijah confronted the sin of *idolatry*. But in 1 Kings 21, Elijah traveled to Jezreel to confront King Ahab for his sin of *injustice*: for stealing a field owned by a man named Naboth and for murdering Naboth. Elijah confronted both idolatry and injustice. If you read through the Old Testament, you will find the prophets confronting these two sins: idolatry, on the one hand, and injustice, on the other. Vertical and horizontal. Both-And.

We see Both-And thinking in that famous verse in Micah 6:8: "He has shown you, O mortal, what is good. And what does the LORD require of you? To act justly and to love mercy and to walk humbly with your God." Toward people we are to act justly and love mercy. Toward God we are to walk humbly. Both-And.

We hear a Both-And message in the preaching of the prophet Jeremiah. Why was God going to destroy Jerusalem through the Babylonian invasion? "For *they have forsaken me and made this a place of foreign gods*; they have burned incense in it to gods that neither they nor their ancestors nor the kings of Judah ever knew, and *they have filled this place with the blood of the innocent*" (Jeremiah 19:4). Worshiping foreign gods *and* murdering the innocent—idolatry and injustice—were the two great sins of Jerusalem. Both-And.

Jesus most clearly taught about the importance of Both-And thinking when he identified the two greatest commandments. "Hearing that Jesus had silenced the Sadducees, the Pharisees got together. One of them, an expert in the law, tested him with this question: 'Teacher, which is the greatest commandment in the Law?' Jesus replied: '"Love the Lord your God with all your heart and with all your soul and with all your mind." This is the first and greatest commandment'" (Matthew 22:34-38).

Jesus could have stopped there. He could have said that people have a single duty in this world: to love and serve God. But he didn't stop there. He went on to say: "And the second is like it: 'Love your neighbor as yourself.' All the Law and the Prophets hang on these two commandments" (Matthew 22:39-40).

You can't just say, "I have wonderful prayer times with God, and I sing my heart out to God in worship. So it doesn't matter how I relate to my parents or my kids or my spouse or my elderly grandmother in a nursing home." There are two Great Commandments, not just one. We followers of Jesus are called to both love God *and* love people. Both-And. There are two beams on the cross: horizontal *and* vertical. This forms a picture of how the cross reconciles us vertically to God and horizontally to each other. Both-And.

All the apostles taught Both-And Christianity. We read in James 1:27, "Religion that God our Father accepts as pure and faultless is this: to look after orphans and widows in their distress and to keep oneself from being polluted by the world." Compassion toward the weak *and* holiness toward God: we are not permitted to choose one over the other. We're always tempted to say, "Which is more important?" God says, "I want both!" The temptation is to say, "I'm making such a great difference in this world by feeding hungry people that God no longer cares about what I do sexually." God wants hungry people fed *and* he wants your sex life cleaned up. Both-And. It is wonderful that you've adopted a child through World Vision, but God also cares about your gossip. With God it is always Both-And.

THE ONGOING JOURNEY OF VINEYARD COLUMBUS

Both-And is what makes a church great. Both-And is what makes a church alive, healthy and vibrant. At Vineyard Columbus, we want to do and believe everything that the Bible tells the church to do and believe. We believe that a church's vision should be the vision of the kingdom: God's whole will done in and through the church. We don't believe in just being a healing church, or an evangelistic church, or a preaching church or a worshiping church. We believe in a church that runs on all eight cylinders. We want to grow the biggest church possible in our city and reach tens of thousands of people who are within driving distance with the gospel. And we want to plant hundreds of churches and send out dozens of missionaries all over the world. We want to be a church that is also involved in the great justice issues of our city. We want to be a church that is racially diverse and is involved in racial reconciliation. We want to be a church that pushes both extremes all the time and doesn't cut the tensions. We want to be a church that does everything with great passion, great intelligence and great integrity. We want to embrace the message of the kingdom of God and see people experience salvation both in their spiritual and material lives. We want to see the *shalom* of God come to our city, our nation and the world! We are absolutely committed to being a Both-And church.

We celebrate the diversity of our congregation, represented by members who were born in over one hundred different nations, and we also celebrate the fact that 40 percent of our attenders have given their lives to Christ after they started attending our church because we are a Both-And church. We tutor kids every day in our afterschool program and also introduce them to Jesus because we are a Both-And church.

We have a community center that offers free medical and dental care and also healing prayer because we are a Both-And church. We have a food pantry that feeds hundreds of people a month and also holds weekly worship services because we are a Both-And church. We have planted churches throughout Africa, Asia, Europe and South America and also are involved in significant community development projects throughout the world because we are a Both-And church.

One objection to this vision might go something like this: "But our church is not a Walmart Superstore where you can buy a snow shovel and a parrot at 2:30 in the morning! We have only 75 people in our church!" That's great! Perhaps God is calling your church to be more of a specialized bakery: to make the very best bread and pies in your community. In other words, your church is probably called to do a few things with excellence. But the vision of the kingdom and its fullness should be held up in front of every church, whatever its size. God cares about poor people. Can a few people in the church volunteer every Saturday morning at a community-wide food pantry? God cares about unreached people across the globe. Can the church join in a mission partnership with other churches to support a missionary family or a water-drilling project overseas? While no church can do everything, God's heart for everything ought to be on the radar screen of every church.

If we preach the central Christian message that "Jesus Christ is Lord," that means that Christ really is Lord of the whole universe and that he came to redeem both the spiritual and material realms. So when we talk about spiritual concerns, it is because we believe Christ is Lord of the spiritual realm. And when we talk about material concerns, it is because we believe that Christ is Lord of all.

LIVING IN TENSION

Both-And is what makes a church great. But Both-And is also the source of most of the conflicts that we experience as a church. These conflicts typically concern a group of people outside the church or an individual on staff or a group within the church trying to pull the church in one direction or the other, away from the Both-And commitment. They say, "You can't do justice; you must do mercy. You can't be large; you must practice authentic community. You can't be evangelical; you must be charismatic. You can't be culturally relevant; you must be orthodox. You need to be an Either-Or church!"

Philippe Petit was a street performer whose big dream in life was to walk between New York's twin towers on a wire. On August 7, 1974, at 7:15 a.m., Petit stepped off the edge of the North Tower onto a wire that was hanging 1,350 feet above the sidewalks of Manhattan. With nothing but a long balance stick in his hands, he mystified onlookers by kneeling, lying down and even dancing on the wire for forty-five minutes. For those forty-five minutes Petit lived in a state of tension that few of us will ever experience.[2]

To be a disciple of Jesus is to live in tension. We worship one God who exists in three persons. We serve Jesus who is both fully God and fully man. We live in a world that is both good and fallen. And the kingdom of God that Jesus announced is both already here and is still yet to come. This tension exists not only in what we believe and experience but in who we are: both sinner and saint.[3]

But here is the rub: gale-force winds are always threatening to knock us off of the wire. As disciples of Jesus, we live in the Both-And tension while always being pulled by forces to relieve the stress and to go back to our "normal" Either-Or state. But the moment the tension is relieved, there is no longer any power. It's like the string on a violin: no matter how wonderful and expensive the instrument itself may be, it is the tension on the strings that enables it to make music.

Power, energy and life reside in tension. What preserves this tension is the kingdom of God. Every other organizing principle pushes you one way or the other and off of the high wire. Only the kingdom of God is large enough to keep the tension.

Paul Krugman was right to note that we are a deeply divided nation. But we need not be a deeply divided church. In the midst of this great division, the body of Christ, the *sanctorum communio*, or "communion of the saints," must be of one heart and mind. We must embrace the fact that we are called to be Both-And Christians, to serve a Both-And God and to preach a Both-And gospel. Both-And: this is the way out of our partisan divide. This is our calling.

1

What Is Our Identity?

EVANGELICAL . . .

I grew up in a Jewish family in New York City and attended a Jewish parochial school for a few years as a child. After my parents transferred me to public school, I attended Hebrew school and Hebrew high school. Like most Jewish boys, I was *bar mitzvah* at age thirteen. When I attended college, I heard about Jesus for the first time in my life. After hearing about him for months and seeing how some of his sincere followers lived, I came to believe that Jesus was, indeed, the Jewish Messiah sent by God to save not only the Jewish people but also the world.

Following my saving encounter with Christ, I was plunged into the evangelical and charismatic worlds. The woman who first spoke to me about Jesus, Marlene (who later became my wife), took me to an InterVarsity Christian Fellowship group a few days after my conversion experience. She also took me to an evangelical church, part of the Evangelical Covenant Church denomination, which was pastored by a Pentecostal preacher. All of my new heroes were drawn from the evangelical and charismatic worlds. I devoured books by C. S. Lewis, John Stott, J. I. Packer, Francis Schaeffer and Elisabeth Elliot. In addition to InterVarsity, I also participated in a charismatic fellowship, where I first encountered vibrant worship and heard about spiritual gifts such as tongues and prophecy.

WHAT EVANGELICALISM IS *NOT*

In 1994, I coined the term *empowered evangelical* to describe the merger that I saw taking place between the evangelical and charismatic worlds. Along with Ken Wilson, I wrote a book titled *Empowered Evangelicals* to describe the merger of these two streams.[1] But over the last decade I have wondered whether the terms *evangelical* and, to a lesser degree, *charismatic* have outlived their usefulness, at least in the United States, because of all of the baggage associated with them.

Unfortunately, no widely accepted alternative term exists to describe the distinctive spiritual and theological commitments held by those who have historically called themselves evangelicals. But anyone identifying with the evangelical movement must be prepared to distinguish between what forms the theological and spiritual core of evangelicalism and what the term *evangelical* has come to mean. Examining what evangelicalism is *not* can ultimately help us understand what it *is*.

Evangelicalism is not a political label. In the 2004 United States presidential election, more than three-quarters of all white evangelicals voted for Republican candidate George W. Bush. In 2012, the media continually referenced the importance of the "evangelical vote" to the success of Republican candidates in both national and local races. (When the media uses the term *evangelical*, they almost always mean *white* evangelicals.[2]) In many people's minds, the evangelical church is simply the "Republican Party on its knees." But evangelicals have not always lined up so decisively for one political party in America. Indeed, until 1976, evangelicals in America were evenly split between Democrats and Republicans.

In 1946, Winston Churchill and President Harry Truman paid a visit to my city, Columbus, Ohio. Truman met with church leaders seeking their support for his legislative agenda. He said, "A truly religious fervor among our people would go a long way to obtaining a national health program, a national housing program, and an extended and improved

Social Security program."[3] In the current religious and political climate, can anyone imagine that an evangelical revival in America would result in greater support for a national health program, a national housing program and an extended and improved Social Security program? In other words, what would be the most likely result of evangelical domination of the public square in the twenty-first century: national healthcare or the repeal of national healthcare? Greater government benefits for the poor or fewer government benefits for the poor? A greater degree of nationalism and militarism or a lesser degree of both? It is important to think about these things whenever we pray for revival. What might the growth of the church actually bring us? In every age and in every country, this question might be answered differently.

Almost certainly, the major issue that created the great partisan divide is abortion. Believing that life is a sacred gift from God and is to be protected from conception until natural death, evangelicals are overwhelmingly pro-life.[4] After the *Roe v. Wade* decision, evangelicals got involved in politics in order to support pro-life legislation. That Supreme Court decision overturned the abortion laws of all fifty states in America and declared abortion to be a woman's unrestricted right until the point of the fetus's viability, and after that to be legal if a mother's health was in danger.[5]

The Republican Party was quick to co-opt evangelicals' pro-life commitments in the late 1970s by adding a pro-life plank to its party platform. Many Republican politicians, some of whom had been noncommittal about the issue of abortion, suddenly went through a "born-again experience" concerning the life issue. The abortion issue, and to a lesser degree the issue of gay marriage, cemented the link between evangelicals and the Republican party in the United States.

It is absolutely legitimate for a Christian to hold the view that abortion is *the* moral issue of our time. However, millions of Christians would reasonably argue that either poverty or immigration is just as important of a moral issue as abortion. Of course, millions of evangelicals are strongly pro-life but still vote for Democrats. Why do they do this? First, they do not believe that making abortion illegal will eliminate abortion any more than Prohibition eliminated the drinking of alcohol. Some evangelicals believe that making abortion illegal will simply drive the practice underground.

Second, because abortion is heavily linked to economics, many evangelicals support Democratic Party proposals for government-assisted daycare programs, minimum-wage legislation, guaranteed maternity leaves with pay, and government-provided contraception as more effective means of protecting life than simply making abortion illegal. Republicans are often opposed to these economic remedies to the abortion issue.[6] But the reasoning of Democrats and some Republicans appears to be sound. Women are biologically wired (I believe from God) to not kill the life in their wombs. If economic impediments are removed, many (although certainly not all) women would choose to not abort.

Third, electing a pro-life congressperson does not guarantee that he or she will promote pro-life legislation; similarly, a pro-life president will not necessarily appoint pro-life justices to the Supreme Court. Many in the pro-life community were sorely disappointed when Republican presidents such as Ronald Reagan and George H. W. Bush appointed Supreme Court justices who consistently rendered pro-abortion verdicts.

And fourth, one of the major issues in voting has to do with prioritization. Many evangelicals see abortion as one of many significant issues to be sorted through when voting. Other moral issues include war, poverty, creation care, promotion of religious freedom across the globe, protection of the rights of minorities and the care of immigrants and refugees. Nevertheless, the reality is that white evangelicalism is strongly associated in the public mind with the Republican Party and often with nationalistic politics. Polls indicate that young people view Christianity as a whole and evangelicalism in particular as "too political."[7]

Evangelicalism is not fundamentalism. In the early part of the twentieth century, a series of twelve books titled "The Fundamentals" appeared. People who subscribed to the positions laid out in these books were called *fundamentalists*. These fundamentalists saw themselves as simply returning to biblical orthodoxy at a time when orthodox Christian doctrine—such as the infallibility of the Bible, the virgin birth, the substitutionary atonement of Christ and his physical resurrection—were all under attack. So-called modernists suggested that the Bible was filled with historical and moral errors, that Jesus never said or did what the Bible claimed he said or did, that he was not born of a virgin and that he did not physically rise from the dead. But the term *fundamentalist* quickly took on a different shade of meaning than merely a person who subscribed to certain historically orthodox positions. As James Davison Hunter points out: "Orthodoxy as a cultural system represents what could be called a 'consensus through time'— more specifically, a consensus based upon the ancient rules and precepts derived from divine revelation. Its authority and legitimacy came from an unfaltering continuity with truth as originally revealed—the truth in its primitive and purest expression. *Fundamentalism is orthodoxy in confrontation with modernity*."[8]

Martin Marty, one of the most distinguished scholars of modern American Christianity, has defined fundamentalism this way: "The fundamental theological feature of modern fundamentalisms which are religious is *oppositionalism*. Fundamentalism in any context takes form when members of already conservative or traditional movements experience threat."[9]

So fundamentalism is primarily a countercultural movement in the United States. The contours of this countercultural movement have included a rejection of many features of modern science, including the age of the earth and evolution as an explanatory scheme for biological diversity.[10] But fundamentalism wasn't only oppositional in response to modern science. It stood against such things as women's changing roles in society, civil rights for minorities and contemporary music and art. After the famous Scopes trial, fundamentalism adopted a siege mentality. As Alister McGrath points out, fundamentalists view themselves as walled cities, or circles of wagons, defending their distinctives against an unbelieving culture.[11]

In the 1940s, however, a new evangelicalism emerged in America, one that sought to engage and even transform culture rather than separate from or simply oppose culture. Leaders of the new evangelical movement, such as Carl F. H. Henry, called people who subscribed to orthodox tenets of the Christian faith to cultural and intellectual engagement. According to these new evangelicals, pursuing academic degrees at secular universities was not only *not* off limits to Christians, but such a trajectory was considered a good way for Christians to be salt and light in every sphere of life.

Benjamin Warfield, a conservative Presbyterian theologian of the late nineteenth and early twentieth centuries, captured this call to Christians to be fully engaged with the world that God created when he said: "We must not, then, as Christians, assume an attitude of antagonism toward the truths of philosophy, or the truths of science, or the truths of history, or the truths of criticism. As children of the light, we must be careful to keep ourselves open to every ray of light. Let us, then, cultivate an attitude of courage as over against the investigations of the day. None should be more zealous in them than we. None should be quicker to discern truth in every field, more hospitable to receive it, more loyal to follow it, wither soever it leads."[12]

J. I. Packer, one of the most influential theologians within American evangelicalism over the past half century, addressed the question of evolution and the book of Genesis this way: "I believe in the inerrancy of Scripture . . . but exegetically I cannot see that anything Scripture says, in the first chapters of Genesis or elsewhere, bears on the biological theory of evolution one way or another. . . . Scripture was given to reveal God, not to address scientific issues in scientific terms, and . . . as it does not use the language of modern science, so it does not require scientific knowledge about the internal processes of God's creation for the understanding of its essential message about God and ourselves."[13]

Many of the new evangelicals began to dream about masses of Christian young people with courage and intellectual firepower who would pursue graduate degrees and fill secular university departments.

They began to wonder what would happen if the head of the philosophy department at a state university, or the chairperson of the English department at a prestigious private college, were an evangelical Christian. They wondered what would happen if a state senator, a star athlete, a Hollywood director, the head of a local dance troupe or the editor of a local newspaper were a committed Christian who sought to live out her or his faith in an exemplary way. After all, young people are always searching for models. What if a student, upon graduation, were to say, "You know, the person I respected most in college was my journalism professor, and she was a committed Christian." "Imagine what would happen," the new evangelicals said, "if instead of raising our kids to be defensive about and afraid of academic disciplines, we raised confident kids who could fully engage with the best and brightest, with one advantage. Our children have the Word of God to serve as a lamp for their feet and a light for their paths; our kids don't have to stumble around searching for ultimate meaning or ultimate purpose. They have found these in Christ."

Evangelicalism is not a stance toward Israel. According to the dispensationalist interpretation of the Bible, the secular state of Israel is the fulfillment of the biblical promise of the land to the descendants of Abraham.[14] Most American evangelicals have been utterly one sided in their support of Israel, even when Israelis build settlements on land upon which Palestinians have lived for hundreds of years. Many evangelicals have supported Israel even when those Israeli settlements are in violation of international law, America's stated policy and the Israeli government's stated policy. Evangelical opposition to Palestinian rights has dismayed the Palestinian people, 20 percent of whom have Christian backgrounds.[15]

In recent years many evangelicals, including the leadership of the National Association of Evangelicals (NAE), the most prominent umbrella organization for evangelicals in the United States, have called into question evangelicals' unconditional support for Israel and its policies.[16] First, they have argued that the land was never owned by the

Jewish people; the land always belonged to God. The Jewish people were simply tenants in the land. We read in the Old Testament, "The land must not be sold permanently, because *the land is mine* and you reside in my land as foreigners and strangers" (Leviticus 25:23). The land promised to the descendants of Abraham in the Old Testament was always thought of as a gift to Abraham's descendants, *not* as a legal right or a claim for future descendants to assert.

Second, if Israel disobeyed God, she would lose her right to the land. This is repeated over and over again in the Old Testament. For example, we read:

> Do not defile yourselves in any of these ways, because this is how the nations that I am going to drive out before you became defiled. Even the land was defiled; so I punished it for its sin, and the land vomited out its inhabitants. But you must keep my decrees and my laws. The native-born and the foreigners residing among you must not do any of these detestable things, for all these things were done by the people who lived in the land before you, and the land became defiled. And if you defile the land, it will vomit you out as it vomited out the nations that were before you. (Leviticus 18:24-28)

God always threatened exile from the land as a punishment for Israelite disobedience. The Old Testament never separated obedience to God's law from the gracious gift of being able to live in the Promised Land. In other words, when people turned their backs on God, they forfeited the land.

Third, all of the promises in the Old Testament, and especially the promises given to Abraham, need to be interpreted in light of Jesus' coming. Because Jesus of Nazareth is the Jewish Messiah, every single promise in the Old Testament must be read in an entirely new light. The coming of Christ changes our vision of everything and sheds an entirely new light on the whole of the Old Testament. For example, in light of the coming of Jesus into the world, who are the children of

Abraham today? Specifically, who can say today, according to the New Testament, "I am a descendent of Abraham and an heir to the promises made to Father Abraham?" Here is what the apostle Paul said about who the true children of Abraham are today: "Understand, then, that *those who have faith* are *children of Abraham.* Scripture foresaw that God would justify the Gentiles by faith, and announced the gospel in advance to Abraham: 'All nations will be blessed through you.' So *those who rely on faith are blessed along with Abraham,* the man of faith" (Galatians 3:7-9). So it is not the modern state of Israel that constitutes the "children of Abraham" but those Jews and Gentiles who believe in the gospel.

Fourth, what is the inheritance of the true children of Abraham in the twenty-first century? Is it a piece of ground in the Middle East? Does it include the West Bank? The Gaza Strip? The Sinai Peninsula? All of the Middle East from Egypt to the middle of Iraq? (This was the original grant to Abraham, but it is geopolitically impossible today.[17]) Listen to the apostle Paul's answer in Romans 4:13: "It was not through the law that Abraham and his offspring received the promise that he would be heir of the world, but through the righteousness that comes by faith."

All of this means that the Bible does not require evangelicals to view the modern state of Israel as the heir of God's promises made to Abraham and his descendants four thousand years ago. Rather, evangelicals are free to consider the claims of Jews, Christians and Muslims according to principles of biblical justice and biblical peace. We are not required to unconditionally support whatever position the Israeli government takes.

What might biblical justice require? I believe that the world owes the Jewish people a secure nation in their historic homeland in light of two thousand years of the world's treatment of the Jews. We cannot read world history—especially the history of the Russian pogroms and the Holocaust, with its systematic slaughter of six million Jews and the participation of so many countries in the world in that slaughter, including the United States, which shut our borders to Jews fleeing Nazi extermination and sent refugees back to Nazi Germany—without concluding that Jews can never be ultimately secure in a nation ruled by others, whether German, French, Russian, American or Arab. As a matter of biblical justice, Jews must have a nation of their own in their own historic homeland.

But biblical justice cuts in two directions. Justice is owed to the Palestinians as well. When Palestinians who can trace their ancestry back for centuries in the land are pushed off of their land, when Palestinian children are murdered in bombing raids, when houses are knocked down, and when men, women and children are systematically humiliated and abused, biblical justice stands up for Palestinians and says this must not continue. We must have justice for both the Jews and the Palestinians.

So what might be a way forward? How can there be peace in the Middle East? Peace in any relationship begins when two unreconciled people are willing to listen to the hurt and pain of the other person and not just their own hurt and pain. If we simply insist that the other person understand our hurt and pain, and we are unwilling to ever listen to the pain and hurt that we have caused, there is no possibility of true reconciliation. We have to get past only telling our own story. We must listen to the story of the other person. We can't have peace unless we walk in the other person's shoes.

What is true at a personal level is also true at a national level. Palestinians must acknowledge that the Jewish Holocaust changed everything for the Jewish people. The pain experienced through the Holocaust and subsequent terrorist attacks have deeply and permanently affected the Jewish need for security. And Israelis must acknowledge that the discrimination, bombing and displacement of hundreds of thousands of Palestinians have deeply affected the way Palestinians relate to the state of Israel today. Here is where Christians have an opportunity to be bridge-builders and peace-wagers.

If we Christians become even-handed arbiters; if we stop communicating to Palestinians that none of their claims are legitimate, or that all Palestinians are terrorists, or that Christ has no good news for the Palestinians but only for the Jewish people; if we American Christians repent of our biases and our prejudices and offer ourselves as possible bridge-builders, I believe that, in Jesus' name, we could encourage the process of reconciliation and peace. I have hope for peace in the Middle East. I believe that if Christians repent, if we become people who love justice and love peace for both Jews and Palestinians, there is good reason to hope!

Evangelicalism is not a stance toward the end of the world. John Nelson Darby was an early nineteenth-century Anglican priest who broke away from the Church of England and created a new Christian movement called the Plymouth Brethren. Darby introduced a brand-new doctrine into Christianity called "the rapture." Darby and his followers taught that the world would become increasingly dark and degenerate before the return of Christ. But he said that Christ would secretly return to "rapture" out of the world true Christians who would meet him "in the air." Nonbelievers and apostate Christians would be left behind to endure a seven-year period of horrific suffering known as "the Great Tribulation." After that, according to Darby, Christ would return to establish his kingdom on earth and, following a thousand-year reign upon the earth, send all non-Christians into "the lake of fire."

The word *rapture* does not appear in the Bible. Nor did anyone in the first 1,800 years of the Christian church's history ever refer to a secret coming of Christ to rapture his church. Many evangelicals today do not believe in a secret coming of Christ to remove true Christians before some Great Tribulation. Instead of three comings of Christ (first, to die and rise again; second, a secret, invisible coming to rapture Christians out from the world; and third, to establish his kingdom), many evangelicals believe in only two comings of Christ: first, to die for sin and to rise from the dead, and second, to judge the world and bring his kingdom to earth.

The most troubling aspect of Darby's rapture theology is that, as a result, many evangelicals do not believe that working on issues such as social justice, global peace or creation care is worth the effort. They see the world as a massive version of the Titanic: we've hit an iceberg called sin, and we are certainly going down. Why should we rearrange the deck chairs on the Titanic when men and women are drowning and need to be pulled into lifeboats? For many who hold a rapture theology, the only proper activity of the church is evangelism, which will result in more people being raptured when Christ secretly returns. This bleak vision of the future ultimately eliminates any constructive engagement by Christians with society and its institutions. It provides no meaningful ethic and is often rightly labeled as callously otherworldly, anti-environment, anti-peace and anti-human.

WHAT IS EVANGELICALISM?

With so much political, cultural, antiscientific and otherworldly baggage, the question must be asked: can the term *evangelical* be saved? While I doubt that the term itself can be saved, I do hold out the hope that the *principles* of evangelicalism can be retained. Historian David Bebbington provides a helpful summary of evangelical distinctives by identifying four primary characteristics of evangelicalism.

- *Conversionism*: The belief that lives need to be transformed through a "born-again" experience and a lifelong process of following Jesus.

- *Activism*: The expression and demonstration of the gospel in missionary and social reform efforts.

- *Biblicism*: The high regard for obedience to the Bible as the ultimate authority

- *Crucicentrism*: The stress on the sacrifice of Jesus Christ on the cross as making possible the redemption of humanity.[18]

Now that we have considered what evangelicalism is not, let's consider several of the main principles and attributes of evangelicalism.

Evangelicalism is the dominant form of Protestant expression. By way of percentages, so-called mainline Christianity in the United States is no longer the dominant Protestant expression of Christianity. Martin

Marty has said that evangelicalism has been so effective in dominating the Protestant religious landscape in the United States that mainline denominations ought to be referred to as "the sidelined denominations."[19] The statistical drop of mainline denominational attendance has been as dramatic as evangelical gains in membership. According to the National Council of Churches, mainline Protestant churches have seen a fall in membership since the 1970s. Membership in the United Church of Christ was down 2.83 percent, and membership in the Presbyterian Church (USA) was down 2.61 percent. The Episcopal Church was down 2.48 percent. The Evangelical Lutheran Church in America was down 1.96 percent, and the American Baptist Churches USA was down 1.55 percent.[20]

Evangelical domination of the Protestant church has been the product of many religious leaders, but most prominently Billy Graham in the United States and John Stott in the United Kingdom. When people turn on Christian radio, they are most likely to hear evangelicals or charismatics preaching, teaching and hosting talk shows. Many of the most influential pastors in America are evangelicals, including Bill Hybels, Rick Warren and Andy Stanley. Others are from the charismatic stream, a subset of evangelicalism, such as Joel Osteen and T. D. Jakes. The largest seminaries in America are evangelical seminaries. The most prominent religious publishing houses within the U.S. are evangelical, as are America's highest-circulation Christian magazines. Millions of Americans have been, at some point in their lives, involved in evangelical parachurch organizations such as Young Life, Youth for Christ, InterVarsity Christian Fellowship, Campus Crusade, the Navigators, Promise Keepers and Women of Faith.

But it is evangelicalism's theological commitments that make it eminently worth saving. Where else do you find the following expressed with so much fervency? Consider these evangelical distinctives.

Evangelicalism is Christian orthodoxy with a focus on the cross. Evangelicalism is about a set of beliefs—specifically, the historic orthodox beliefs affirmed in the Apostle's, Nicene and Athanasian Creeds.

Evangelicals are orthodox, Christ centered and cross centered. Alister McGrath puts it this way:

> Whatever grasp we have upon the knowledge of God, and whatever hopes of salvation we may possess, are totally dependent upon the identity of Jesus Christ our Savior and our Lord, the only Son of God, God Incarnate. [And it is] Christ's death on the cross [which is] . . . the unique, necessary and sufficient basis of salvation. It is no accident that many of the greatest hymns within the evangelical tradition focus on the sufferings of Christ on the cross, emphasizing both the costliness and the reality of the redemption which has been won through him, and is offered to us and to the world.[21]

Evangelicalism prioritizes a high view of Scripture and a born-again experience. Whatever else evangelicals are, we are a Bible-centered people. Evangelicals look to the Bible as the ultimate authority for our faith and practice. As a result, evangelical spirituality almost always involves Bible study as a central feature and scriptural meditation as part of a daily time of devotions. Evangelicalism is not simply a matter of holding to a certain set of orthodox doctrines. To be an evangelical is also to "participate in a special kind of experience."[22] Thus, we evangelicals believe that a person must surrender his or her life to Jesus Christ and be transformed through a born-again experience and through the lifelong process of following Jesus. The need for personal conversion is central to evangelical spirituality.

Paul writes in Galatians 2:20, "I have been crucified with Christ and I no longer live, but Christ lives in *me*. The life I now live in the body, I live by faith in the Son of God, who loved *me* and gave himself *for me*." Martin Luther, the father of the Protestant Reformation, said this in his commentary on this verse:

> Who is this "me"? I, wretched and damnable sinner, dearly beloved of the Son of God. If I could by work or merit love the Son

of God and come to Him, why should He have sacrificed Himself for me? . . . Read the words "me" and "for me" with great emphasis. Print this "me" with capital letters in your heart, and do not ever doubt that you belong to the number of those who are meant by this "me." Christ did not only love Peter and Paul. The same love He felt for them He feels for us. If we cannot deny that we are sinners, we cannot deny that Christ died for our sins.[23]

Evangelicalism prioritizes witnessing. Evangelicals place primary importance on bearing witness to Christ through word and deed. Tony Campolo, in his wonderful *Letters to a Young Evangelical*, recounts the story of Martin Niemöller, a Lutheran pastor and head of the German confessing church movement, which opposed Nazism during World War II. Niemöller told of a nightmare in which he saw Hitler standing before God's judgment seat: "In this nightmare, Jesus came off his throne, stood alongside Hitler, and put his arm around Hitler's shoulders. Then with pain and sorrow in his voice, Jesus asked, 'Adolf! How could you have done the incredibly cruel and evil things you did?' In the dream, Adolf Hitler answered, 'Because no one ever told me about your love for me and what you did for me.'"

Niemöller said, "At that point I would wake up in a cold sweat and remember that, in all the meetings I had with Hitler, I could not remember once having said anything like, 'My Führer! Do you know how much Jesus loves you? And that he gave himself in a crucifixion to save you? Do you realize that if you were the only person that ever lived in history, his love for you is so great that he would have come into the world and would have died just for you?'"[24]

Evangelicals take seriously our identity as Christ's ambassadors. The apostle Paul said, "We are therefore Christ's ambassadors, as though God were making his appeal through us. We implore you on Christ's behalf: Be reconciled to God" (2 Corinthians 5:20). As a consequence, not only do we evangelicals feel a personal responsibility to share our faith with whomever we can; we also send out tens of thousands of missionaries around the globe.

One of the most encouraging developments of the last thirty years is the extraordinary deployment of missionaries from countries that used to be viewed as targets of mission work by Western Christians. In fact, an emerging missionary movement, called the *majority-world mission movement*, is about to eclipse centuries of Western-dominated Protestant missions. This new term is necessary to replace the aging terms *third world* and *developing world*. The radical change in world missions is forcing scholars and missionaries to create new ways of talking about the global scene. The global majority, 5.2 billion people, live in less developed nations. Of the world's 7 billion people, less than 18 percent live in developed nations. Scholars say the church's future in large measure rests in the hands of the global majority.

Time will tell whether the term *evangelical* continues as a useful designation of this faith that focuses on the cross, holds a high view of Scripture and prioritizes a born-again experience and witnessing. In any case, evangelical principles offer an array of gifts to the body of Christ, especially when held together with a charismatic experience, which we explore next.

2

What Is Our Identity?

. . . AND CHARISMATIC

I read an interesting article in *Sports Illustrated* about a big wave event at Maverick's, a spot twenty-two miles south of San Francisco. A surfing competition takes place at Maverick's every year, right there off of Highway 1. Here is what the reporter writes about a surfer named Virostko:

> For his first wave, a 40-footer, he made a beautiful drop, essentially skiing down the face of the wave. The breaking wave exploded in a huge whitewash and Virostko raced ahead of it to safety. The judges were impressed: 83 points. On his second ride, Virostko did something few surfers in the world can do. Rather than ski down the face of the 35-foot wave, he used his feet to point the nose of the board straight up and went free-falling. Two helicopters were rumbling above his head. The contestants on the boat were hooting, and the surf was roaring, but Virostko never lost focus. He positioned himself to catch the oncoming barrel and rode inside it. When he emerged from the tube, he surfed the wave to its terminus. The judges were awed: 98 points. On his third wave, Virostko showed that he could be a classicist too. He took off right at the peak of a 40-footer, made a graceful

drop and rode it serenely. His arms and his legs, even his polka-dotted head, looked utterly relaxed though he was being chased by a wave big enough to kill. The judges were moved: 86 points. He had 267 points total, good enough for $10,000.[1]

Imagine sitting on a little board and having a forty-foot wall of water roaring at you and then deciding to stand up on that little board so that you can get eighty-six points. I don't think anyone who surfs at Maverick's comes away thinking, "Well, that was boring. Maybe tonight I can do something exciting like watch TV!"

Rick Warren, the bestselling author of *The Purpose Driven Life*, once said that human beings can't build a wave; only God can. But when God builds a wave, we can accommodate the wave by surfing on it and riding it all the way in.[2] At different times in history, God has built a wave. About thirty years before our nation's founding, a wave swept across the American colonies. Many people were converted, and churches came alive. People became passionate for the things of God. The wave came to be known as the First Great Awakening.

At the turn of the twentieth century, another great wave swept across much of the world, including North America, Europe, South America, South Africa and India. It came to be known as the Pentecostal Revival. And in the late 1960s and early 1970s, another wave hit in the United States; it was called the Jesus Movement.

Are we on the verge of another great wave of God's activity? God works in history and uses things in our culture to create a surge in spiritual interest. During times of global uncertainty, people often begin to reach beyond this world for answers. We are living at a time of great uncertainty. We can't build a wave, but we can accommodate what God is doing by riding the wave God is building.

For so many people, Christianity can be described by one adjective: *boring*. People go to church all across the Western world and sleep through the sermon. Millions of people have left churches because they believe that churches deal with trivial issues. They imagine a bunch of blue-haired ladies arguing about the color of carpeting in the fellowship hall.

But what if God is building a wave? And what if he is inviting you and me to surf the wave? What if God, for reasons known only to God, has decided to take this moment to create a surge of spiritual interest across this country and around the world? What if the wave is building and the church begins to awaken from its long slumber? What if churches across America and the West were suddenly not characterized by dead orthodoxy or dead liberalism but by conversions and miracles and transformed lives?

Billy Graham, one of the great Christians leaders of our time, has traveled all over the world, preaching the gospel and seeing millions of lives transformed by Jesus. He has said this: "Everywhere I go I find that God's people lack something. They are hungry for something. Their Christian experience is not all that they expected and they often have recurring defeat in their lives. Christians today are hungry for spiritual fulfillment. The most desperate need of the nation today is that men and women who profess Jesus be filled with the Holy Spirit."[3]

According to David Barrett, the leading expert on the growth of Christianity in the twentieth century, about six hundred million people worldwide are part of the Pentecostal, charismatic or empowered evangelical wings of the Christian church. In other words, 30 percent of all the people in the world who identify themselves even loosely with Christianity are Pentecostal, charismatic or empowered evangelicals. That number is growing much faster than the world's population is growing, and it is growing faster than Islam. That number is growing faster than any other segment of Christianity. If you want to invest in a growth stock for the twenty-first century, a sure bet is to cast your lot with the Holy Spirit wing of the Christian church.

Charismatics are, unfortunately, freighted with many of the same issues that have plagued the evangelical church.[4] Like evangelicals, charismatics in the United States have become associated with right-wing, ultranationalistic, pro-American politics. Like evangelicals, many

charismatics have bought a rapture theology and have offered unconditional support for Israel and its policies. Even more than evangelicals,
charismatics have historically been biased against modern science and
against the life of the mind.

Despite the negatives, the charismatic movement has been an overwhelmingly wonderful blessing to the worldwide church. While certainly not confined to the charismatic or Pentecostal movements, the
Third Lausanne Congress on World Evangelization that met in Cape
Town, South Africa, in 2010 (and may have been the largest gathering
of Christian leaders in world history) emphasized the importance of
the Holy Spirit to the mission of the church.

> We love the Holy Spirit within the unity of the Trinity, along with
> God the Father and God the Son. He is the missionary Spirit sent
> by the missionary Father and the missionary Son, breathing life
> and power into God's missionary church. We love and pray for
> the presence of the Holy Spirit because without the witness of the
> Spirit to Christ, our own witness is futile. Without the convicting
> work of the Spirit, our preaching is in vain. Without the gifts,
> guidance and power of the Spirit, our mission is mere human
> effort. And without the fruit of the Spirit, our unattractive lives
> cannot reflect the beauty of the gospel.[5]

The charismatic movement has borne witness to the larger church
regarding the person and work of the Holy Spirit. Among many other
things, the charismatic movement has addressed our need for the
Holy Spirit's gifts, for an experience of God, for God's power and for
inclusion.

OUR NEED FOR THE HOLY SPIRIT'S GIFTS

The Holy Spirit is the star of the book of Acts. Some commentators
have said that rather than "Acts of the Apostles," the book should be
titled "Acts of the Holy Spirit." As people discover the Holy Spirit and
allow the Holy Spirit to star in their own lives and to star in their

churches, the church becomes irresistible. Luke, who wrote the book of Acts along with the Gospel of Luke, is often called "the theologian of the Holy Spirit," because the Holy Spirit shows up so prominently in both Luke and Acts. As Luke writes about Jesus of Nazareth, what stands out most about Jesus of Nazareth is that he is a Holy Spirit–saturated man.

Jesus' human life was created in the womb of the Virgin Mary by the Holy Spirit. Then we read in Luke 4 that Jesus was led by the Spirit to the wilderness and that he came back in the power of the Spirit. His entire ministry was done in the power of the Spirit. When Jesus talks about his ministry in the Gospel of Luke, he says,

> The Spirit of the Lord is on me,
>> because he has anointed me
>> to proclaim good news to the poor.
> He has sent me to proclaim freedom for the prisoners
>> and recovery of sight for the blind,
> to set the oppressed free,
>> to proclaim the year of the Lord's favor. (Luke 4:18-19)

Jesus was raised from the dead by the power of the Spirit, and the final activity of Jesus was to pour his Spirit out upon people from heaven. Jesus' whole life—his death, resurrection and ascension—is all under the leadership and empowerment of the Holy Spirit. That's why he is called *Christ*. Christ is not Jesus' last name. *Christos* is the Greek translation of the Hebrew word *Messiah*, which means "anointed one." Jesus was the one anointed to be the bearer of the Holy Spirit. And when people become Christians, Jesus invites them into his Holy Spirit–anointed community. Christ, who is the bearer of the Spirit, pours out his Holy Spirit on human beings, and we become the bearers of the Spirit in the world.

Apart from the Holy Spirit, we Christians have nothing. Our coming to Jesus is the product of the Holy Spirit. Our Christian growth is a result of the Holy Spirit, and our unity in the church is created by the

Holy Spirit. Our evangelism is empowered by the Holy Spirit, and our knowledge of God's Word is a result of the Holy Spirit. Our healing, our casting out of demons, the restoration of marriages and families, our insight into the things of God, our servanthood, our Christian character: these things all come from the Holy Spirit. The Christian life is life "in the Spirit."

OUR NEED FOR AN EXPERIENCE WITH GOD

In the thirteenth century, a German emperor named Frederick the Second wanted to know what language children would speak if no one ever spoke to them. He chose several newborns and instructed nurses to feed them but to provide them with no cuddling or talking. What language do you think the children grew up speaking?

They didn't grow up at all. All the babies died before they could talk. The rate of infant mortality among orphans has sometimes reached incredible proportions. In 1915, a doctor who was investigating infant mortality in American orphanages found that 90 percent of American orphans died in childhood. After World War I, physician Fritz Talbot studied marasmus, or failure to thrive, in German orphanages. He watched an elderly German woman carrying babies on her hip. One of the hospital workers said, "Oh, that's old Anna. When we have done everything medically we can do for a baby, and it is still not doing well, we turn it over to old Anna, and she is always successful."

Talbot published his findings, in which he taught orphanage workers to touch, hold, carry and mother every baby in the orphanage several times every day. As this message of "touch" was spread to American orphanages, infant mortality went from 90 percent to 10 percent. Today nurses who work with premature infants in neonatal units are taught how to therapeutically touch babies.

The apostle Paul wrote in Romans 5:5, "And hope does not put us to shame, because God's love has been poured out into our hearts through the Holy Spirit, who has been given to us." The apostle Paul says that the thing that secures us, that gives us joy in the face of incredible trials, is this direct experience of love poured out in our hearts by the Holy Spirit. We need to be reassured that God is real and that God loves us, that the Christian story is true and that there is a reason to hope. We need something that goes beyond our intelligence, our deducing and our reasoning. The way God touches us is by the Holy Spirit. The way that anyone in the twenty-first century experiences God is by the Spirit.

Gordon Fee, a New Testament scholar, wrote a massive book on the Holy Spirit called *God's Empowering Presence: The Holy Spirit in the Letters of Paul*. He opens his book this way: "I am convinced that the Spirit in the apostle Paul's experience and theology was always thought of in terms of the personal presence of God. The Spirit is God's way of being present, powerfully present, in our lives and communities as we await the consummation of the kingdom of God. Precisely because Paul understood the Spirit as God's personal presence, Paul also understood the Spirit always in terms of an empowering presence and an *experiential* presence; whatever else, for Paul the Spirit was an *experienced* reality."[6]

Fee uses the term *experience* very appropriately and deliberately, because throughout the New Testament, the Holy Spirit is not presented to us simply as a doctrine to be added to the end of a creed. The reason that Christianity has so little real impact on the way that Christians live is because for many Christians, Christianity is simply presented as a series of propositions to be believed.

What does it mean to be a Christian? For many people, it simply boils down to whether you can put a check next to certain propositions. Do you believe that God is a Trinity: Father, Son and Holy Spirit? Check. Do you believe in Jesus Christ, God's only Son, our Savior? Check. Do you believe that Christ died for your sins? Check. Do you believe that Christ rose from the dead? Check. Do you believe in the Holy Spirit? Check. Many of us have been told that if we believe these things, our life will change. But then we look at our lives and we say, "But my life hasn't changed." What's wrong? There is more to Christianity than *something* to believe; there is also *someone* to receive and to experience.

Biblical Christianity goes beyond creeds and propositional statements; it involves the experience of the Holy Spirit. The church today needs to regularly invite people to experience the Spirit. There is a growing hunger inside of people for experience. Hundreds of thousands of people have looked to the New Age movement because it promises some kind of experience. People have gone into the woods and pounded drums, sat in sweat lodges and then jumped into icy water. Why? Because they have wanted some kind of experience. People want to feel something.

Other people have sought experiences through some sort of altered state of consciousness or the use of alcohol or drugs. Still others have sought experience through ever more exotic sexual practices. Many seek near-death experiences through cliff jumping, rock climbing without rope, paragliding, wingsuit flying and extreme snowboarding. The Christian faith offers an experience: not just a creed, but an experience of God through the Holy Spirit!

OUR NEED FOR GOD'S POWER

There was once an old guy in the backwoods of Kentucky who showed up at revival meetings whenever an evangelist came to town. At the end of each service, when the evangelist gave an invitation, he would come down the aisle, get down on his knees, raise his arms to heaven and cry out, "Fill me, Jesus! Fill me! Fill me, Jesus!" Then, within a week or two, he would slip back into his old ways of living. But when the next round of revival meetings was held, he would once again go to the meetings, walk down the aisle and pray the same prayer over and over. One time, he was down on his knees yelling to the ceiling, "Fill me, Jesus! Fill me! Fill me, Jesus! Fill me!" Suddenly, from the back of the church, an old woman yelled, "Don't do it, Lord! He leaks!"

Of course, the truth is that we all leak. Being filled spiritually is not a once-and-done thing. We must be filled with the Holy Spirit over and over again.

In Acts, when the Spirit of God descended on Pentecost, Luke records that the Spirit came in "what seemed to be tongues of fire" (Acts 2:3). A Christian is someone who is set on fire by God's Spirit. Danish theologian Søren Kierkegaard put it powerfully when he said, "Christianity is fire setting!" Considering all the problems facing the church in the West in the twenty-first century—declining church attendance, attacks from without, cynicism concerning all institutions (especially religious institutions), moral corruption from within—it is clear that what the church needs is men, women and children who are set on fire by God. Our supreme need is not better techniques or a more powerful website or better marketing or graphics or a slicker presentation on Sunday morning. Our supreme need as individuals and as the church worldwide is to be set on fire by the Holy Spirit.

Jesus did not leave us in the trenches to slug it out on our own. We read in Acts 1:8, "But you will receive power when the Holy Spirit comes on you; and you will be my witnesses in Jerusalem, and in all Judea and Samaria, and to the ends of the earth." Jesus did not simply give us marching orders to go out into the world and spread the gospel. He basically said, "I'm going to go with you. I'm going to give you power to perform the mission that I gave you. I'm going to fill you with the Holy Spirit so you can carry out my marching orders in this very difficult world."

According to Jaroslav Pelikan, one of the world's foremost church historians,

> The history of the church has never been altogether without the spontaneous gifts of the Holy Spirit. From the first century to the twentieth, from Antioch to Azusa Street, the accounts have been gathered and preserved to challenge the skepticism of unbelievers and to build the faith of believers. In the light of such overwhelming evidence, the church today can look to the past with gratitude for what God has done, to the present with faith in his still-awesome power, and to the future with hope for the great miracles he will yet accomplish.[7]

OUR NEED FOR INCLUSIVITY

Inclusivity is the welcoming of people regardless of their nationality, race or gender. When the gift of the Holy Spirit was poured out on the day of Pentecost, Peter explains the Spirit's coming by quoting from the Old Testament prophet, Joel:

> In the last days, God says,
>> I will pour out my Spirit on all people.
>
> Your sons and daughters will prophesy,
>> your young men will see visions,
>> your old men will dream dreams.
>
> Even on my servants, both men and women,
>> I will pour out my Spirit in those days,
>> and they will prophesy. (Acts 2:17-18)

According to the prophet Joel, God says, "I will pour out my Spirit on *all people*" (Joel 2:28).

Not racist. The gift of the Spirit is not racist. For a recent illustration of this, one need go no further back in history than the beginning of the Pentecostal movement at the turn of the twentieth century. In the decade prior to 1906, lynchings of blacks in America had skyrocketed. It is estimated that well over one thousand blacks, mainly black men, were lynched—hanged, shot or sometimes buried alive—in the United States. Millions of people in the United States had joined the Ku Klux Klan. In 1906, the Spirit of God was poured out in a powerful revival in Los Angeles that has come to be known as the Azusa Street Revival. Under the leadership of a black man, William Seymour, tens of thousands of people from all over the world and all walks of life—rich, poor, men, women, Americans, non-Americans, black, white, Asian, Latino—came by car, by horse and buggy, by train and by boat. They all encountered the Spirit. In a year of lynchings, blacks and whites were embracing each other as beloved brothers and sisters in Christ. Frank Bartleman, a historian of the Azusa Street Revival, said, "The color line is washed away by the blood of Jesus Christ!"

Not sexist. Not only is the Spirit not racist; Acts 2:17 shows that the Holy Spirit is not sexist. Wherever the Spirit of God is poured out, women are set free to be and to do all that God intends individual women to be and to do. Fawn Parish, a researcher of women's ministries in the twenty-first century, writes, "Two-thirds of the pastors in the unregistered church in China are women. A majority of effective missions in North Africa is being conducted by single young women. Historically, single women missionaries have courageously braved death, spoken hard truths, been the recipient of hard criticism, and have many sheathes [sic] of harvest to lay at the feet of Jesus."[8]

Not ageist. According to Acts 2:17, the Spirit of God is also not ageist. The Spirit of God is not given as a gift just to adults; God's Spirit comes on children. Many Christians are familiar with what has been called the 10/40 Window: the region where most of the unreached people in the world live.[9] But did you know that there is also a 4/14 Window? The people who are most open to God and with whom the gospel gets the warmest reception are between the ages of four and fourteen. In virtually every church around the world, the vast majority of church members receive Christ before age fourteen.[10] The older people get, the more resistant they are to God and to an experience with the Holy Spirit.

Not elitist. Finally, according to Acts 2:17, the Spirit of God is not elitist; the Spirit is poured out on male and female slaves. The Spirit of God does not show favoritism for those who are well off. In fact, the Bible is full of stories that demonstrate that the heart of God is tilted toward those who are the least and the last. The Spirit is near to those who have been marginalized in our world.

PLUG IN TO THE POWER OF GOD

The power of the Holy Spirit is what makes the kingdom of God spread. We need power. Craig Keener uses the following illustration to describe the activity of the Holy Spirit in our lives. He says, "Imagine visiting a town at night that has no lights, no television, no alarm clocks, no radios, no air conditioning, no refrigerators. And then imagine learning that the town's power supply is virtually infinite, but no one in the town had thought to plug in any of their electric appliances. Wouldn't that town seem silly?"[11]

That's the way much of the church is. We are promised a virtually infinite supply of the power of the Holy Spirit, but most of the church is not plugged in. The Christian faith becomes exciting when you plug in to the power of God.

Christians debate the timing of this experience of the baptism of the Holy Spirit. Some parts of the church say that it happens at conversion; others say that it happens after conversion. But I think every single Christian, regardless of his or her perspective on that issue, could agree that we need more power in our lives. Do any Christians believe that they have appropriated all of the power of the Holy Spirit that they could possibly ever use? Would you really believe that you are as yielded as you could possibly be to the direction, leading and initiation of the Holy Spirit? All of us need more power.

I believe that God is building a wave right now in the United States. We have a choice: we can miss it, or we can ride the wave by saying, "Lord Jesus, fill me with your Holy Spirit. Lord Jesus, I want to surrender more of my life to you. Lord Jesus, I want to be available for your activity in this world. I don't want to just watch what you are doing from the safety of the beach or admire other surfers. Lord Jesus, I want to paddle out." What will you choose?

WHAT GOD HAS JOINED TOGETHER

The historic animosity that existed between charismatics and evangelicals has faded almost to the disappearing point in the last few decades. A number of factors have conspired together to promote reconciliation between the camps. Baby boomers and their children are much less institutionally loyal than earlier generations, and evangelicals and charismatics have found themselves enjoying one another's fellowship through parachurch campus ministries, neighborhood Bible studies and global mission partnerships. Charismatics and evangelicals have stood together in the public arena concerning issues such as the sanctity of life. The Internet and radio and TV ministries have made it impossible to avoid being exposed to the best (and sometimes the worst) of the "other side." Historically evangelicals emphasize the Word over the Spirit, while charismatics have emphasized the Spirit over the Word. But the Word and Spirit belong together.

If we emphasize the Word without the Spirit, we *dry up*. If we emphasize the Spirit without the Word, we *blow up*. If we hold the Word and the Spirit together, we *grow up*. We won't gain more of the Spirit by having less of the Word, and we won't depend less on the Word by having more of the Spirit.

The most exciting aspect of the Both-And marriage of evangelical and charismatic Christianity is the bringing together of evangelicals' historic focus—the salvation of the lost—with charismatic power to get the job done. Imagine churches that experience joyful intimacy with God, regularly see sick people healed, tune into God's voice and worship with bodies, emotions and the Spirit's presence. Imagine churches that employ the power of the Spirit not for a "spiritual buzz" but for evangelism, world missions and deeds of justice and mercy. Imagine churches that experience powerful spiritual life channeled not toward themselves but toward the world. This is the genius of Both-And!

3

What Is Our Community?

In one of my favorite *Peanuts* cartoons by Charles Schultz, Linus is watching a show on television when Lucy comes into the room and demands that he change the channel. Lucy threatens Linus with her fist if he doesn't comply with her demands. Linus asks Lucy, "What makes you think you can walk right in here and take over?"

"These five fingers," says Lucy. "Individually they're nothing. But when I curl them together like this into a single unit, they form a weapon that is terrible to behold!"

Linus reluctantly concedes, "Which channel do you want?" Then, turning away, he looks at his fingers and says to them, "Why can't you guys get organized like that?"

UNITY OUT OF DIVERSITY

The issue of creating unity out of diversity raises one of the most pressing questions facing the world today: How can we all get along? How do we in the United States continue to absorb millions of immigrants, many with different cultures, customs and languages?

There are basically three main answers to the question of relational healing and unity among people. These represent three radically competing visions for how we can all get along.

Pluralistic tolerance. The first option for how we can all get along is the option of pluralistic tolerance. In a world in which some people are willing to engage in suicide bombings and assassinations to achieve their political or religious goals, this approach says that the only way we're all going to get along is for no one to believe anything too strongly.[1] In other words, from this perspective, non-Christian Christians should meet non-Jewish Jews and non-Muslim Muslims, with none of us caring very deeply about anything, especially our faith traditions. This is the vision in John Lennon's classic song, "Imagine." Get rid of countries, nationalism and religious convictions, and then we'll all get along.

What John Lennon missed is that such a vision of the world, without religion and without countries, is itself a strongly held belief. In other words, Lennon was saying that his view of reality was superior to religious worldviews. The pluralistic tolerance view, which grows out of postmodernism, can itself be deconstructed as an assertion of power over less privileged viewpoints.

Ruthless domination. The second option for getting along is ruthless domination: the smashing of all opposition and restricting of individual freedom. It's what Marshal Tito did in the former Yugoslavia, and it's the approach Joseph Stalin took in the former Soviet Union: "We can get along when I destroy you!" It was the option taken by Saddam Hussein: "Our country can hang together with all of its tribalism only if all opposition is suppressed." It was the option of Vladimir Lenin in the Bolshevik Revolution: "When one makes a Revolution, one cannot mark time; one must always go forward—or go back. He who now talks about 'the freedom of the press' goes backward, and halts our headlong course toward Socialism."[2] No freedom of the press or freedom of any kind. This is the Taliban vision for uniting Afghanistan. How is Afghanistan, with all of its conflicts, going to get along? The Taliban's answer is by destroying all opposition and especially by restricting women's freedom.

The world into which Jesus was born was ruled by *Pax Romana*,

Latin for "Roman Peace": an unprecedented time of peace throughout the world. Certainly it was a time of peace, prosperity and justice for the privileged. Yet for the majority, it was a time of great oppression, misery and suffering. As Klaus Wengst notes in *Pax Romana and the Peace of Jesus Christ*, "In the eyes of the Roman provincial administration Jesus was a rebel who endangered the existing peace. A disturber of the peace was done away with, by legal means, by the power responsible for peace."[3]

Christian peacemaking. The third great vision for unity and the healing of our relationships with each other is *Christian peacemaking*. Creating unity out of diversity through Christian peacemaking ought not to be a marginal or peripheral activity for the Christian, because peacemaking is at the heart of the gospel message. We read this in Ephesians 2:13-18:

> But now in Christ Jesus you who once were far away have been brought near by the blood of Christ. For he himself is our peace, who has made the two groups one and has destroyed the barrier, the dividing wall of hostility, by setting aside in his flesh the law with its commands and regulations. His purpose was to create in himself one new humanity out of the two, thus making peace, and in one body to reconcile both of them to God through the cross, by which he put to death their hostility. He came and preached peace to you who were far away and peace to those who were near. For through him we both have access to the Father by one Spirit.

According to the apostle Paul, the mission of Christ in the world is a peacemaking mission that breaks down dividing walls between Jews and Gentiles, blacks and whites, Americans and internationals, native born and immigrants, the wealthy and the poor, men and women, husbands and wives, parents and children and, of course, God and us. Breaking down dividing walls is not marginal to the gospel. Peacemaking is at the heart of the gospel! Peace is the good news. Jesus came *to be* our peace. He died on a cross *to make* peace. And he came *preaching* peace. So when someone is involved in peacemaking activities and is trying to heal divisions between people, nations and ethnic groups, or when someone labors to achieve racial reconciliation or bridge building, this is not a politically liberal agenda. This is our Christian heritage. This is the gospel in action. Peacemaking is at the heart of who we are as Christians.

MAKING PEACE

So how do we make peace? In Ephesians 4:3 we read, "Make every effort to keep the unity of the Spirit through the bond of peace." What the apostle Paul is speaking about is the deliberate intentionality required to make peace. Paul says we must make *every* effort! Here is where Christian peacemaking activity moves from theory to practice. If you claim to be a gospel person, the question for you is: "Are you making *every* effort to have healthy relationships with other Christian believers?"

I am so challenged by this phrase: "Make every effort." It's almost as if the apostle Paul were saying, "Spare no expense. Be urgent. Be passionate. Don't settle for being just okay in your relationships." Many of us settle for a low standard of unity in our relationships with others or even in our own families. If we were honest, we would have to admit that we are satisfied with a certain level of disunity and broken relationships with each other.

Imagine if someone said, "Nobody can keep all Ten Commandments. That's a lot. So I will keep eight of the commandments and forget about the one regarding not stealing. I steal copyrighted music off the Internet. I steal stuff from my job. Stealing is so hard to define anyway. I will also forget the commandment about not lying and regularly exaggerate. I lie on my income tax return and to clients, and I cheat a little bit on exams. But at least I am not bowing down to idols, and I do try to honor my parents!" That's the way many of us are in our relationships, isn't it? We say, "Well, I know that I am at odds with these two roommates, but that's okay because I have eight other good relationships. Isn't that enough?"

Paul says, "Make every effort! Stop settling for a certain amount of relational disharmony. Aim to be at peace with every single person you know. Aim at total unity, just as you would aim at obeying all the commandments of God." Churches must aim to become a reconciled and reconciling people. We must make every effort to keep the unity of the Spirit and the bond of peace.

How far should you go in making every effort to be at peace with your siblings? With your parents? With your spouse? With another person in the church? With folks outside the church? Between churches? How much time, effort and energy should we expend?

The Bible teaches that we should worship God above our desire to make money. Worshiping God should come before the pursuit of leisure or anything else. But Jesus also says, "If you are offering your gift at the altar and there remember that your brother or sister has something against you, leave your gift there in front of the altar. *First go and be reconciled to them; then come and offer your gift*" (Matthew 5:23-24). In other words: first make every effort to be at peace, and then come and worship God. Reconciliation between people is so important that Jesus teaches us, in a sense, to keep God waiting until we have been reconciled with each other.

The priority of making peace runs all through the Scriptures. The prophets regularly challenged the people of God regarding what they called *phony worship*. The people of God would come to the temple and make a big show of their worship by offering sacrifices and singing songs. But their lives held many areas of disobedience—places of darkness, oppression of the poor and unjust divorces of spouses. They said, "I will still lift my hands and worship God. I will sing and clap and that will take care of everything. I don't need to repent." But the Lord says, "No! Worship can wait. First straighten out your relationship with the person you are at odds with. Then you can come and worship me."

Peacemaking is more than just the healing of interpersonal relationships. Peacemaking is also about engaging in the pursuit of global peace. Rick Love is the president of Peace Catalyst International, an organization dedicated to peacemaking between individuals and between peoples. Because two of the greatest areas of conflict in the world today are between Christians and Muslims and between the West and the Muslim world, the organization places high priority on these relationships. Love lays out the following eight practices of peacemaking:

- Pray for Peace
- Pursue Peace with All
- Take Responsibility
- Lovingly Reprove
- Accept Reproof
- Ask for Forgiveness
- Forgive Others
- Love Your Enemies

Rick Love notes, "Jesus is the promised Prince of Peace. His kingdom will be a kingdom of shalom. His peace will be a comprehensive peace (including justice and righteousness). His peace will be multidimensional (peace with God, social harmony, welfare, health, prosperity and human flourishing). His peace movement is expanding and will endure forever. God is on a mission to bring peace to earth. Contrary to popular opinion, he will be successful. For Isaiah says: 'The zeal of the Lord Almighty will accomplish this!'"[4]

MAINTAINING PEACE

The apostle Paul says that the unity of the Spirit is a gift given by the Holy Spirit. The Holy Spirit breaks down dividing walls and makes peace between people. But Paul teaches that this peace must be maintained. He wrote, "Make every effort to *keep the unity of the Spirit* through the bond of peace" (Ephesians 4:3). Some translations speak of "maintaining" the unity of the Spirit. In other words, peace between people is a gift given to us by the Spirit, but it must be maintained.

Imagine for a moment that you were chosen to get a complete home makeover on *Extreme Makeover: Home Edition*. After the television show has been aired, you sit back in your amazing new house, with its many bells and whistles, and say, "Great! I've been given this sweet house as a gift. Now I can kick back and enjoy it!" But after a few months of kicking back, your neighbors start circulating a petition against you because you never mow your grass. After a year, little trees are growing out of your gutters. Your garage door stops working, your furnace goes out and your driveway needs to be repaved. The house was a free gift, but a lot of ongoing work is necessary to maintain the house.

Everything in the universe moves toward entropy, toward disintegration. It's like my wife's car: she hauls around a bunch of children, so if I don't clean out her car regularly, she would be driving a gasoline-powered dumpster! Maintenance: you have to do it with your house and your car, and we need to do it with our relationships as well. Our marriages need constant maintenance; Marlene and I have a date night every week. Friendships and small groups need maintenance, too. In relationships, we have to constantly apologize, and we have to constantly grant forgiveness. Yes, unity is a gift, but the gift needs to be constantly maintained. The gospel is all about peacemaking and making every effort to *maintain* the unity of the Spirit.

PRIDE GETS IN THE WAY

Imagine a husband and wife who are at odds with each other. They have settled into a cold war of virtual noncommunication about anything that is really significant, because whenever they move beyond the superficial, anger flares up and creates more hurt. If they don't want to live in that cold war anymore, what should they do?

No amount of counseling, reading or churchgoing will ever bring this couple together unless something happens in their hearts. Unless there is an attitudinal change, they can schedule date nights from now until forever, and they can go through all of the motions. Without an attitudinal change, however, their relationship will not change.

In Ephesians 4:2, Paul writes, "Be completely humble and gentle; be patient, bearing with one another in love." Pride is behind so much of the discord and the disunity that we find in our relationships and the criticisms that we level at other Christians.

This arrogant criticism has been multiplied exponentially through blogs and the Internet. I once received an email from a man who wrote, "Rich, I like your church and I'm thinking about coming over to Vineyard Columbus. But I am concerned about a blog that a friend sent to me. Would you please respond to this blog?"

The blog said that a church that was pastored by a friend of mine was engaged in a "dangerous" practice of prayer called *contemplative prayer.* The blog said that this church was following in the footsteps of a dangerous writer named Richard Foster, who they claimed was mixing Christianity and Buddhism.

I wrote this guy back and I said, "This church is pastored by one of my oldest and dearest friends. He is a godly, wonderful man, and I would recommend that church to anyone. Richard Foster is one of my favorite Christian authors, and I have regularly recommended his books to anyone seeking a deeper life of prayer." I went on to say to this person that the writer of the blog would hate our church because we don't appreciate sowing discord and suspicion regarding other Christians. We understand that peacemaking is at the heart of the gospel.

In another instance, a dear Christian woman who has been part of our church for years said to me, "Rich, I was listening to Christian radio, and the person said that pastor Rick Warren was involved in the dangerous practice of blending Christianity and Islam into a new religion called *Chrislam.*"

I was furious, but I tried to respond with grace: "Rick Warren is a godly, orthodox Christian who completely understands what it means to live the Christian life. He's not trying to blend Christianity and Islam, or Christianity and any other religion. Rick Warren is simply attempting to lovingly reach out to Muslims so that we can live at peace with each other and hopefully help someone find faith in Christ. That's exactly what we try to do at our church. We build bridges to people. That doesn't mean that we agree with everyone else's religious views or everyone else's practices. But we believe that we are supposed to share the love of Jesus with all of creation."

Apparently, Rick Warren has been so criticized by people claiming that he's making up a new religion that he felt it necessary to write a long blog announcing his orthodox Christian views. When I read his blog, I thought to myself, "What is wrong with American Christians that some self-appointed critics demand that we show our orthodox credentials to them in order to stop their criticism?" It's like requiring people who have driven a car for thirty years to show their driver's licenses at every stoplight.

The unity of the Christian church in America today is being destroyed by a proud, pharisaical spirit. Self-appointed judges, especially on Christian radio and in the blogosphere, attack godly, Bible-believing Christians and raise question marks over them. This is what pride always does: we presume to be above other people, and we look down on them and we judge them.

I'm not saying that there cannot be robust discussion in which people of goodwill and honest conviction disagree with one another. I'm writing about a spirit that is foreign to the gospel: a lack of charity and humility, and a haughtiness that calls into question women and men whose devotion to Christ may actually exceed our own. For unity to thrive, everything we do and say must be undergirded by a spirit of humility!

THE FOUNDATION FOR PEACE

What unites us is not our political opinions. Christians don't all vote the same way. Our unity is not found in our worship preference or favorite sports team. What unites us—Jew and Gentile, black and white, Asian and Hispanic, women and men, old and young, rich and poor,

American and immigrant—is the gospel. We may have different cultural ways of expressing our faith, but our fundamental unity is around the triune God.

The gospel tells us that there is level ground only at the foot of the cross. We have a huge amount in common. Being sinners, being lost without Christ, standing condemned under God's wrath: we share these things in common. But we share other things in common, too: a common way to salvation through trust in Jesus, a common baptism in water and the Spirit and a common new identity in Christ as children of God. We share together as priests in God's temple and heirs of the coming kingdom.

In Ephesians 4:4-6, Paul is clearly referencing the three persons of the Trinity. He writes, "There is one body and one Spirit, just as you were called to one hope when you were called; one Lord, one faith, one baptism; one God and Father of all." He is saying that God, who eternally exists as three persons—God the Father, God the Son and God the Holy Spirit—is always one God. This unity of the Godhead is the foundation for the unity that should exist among God's people.

John Stott, one of the greatest Bible teachers and evangelical leaders of the last generation, wrote in his commentary on Ephesians:

> We are now in a position to repeat the three affirmations, this time the other way round and in the order in which the Persons of the Trinity are normally mentioned. First, the one Father creates the one family. Secondly, the one Lord Jesus creates the one faith, hope and baptism. Thirdly, the one Spirit creates the one body. Indeed, we can go further. We must assert that there *can* be only one Christian family, only one Christian faith, hope and baptism, and only one Christian body, because there is only one God, Father, Son and Holy Spirit. You can no more multiply churches than you can multiply Gods. Is there only one God? Then he has only one church. Is the unity of God inviolable? Then so is the unity of the church. The unity of the church is as indestructible as the unity of God himself. It is no more possible to split the

church than it is possible to split the Godhead.[5]

Some might object and say, "Well, churches split all the time. We've got thousands of denominations. How do you reconcile this with the perspective that there can only be one church?" Here's how Stott responds:

> Perhaps the analogy of a human family will help us to grasp our responsibility more clearly. We will imagine a couple, called Mr. and Mrs. John Smith, and their three sons, Tom, Dick and Harry. They are one family; there is no doubt about that. Marriage and parenthood have united them. But in the course of time, the Smith family disintegrates. Father and mother quarrel . . . and finally get a divorce. The three boys also quarrel, first with their parents and then with each other, and separate. Tom goes to live in Canada. Dick in South Africa. And Harry in Australia. They never meet, write or telephone. They lose contact with each other all together. More than that, so determined are they to repudiate each other that they actually change their names. It would be hard to imagine a family which has experienced a more disastrous disintegration than this.[6]

Stott asks, "What if you were one of their cousins? Should you shrug your shoulders and say, 'Well, I guess in God's sight they're still a family even though it's all disintegrated. Their disunity is not so bad. They're doing fine. They've formed other families. So what if none of them talk to each other? It's none of my business!'"

It is precisely in a situation like this in which peacemaking, which is at the heart of the gospel, must be considered. In situations of discord, "making every effort to keep the unity of the Spirit" has to have some practical application. What role must we take to heal divisions? What would God have us do to reconcile people? What level of importance should we place on assisting folks to understand each other and to get along? How can we help Christians who disagree?

WHEN CHRISTIANS DISAGREE

Imagine that a woman named Amy walks into a meeting of her women's group that meets on Saturday morning. She announces, "I am not going to come back to this group anymore. I don't need to spend Saturday morning in a nursery changing diapers and holding crying babies. I could do that at home with my own baby. The reason I come here is to get a break. By the way, I am not the only one who feels this way. I have talked with several other women and they said that if they are put in the nursery to watch the babies during Bible study time, that they are not coming back to this group either."

Immediately, five other women in the group respond to Amy's attack. One of the women, Betty, tries to solve the problem right away. She says, "Well, the reason why we are not hiring babysitters is because some of the women in the group can't afford to pay. But how about this? How about if one week we hire babysitters and the next week some of the women rotate through?" Betty tries to split the difference.

Amy is not satisfied. She says, "Forget it! There won't be any splitting the difference here. Either we are put off the nursery team, or I am walking."

A second woman, Carmela, raises her voice and says, "I really don't think that we should be disagreeing here." She looks down at the floor and nervously around the room. "I think that perhaps it would be better for us to focus our attention on the women's breakfast that is coming up." After several more minutes of the women still arguing with each other, Carmela finally says, "I have to get out of here," and scurries out of the room.

A third woman, Denise, says nothing. She smiles pleasantly at everyone in the group. She says nothing through the discussion and disagreement. When she leaves the meeting, however, she immediately gossips about the problems in the group with a friend who is not part of the group.

The leader of the group is an older woman named Emma. She is sweet and mild. Emma immediately takes the whole problem on herself and says, "Amy, this is my fault. I really haven't been a good leader. I should have planned last year for raising money for babysitting this year. I will pay for the babysitting for the year for the group."

Finally, Felicia, who is a seasoned veteran of church conflict, stands up and says, "No, I don't think it would be appropriate for you to pay for everyone else's children. But I do think we need to talk here. Amy, what exactly are you upset about?"

This conflict is very typical of the kind that comes up in a group setting. Think about how these women related to each other. Amy comes in with her ultimatum. Essentially she's saying, "It's my way or the highway." She is a *lion*: "If you don't do what I say, I am going to bite your head off. Even if everyone else has to lose, I get to win. I am not interested in discussion." Amy is the *conflict instigator*.

Then there is the *fox*, who tries to finagle a deal. Betty says, "Well, maybe we can split the difference here." Sometimes it is right to split the difference, but sometimes that is just a way for us to not hear people's real problems. Betty is the *conflict compromiser*.

There is Carmela, the *turtle*. Carmela can't stand any sort of conflict and just wants to end it right away. Turtles have learned to pull in and withdraw whenever a disagreement arises. Carmela is the *conflict avoider*.

Denise is the *snake*. She is the woman who sits and smiles, says nothing and lets everyone believe that she is on their side. She then goes out and attacks the other women in the group to anyone who will hear. She is the *conflict spreader*.

Emma, the Bible study leader, is a *teddy bear*. She comes to the rescue of every person in her group and takes everyone's weight upon herself. Emma is a *conflict absorber*.

Finally, Felicia, the woman who gently confronts Amy, doesn't think that the sky will fall just because there is a disagreement. She understands that conflict is often the result of God wanting to do something in a group. She also understands that conflict is sometimes inevitable, because people come from different places and have different perspectives and gifts. She knows that there is a godly way to resolve conflicts. Felicia is the *wise owl*. She is a *conflict healer*.[7]

Because of Felicia's gentle confrontation, the women discover that one of the reasons that Amy is so upset is that she has been awake half the night with her baby, who is colicky. She can barely drag herself through the day, and she really does need a break from spending a third of her time in a nursery. Small-group fellowship is a necessity for her. They also discover that women in the group really can't afford to pay more. The wise owl proposes a solution. "Let's put together a fundraiser for this group. We will hold a garage sale together at my home. Let's bring over all of our stuff, and we should be able to afford to pay for childcare for everyone." The garage sale is held, and they raise six hundred dollars.

What is your basic conflict management style? Are you a conflict instigator like Amy? Are you a conflict compromiser like Betty? Are you a conflict avoider like Carmela? Are you a conflict spreader like Denise? Are you a conflict absorber like Emma? Or are you a conflict healer like Felicia?

Years ago when I was in college, for two years I made money by tarring flat roofs. One time while I was putting tar on the flashing of a roof, a little piece of metal flicked up and went under my eyelid and began to scratch the surface of my eye. Madly blinking my eye, I tried to dislodge this thing. The feeling of it scratching the surface of my eye was driving me crazy.

I was about two stories up, and I had to walk down a ladder, virtually blind, and then a couple of blocks to the student infirmary. In agony from the little speck in my eye, I ran into the student infirmary and to the front desk. I cried out, "There is something in my eye!" A wonderful doctor brought me into one of the waiting rooms. She had me lie down on the table and put a huge magnifying glass over my eye. Then she put a tiny cotton swab in my eye and gently and patiently pulled the piece of metal out.

This experience gave me a new appreciation and understanding of Jesus' Sermon on the Mount, in which he speaks these words:

> Do not judge, or you too will be judged. For in the same way you
> judge others, you will be judged, and with the measure you use, it

will be measured to you. Why do you look at the speck of sawdust in someone else's eye and pay no attention to the plank in your own eye? How can you say, "Let me take the speck out of your eye," when all the time there is a plank in your own eye? You hypocrite, first take the plank out of your own eye, and then you will see clearly to remove the speck from the other person's eye. (Matthew 7:1-5 TNIV)

When we handle conflicts and disagreements among Christians, we must realize that many times we are essentially performing eye surgery. Thus, we must handle the situation with great care, gentleness and patience.

Making peace is such an important issue for our congregation that we ask everyone who wants to become a member of our church to agree to handle conflicts in a biblical way. We expect that, whenever members of our church have a dispute of any kind, the conflict will be settled by Bible-based mediation and, if necessary, legally binding arbitration.

THE RESOURCE FOR PEACE

Christian efforts for peace would be utterly futile without the peace-making resources we find in Christ. How does the incarnation of Christ and his death on the cross provide the resources necessary for Christians to help the world get along? Pastor Tim Keller, in *The Reason for God: Belief in an Age of Skepticism*, reminds us that the Greco-Roman world into which Christianity came was very open and tolerant about beliefs. Everybody could worship their own god. But it was also a world that was really brutal; there was a huge distance between rich and poor and be-tween slave and free. Christianity, on the other hand, said that there is only one true God, and that he sent his Son, Jesus Christ, to descend to the cross, where he died for the world. And Christians—even though they had this strong conviction about there being only one God and one Savior—were incredibly welcoming of others who held different beliefs. They had a resource in the example of Jesus, which enabled them to create peace in the midst of a hostile world. As Keller writes, "Christians had within their belief system the strongest possible resource for practicing sacrificial service, generosity and peacemaking. At the very heart of their view of reality was a man who died for his enemies, praying for their forgiveness. Reflection on this could only lead to a radically different way of dealing with those who were different from them. It meant that they could not act in violence and oppression toward their opponents."[8] Following the example of Jesus—especially the sacrifice of self in dying for his enemies—led the early Christians to not only care for those who were inside the church but to reach out in self-sacrificial love to those outside the church. Becoming instruments of peace and healing in this world is possible through devotion to our self-sacrificial Savior, Jesus Christ, and the empowering gift of his Holy Spirit. The cross of Christ and the gift of the Holy Spirit is the answer for how we can all get along.

In 1976, Bill Bright, who was the founder and president of Campus Crusade for Christ, met with a few evangelical leaders to form a conservative, right-wing political organization. A magazine called *Sojourners*, published by Jim Wallis, reported on this plan to mix Christianity with Republican politics. *Sojourners* carefully documented all their sources, and then they invited Bill to respond to their reporting and offer his side of the story.

Bill was hurt and angry, and he denounced the magazine and Jim. This heated exchange between Bill and Jim led to two decades of hostility between them.

After all that time, they ran into each other again. By this time, Jim had decided that the healing of their relationship was long overdue, so he approached Bill and he said, "Bill, I need to apologize to you. I should have . . . tried to mend the painful breach between us after all these years. I didn't do that, and I should have. I'm sorry."

Bill, who was an old man by this time, wrapped his arms around Jim and said, "Jim, we need to come together. It's been so long, and the Lord would have us come together. Jim, I'm so worried about the poor about what's going to happen to them. You're bringing us together on that, and I want to support you." They hugged each other for a long time with tears in their eyes.

It was a few months after this encounter that they ran into each other again and had the opportunity to go for a walk on the beach. Bill said, "You know, Jim, I'm kind of a Great Commission guy. And I've discovered that caring for the poor is part of the Great Commission, because Jesus instructed us to 'teach the nations to observe all the things I have commanded you.' And Jim, Jesus certainly taught us to care for the poor, didn't he? Caring for the poor is part of the Great Commission!" After the walk, Bill and Jim got back to the hotel where they spent time praying for each other and their ministries.

Some time after that, Jim got a surprise in the mail from Bill, who was then eighty years old and quite ill. Bill had written, "Dear Jim, Congratulations on your great ministry for our Lord! I rejoice with you. An unexpected gift designated to my personal use makes possible this modest contribution to your magazine. I wish I had the means to add at least three more zeros to the enclosed check. Warm affection in Christ. Yours for helping to fulfill the Great Commission each year until our Lord returns. Bill."

Inside the envelope was a check for one thousand dollars! As Jim was reading Bill's letter, one of Jim's colleagues came in and said, "Jim, did you hear that Bill Bright just died?" Comparing the postmark on the letter with the news report of Bill's death, they concluded that one of the last things that Bill did before he died was to write this letter to Jim.[9]

Jim approached Bill, who had called him a liar, and apologized for not trying to heal the breach of their relationship sooner. And Bill sent one thousand dollars to a magazine that had published a very painful and embarrassing article about him thirty years before. Both men reached out to someone who had wounded them badly and together made sure to rebuild the bridge of fellowship that had been broken between them.

Is there anyone with whom you have an unhealed breach of fellowship? Are there any burned-out bridges in your past? How might God wish to use you to "maintain the unity of the Spirit through the bond of peace?"

4

What Is Our Community?

...AND DIVERSITY

The issue of diversity hasn't been far from my mind ever since I became a follower of Christ. As a Jew who did not fit into the majority white Protestant culture into which I was thrust, I have always been aware of God's plan for unity and diversity. For years I've lived as both an insider and an outsider in the church. I've learned to understand the evangelical culture, but there are communication patterns and cultural features that have never become entirely mine.

One night about twenty-five years ago, I had a series of vivid dreams that made me extremely joyful. In the dreams, I saw myself preaching in our church, but the congregation that I was preaching to was very diverse. Over the course of that one evening, this dream was repeated to me several times. I felt that these dreams were from the Lord, and my response was to regularly pray for the fulfillment of these dreams.

Despite these dreams and my fervent prayers, however, our church didn't change much. We made great efforts to reach out to other ethnic groups through our outreaches, food pantry and free medical clinic, but we continued to be a predominately white church. It would be years before we saw any changes. But after years of praying together as a church and being very intentional about becoming diverse, we began to sense God moving in our midst in incredible ways. Today, by the grace of God, individuals from over one hundred different nations worship together at our weekend services. What you are about to read is the story of our journey.

Before I share our story, however, let's take a quick look at the history of race relations in America.

THE HISTORY OF EVANGELICALS AND RACISM

Why begin this chapter with a look back at history? According to surveys by sociologists Michael Emerson and Christian Smith, white evangelicals in America tend to be *ahistorical*: that is, they do not grasp how history has an influence on the present. Emerson and Smith's research indicates that white evangelicals in America feel that many African Americans are to blame for their problems. Many white evangelicals think, *Things are the way they are because African Americans cannot forget the past. They are overly sensitive, and they are incited by black leaders. They are just exaggerating the problems of race in America.*

When white evangelicals are asked about where racism exists in America, they find it difficult to cite any concrete examples. People of color, on the other hand, have no trouble producing specific instances of racism. Generally, white evangelicals find structural explanations for the disparity between blacks and whites in America to be either mistaken or overblown. White evangelicals are particularly suspicious of people blaming the American legal system, institutional discrimination or historical segregation as the cause of their problems. White evangelicals feel much more comfortable looking at an individual's personal accountability for her or his success or failure in life.[1]

What does American history tell us about white evangelicals' involvement in the fight for racial justice for African Americans?

George Whitefield, who many regard as having laid the spiritual foundations for the American Revolution, preached to both whites and blacks. But while he preached equality in Christ and preached the gospel to slaves, he was a supporter of slavery. In 1741 Whitefield testified before the British Parliament, where he spoke up in favor of slavery in Georgia. From his perspective, it was better to live in a Christian country as a slave than to live in "heathen" Africa.[2] Cultural and religious legitimation of slavery was very strong, and to overturn slavery was seen as going against God's ordained pattern.

By the time of the American Revolution, many people began saying that it was not enough to Christianize slaves. The rhetoric used to muster support for the Revolutionary War—"All men are created equal and are endowed by their Creator with certain inalienable rights"—condemned the enslaving of fellow human beings. Within a few decades of the revolution, most Northern states outlawed slavery. In 1808, the importing of slaves was abolished nationwide.

White evangelicals such as D. L. Moody and (later) Billy Sunday simply did not emphasize social reform as part of their Christian message. Their message was entirely focused on evangelism and personal piety. Moody held revival meetings in the South but on a segregated basis. And when Billy Sunday preached in the South after 1900, he also segregated his revival meetings.[3]

In the 1950s, Martin Luther King Jr., Ralph Abernathy and many other African American Christians protested, boycotted and fought for an end to Jim Crow segregation. Their goal was freedom from oppression and unequal treatment as expressed through the Southern laws and practices.[4] The civil rights movement arose in the context of the African American church. Its agenda, tactics, organizing principles and rhetoric were explicitly Christian.

While mainline Protestants and Jews joined African Americans in their historic struggle for freedom and equality, very few white evangelicals participated in the civil rights cause. Many white fundamentalists branded Dr. King and the civil rights movement "communistic." They said, "The only thing that matters is saving souls for heaven!" Some of these "born-again" Christians wrote to Dr. King, urging him to stop focusing on civil rights and to start focusing on God. Dispensationalists could never have created the "I Have a Dream" speech, in which

Dr. King stated his hope that one day his children might play together with white children. When Frank Gaebelein, then coeditor of *Christianity Today*, chose to not only cover Dr. King's march on Selma but also to endorse him and join the movement, other evangelical leaders were scathingly critical.[5]

On June 19, 2012, the Southern Baptist Convention elected its first African American president. The election of Fred Luter Jr., a former street preacher and pastor of a church in New Orleans, was truly a watershed moment for the country's largest evangelical denomination, which separated in 1845 from its northern counterpart in order to defend the right of Southern slaveholders to serve as missionaries. It was not until 1995 that the denomination adopted a resolution of racial reconciliation!

In a poignant *New York Times* article, Molly Worthen, an assistant professor of history at the University of North Carolina–Chapel Hill, notes that even as great strides are being made toward racial reconciliation, there is still a great divide between black and white evangelicals:

> Black Protestants have good cause to eye Republicans warily and mistrust the label "evangelical": the Christian right's concerns do not match their own experience or priorities. . . . Conservative black Protestants and the Christian Right also have different memories of American history. . . . For black Christians, American history is not a narrative of decline from an arcadia of Sunday family devotionals and McGuffey Readers to the godless fleshpots of modern America. It is a narrative of liberation that is not yet complete. These divergent understandings of history have amplified disagreement over what it means to follow Jesus' and the prophets' command to "set at liberty those who are oppressed."[6]

RACIAL RECONCILIATION: OUR STORY

In 2001, I took a sabbatical for ten weeks. During that time, my family and I visited different African American churches each weekend for worship. Over the course of those ten weeks, I became cognizant of several things. First, I discovered a great diversity among African American churches. Contrary to my prior belief, African American churches are not monolithic: the music, preaching style and length of services varies greatly. Some services are about an hour long, while others last almost four hours. Some are contemporary, while others are more traditional. Some of the preaching styles are exactly like what one might expect to find in a mostly white evangelical church, while in others the inflection and timing is so musical that it sounded to me like improvised jazz. In many churches, the congregations answer the preacher verbally at every opportunity, creating a call-and-response pattern that builds in intensity as the sermon progresses. Other congregations are less verbal. I found myself loving the warmer, engaging, more-than-cognitive style of the messages that I heard. My family was uniformly greeted with great affection by members of the various congregations. But I was also keenly aware of our minority status.

The first thing that I did—unconsciously—after taking a seat in the sanctuary was to look around to see whether any other people looked like us. I discovered a little of what it would feel like to be a person of color who chose to attend the church that I pastored. I felt conspicuous by my otherness.

From the earliest days of my Christian faith, I knew that God has only one family because I read passages like this one: "But you are a chosen race, a royal priesthood, a holy nation, God's own people, in order that you may proclaim the mighty acts of him who called you out of darkness into his marvelous light. Once you were not a people, but now you are God's people; once you had not received mercy, but now you have received mercy" (1 Peter 2:9-10 NRSV).

All of God's children fall into that one race—the race of those who have been adopted by God through the atoning death of Jesus Christ. But it took a couple of decades following my conversion to realize that this "one race," "one family" diversity needed to be practically expressed and seen as much as possible in each local congregation.[7]

WORLD-CHANGING CHURCHES

What kind of church does God use today to change the world? To answer that question, we must ask: what kind of church did God use at the beginning of Christian history to change the first-century world? We read in Acts 13:1-3, "Now in the church at Antioch there were prophets and teachers: Barnabas, Simeon called Niger, Lucius of Cyrene, Manaen (who had been brought up with Herod the tetrarch) and Saul. While they were worshiping the Lord and fasting, the Holy Spirit said, 'Set apart for me Barnabas and Saul for the work to which I have called them.' So after they had fasted and prayed, they placed their hands on them and sent them off."

Antioch was the launching pad of world-changing international missions. So what exactly were the features of this world-changing church?

First, we see that a diversity of gifts was welcomed in the church: "In the church at Antioch there were prophets and teachers."

Second, we see that the people in the church spent time seeking the face of God: "While they were worshiping the Lord and fasting . . ." In other words, the leaders didn't merely sit around in strategy sessions, trying to figure out the best way to promote and spread the Christian faith. They sought the mind of God.

Third, we see that they were responsive to God when he spoke: "The Holy Spirit said, 'Set apart for me Barnabas and Saul for the work to which I have called them.' So after they had fasted and prayed, they placed their hands on them and sent them off." The early church listened to the Lord.

Fourth, we see that ethnic and cultural diversity was at the core of the church in Antioch. Let's take a look at the leaders in Antioch. There was Barnabas, who Luke described as a "Levite from Cyprus" (Acts 4:36). In other words, he was a Jewish man from a religiously elite family. There was "Simeon called Niger [black]," who was presumably a black African. Simeon was perhaps Simon from Cyrene, who carried the cross for Jesus and who might have become a Christian believer following his encounter with Jesus. We read of Lucius of Cyrene, who definitely came from North Africa. And there was Manaen, who is said to have been "brought up" with Herod the tetrarch. Scholars believe that he may have been a foster brother of Herod or, at the very least, Herod's intimate friend. Manaen was well connected with the powerful. Finally, we read of Saul, whose family came from the Greek-speaking city of Tarsus but who described himself as "a Hebrew of Hebrews" (Philippians 3:5). These five men symbolized the ethnic and cultural diversity of Antioch.

Isn't it interesting that the term *Christian* first began to be applied to followers of Jesus in Antioch (Acts 11:26)? This was a new human community!

The Christians in Antioch strived to conform their lives to the example and teaching of Jesus. They were Christlike. They not only loved God; they loved other people unconditionally. When Jews loved Gentiles and Gentiles loved Jews and they worshiped together in one integrated local church, it was a witness to everyone around. Observers would have thought, "Obviously, Jesus is someone who breaks down dividing walls between people." And the integration of the Christians told the watching world that God is not just a tribal or ethnic or national God. Jesus Christ is Lord of all people.

REASONS TO STRIVE FOR DIVERSITY

Why is a racially diverse church the will of God? Why are racially and culturally diverse churches such as Antioch precisely the kind of church that God uses to influence communities and to launch world missions? It's not that God values one culture over another. Nor does God care about "political correctness." But God used a racially diverse church at the beginning of the Christian era—and God still uses racially diverse churches today to change the world—for at least four reasons.

Theology. First, there is a theological reason. Christ died not only to reconcile people to God but to reconcile people to each other. The apostle Paul speaks about the cross tearing down the dividing wall of hostility between Jew and Gentile. The ground is level at the foot of the cross.

Every human being—black, white, Asian, Latino and other—approaches God in the same condition: as sinners in need of grace. And every human being is saved in exactly the same way: by grace through faith. Racism, especially against African Americans, has been called "America's original sin." What force is powerful enough to bring blacks and whites together in the twenty-first century? The same force that brought Jews and Gentiles together in the first century: the cross of Christ!

Eschatology. Second, there is an eschatological reason. In theology, eschatology has to do with the doctrine of "the last things" (*eschata*). Eschatology deals with such issues as death, resurrection, the return of Christ, judgment and the new world that is coming. But what will this coming world be like? Revelation 7:9 says, "After this I looked, and there before me was a great multitude that no one could count, from every nation, tribe, people and language, standing before the throne and before the Lamb. They were wearing white robes and were holding palm branches in their hands."

The church today is called to be a pointer to the coming kingdom. When people step into a local church, they ought to experience something of the world to come. Why do we pray for the sick? Because in the coming kingdom, people will enjoy perfect health. Why do we feed the hungry, comfort the grieving, reconcile broken marriages and deliver people from the power of the devil? Because these are pointers to the coming kingdom. Revelation tells us that when the kingdom comes in its fullness, it's not going to look like a white church or a black church. The kingdom of God is going to be thoroughly multiethnic, multilingual and multicultural.

Mission. Third, there is a missional reason. Most people are reached for Christ by people who are like them. Motorcycle enthusiasts reach other cyclists, school teachers reach other school teachers, Jewish believers reach other Jews and young moms reach other young moms. In multicultural settings, if the city is going to be reached, it will only be reached by racially diverse congregations.

Liturgy. Finally, there is a liturgical reason. In English, the word *liturgy* speaks about public or corporate worship. How do we communicate to the watching world the greatness of the God that we worship? I have always believed that the greatness of one's leadership can be measured by the diversity of people who follow the leader. If a leader can only get one toddler to follow, then he or she is probably not a great leader. If a leader can only get people from a narrow socioeconomic or racial group to follow, she may not be a great leader. But if a leader can draw people from every conceivable ethnicity and culture to follow them, we have discovered a great leader!

The chief reason that it is the will of God to have a racially diverse church is that it is God's chief passion to gain glory for himself from all peoples on the earth. When people from over one hundred nations gather to worship Jesus, we proclaim to the watching world, "Behold the King of Kings and Lord of Lords!"

LISTENING TO OTHERS

Racial reconciliation is not simply a matter of numerical diversity. In other words, building a racially diverse church is not simply a matter of recreating Noah's Ark, in which there are two of every kind in the church. True reconciliation takes place in the heart. We need to be able to empathetically hear the stories of people who are different than us and walk in their shoes.

Nearly a decade ago, I joined with an African American pastor, Sam, to start a roundtable for pastors of other large churches in our area. We spent one of our gatherings tackling the subject of race. During one particularly vulnerable session, a white pastor challenged Sam, who had claimed that the marketing of a nationally known evangelical ministry had demonstrated great racial insensitivity. Sam responded to the white pastor's challenge by saying, "You white brothers are utterly unaware of the extent of racism in the American church." He then asked, "How many of you white brothers have taught your sons what to do with their hands when they are pulled over by the police?" None of the white pastors raised their hands.

Then, looking at the other black pastors around the table, Sam asked, "How many of you brothers have taught your sons what to do with their hands when they are pulled over by the police?" All of the African American pastors raised their hands.

"You see, we teach our sons that when you are pulled over by the police, you keep your hands on the steering wheel," Sam explained. "You don't reach for the glove compartment or for something under your seat, because you may get shot. The police may assume that because you are a young black male, you have a gun. But if you are white in America, you don't think about those kinds of things."

He continued, "How many of you white pastors have taught your people what to do with their hands when they go shopping?" None of the white pastors raised their hands. He then asked, "How many of the brothers have taught your people what to do with their hands when they shop?" Most of the African American pastors raised their hands.

He said, "You see, we teach our people that when you go into a white store, you don't touch the items and then reach into your purse. They will assume that you are shoplifting. You use big gestures with your arms so that everyone can see what you have in your hands."

Then turning to me, Sam said, "Rich, here's the issue. When you look into the mirror in the morning, you see a man. When I look into the mirror in the morning, I see a *black* man. You never think about race. I think about race every day of my life. Every part of our existence in America—whether it's shopping, driving, applying for a job or purchasing a home—is affected by our race!"

Listening to Sam share his story was a Holy Spirit moment for me. It was then that I realized that not only did my church have to embrace diversity; I had to embrace it, too.

Of your ten closest friends, how many are not of your race? Of the last five people you shared a meal with, how many were not from your race? I ask this because *friendship always changes our perspectives!*

About a decade ago, my wife started an African American women's group in which she was the only white person. Not to be outdone by

Marlene, I decided to start an African American men's group for about twenty-five African American men in our congregation. My co-leader was a dear friend of mine who is African American. Spending a few years as the only white man in this men's group, I listened to and learned from the life experiences of people who were racially different from me. And I had the opportunity to build long-term friendships.

I started to read everything I could on the subject of diversity and racial reconciliation.[8] I also began to host staff meetings on race and racial reconciliation. Over the last decade, we've had many staff meetings devoted to training about racial and cultural awareness.

BECOMING INTENTIONAL ABOUT DIVERSITY

Many people say they would love to have their church become more racially diverse. I've met very few Christians over the past forty years who would intentionally turn anyone away. Almost everyone I've ever met believes that their church is welcoming of everyone, regardless of race. They would say that if someone from a different racial background showed up, they would feel comfortable in their church. In my interactions with pastors and Christian leaders, however, I have found that few are actually doing anything to *intentionally* draw diverse people to their churches. Most of the time, what people mean by "being welcoming" is that other folks are welcome to join their church so long as they do things "our way." The message they send is, "You can come, but don't bring your culture. Make sure you fit into the way we've always done things. Don't try to change us!"

We must understand that our way of doing things in the past is not necessarily God's way forward for the future. The Bible declares that God's thoughts are higher than our thoughts, and that his ways are not our ways (Isaiah 55:8). And Philippians 2:4 says, "Let each of you look not to your own interests, but to the interests of others" (NRSV). The relevant question is not how my church or your church has always done things; that's an issue of personal comfort! A church that is committed to becoming racially diverse must *become comfortable with being made uncomfortable.* This may mean that we sing a song in Spanish or with a gospel choir. It may mean having someone with an accent do announcements, or being led by someone whose approach to leadership is different from ours. The majority-culture people need to share power and decision making with others. It's not just diversifying the worship songs or the speakers; it's about having a fully multiethnic community working and leading together as stakeholders. All of this may be uncomfortable. But learning to embrace the discomfort—and even to celebrate it as a sign that we are on the right track—is important.

Have you ever noticed how surprised—or even offended—people are by the inclusiveness of Jesus in the New Testament? This, of course, was the subject of debate and consternation on the part of the Pharisees toward Jesus: "We don't understand why you eat with sinners and tax collectors"; "We don't understand why you are touching lepers"; "We don't understand why you are healing people on the Sabbath." The large, inclusive heart of Jesus regularly offended the hearts of the Pharisees. Sadly, his welcoming heart didn't just offend the Pharisees; it offended his own disciples. They found him talking to a Samaritan woman and were offended. Jesus welcomed children who the disciples thought should be excluded.[9]

But the challenge of Jesus' inclusive heart did not stop with his resurrection and ascension. In the book of Acts, Peter was offended by the Lord's direction to take the gospel to the Gentiles (Acts 10). The believers in Jerusalem struggled with how to integrate Gentiles into the church (Acts 15). It is a rare and precious thing when a disciple has the heart of Barnabas—a Jewish Levite—who was able to transcend his own culture. When Barnabas visited the multicultural church in Antioch and "saw what the grace of God had done, he was glad and encouraged them all to remain true to the Lord with all their hearts. He was a good man, full of the Holy Spirit and faith, and a great number of people were brought to the Lord" (Acts 11:23-24).

Personal relationships. Let's look at some specific ways that we can be intentional about diversity. First of all, we must be intentional about our personal relationships. We must ask ourselves, "How many of my ten closest friends are of a race different from mine?" "How many people of a different race have I invited over to dinner in the last six months?" "Have I ever gone out to a movie with a friend or a couple who is racially different than me?"

Illustrations. We must also become intentional regarding the illustrations we use when speaking. As a preacher, I deliberately include examples of great African American heroes in my sermon illustrations. Our church is intentional about who is represented in our graphics, videos and church announcements. When people look at a photo, they are asking, perhaps subconsciously, "Is there someone who looks like me in this picture?" In our videos we don't just have white leaders serving black clients; we show blacks and Hispanics praying for whites. The poor in our videos are not just people of color but are often white.

Goal setting. We have been very intentional in setting goals. One of our goals was to have our congregation reflect the diversity of our city. By the grace of God, we reached this goal in 2009! Having begun as an entirely white church with about 4 percent of its members being people of color, 33 percent of Vineyard Columbus is now of a nonmajority race. We look like our community in central Ohio.

Hiring and leadership development. We have also become intentional in our hiring and leadership development. As a leadership team, we have made a commitment to hire new staff only if there is a person of color in the interview pool. We have achieved this, with only the rarest exception. If we have to keep a job posting open for months in order to find a qualified minority candidate to interview, so be it! Our goal is that our church's leadership team reflects the church's demographics.

CARING FOR IMMIGRANTS

Intentionality about diversity is not simply about creating a multiracial church; it is about creating a multinational church. I have become convinced from Scripture that advocacy on behalf of immigrants is a Christian duty. Throughout Scripture, God urges the nation of Israel to love three groups: widows, orphans and aliens. Deuteronomy says, "For the LORD your God is God of gods and Lord of lords, the great God, mighty and awesome, who shows no partiality and accepts no bribes. He defends the cause of the fatherless and the widow, and loves the foreigner residing among you, giving them food and clothing. And you are to love those who are foreigners, for you yourselves were foreigners in Egypt" (Deuteronomy 10:17-19). The first application of the Great Commandment to love your neighbor as yourself is the call to Israel to love immigrants. We also read, "When a foreigner resides among you in your land, do not mistreat them. The foreigner residing among you must be treated as your native-born. Love them as yourself, for you were foreigners in Egypt. I am the LORD your God" (Leviticus 19:33-34).

Our forebears in the faith were refugees. Abram journeyed to Egypt because there was a famine in the land and he and his family needed to find food (Genesis 12:10). Isaac moved to the land of the Philistines because of a famine, and Jacob and his family moved to Egypt because of a famine in the Promised Land (Genesis 26:1; 47:1-12). The story of Ruth is a story of refugees who moved across national borders to survive. Ruth is also a wonderful story of the care and hospitality provided to an immigrant by Boaz, an ancestor of King David. Joseph, Mary and the child Jesus were political refugees who escaped the murderous troops sent by Herod the Great to kill the baby boys born in Bethlehem (Matthew 2:16-21).

Throughout the Bible, God gives an enormous amount of instruction to the people of Israel concerning how to treat immigrants. Jesus tells Christians that the way we treat immigrants is the way we treat him. In Matthew 25, Jesus tells about the king who is judging the nations, and this king says to those who are being judged, "I was a stranger and you invited me in." Confused by this statement, they ask the king, "When did we see you a stranger and invite you in?" To which the king replies, "Truly, I tell you, whatever you did for one of the least of these brothers and sisters of mine, you did for me" (Matthew 25:35, 38, 40).[10]

Our congregation became convinced from Scripture and from listening to the stories of immigrants in our city and at our church that we need to intentionally welcome the stranger. We do so by offering English as a Second Language (ESL) classes and citizenship classes in our community center. We have multiple fellowship groups for West Africans, East Africans, Hispanics, Hungarians and Filipinos. We work diligently to resettle refugees, and we advocate for comprehensive immigration reform in the political arena. Once every month, our communion meditation is read in another language to remind us that the cross of Christ breaks down dividing walls between ethnolinguistic groups. Congregations that are serious about multinational diversity will put together intentional plans to welcome immigrants into their midst.

OVERCOMING SELFISHNESS

We must be intentional about the way we do worship at our weekend services. Being intentionally inclusive of racially diverse people and worship styles is challenging because we all have a tendency to be selfish. Most people come together on Sunday morning and ask the question, "What am I getting out of worship? How can I personally connect with God and personally experience his blessing?" Most people do not ask the question, "How accessible is this worship experience to my neighbor? How edifying is this to the seeker?" Most people approach worship and God in a very selfish way. We act as if we mean, "*My* Father, who is in heaven" instead of "*Our* Father, who is in heaven."

One way to overcome selfishness is to keep in mind the difference between private and public worship experiences. In private, I am free to sing my favorite songs and to adopt whatever worship posture I desire. I can lie on the floor, or get on my knees, or dance around the room, or jump up and down or shout in tongues. But in public, the apostle Paul calls us to be concerned about edifying and loving our brothers and sisters (1 Corinthians 14). Love is interested in accommodating other people. Love goes beyond asking, "What do *I* like?" or "What do *I* prefer?" or even "Where and in what style of worship have *I* met God in the past?" Love asks, "What would be most helpful in drawing more people—and different kinds of people—into a deep connection with Jesus Christ?" Love is concerned with concepts like accessibility and welcome. Love rolls out the red carpet of welcome to others.

When worshiping with a diversity of cultures, you round out your picture of discipleship. In suburban churches, for example, many songs focus on certain psychological or emotional benefits of knowing Jesus Christ. Those in suburban churches sing little about overcoming death, heaven, pain in this life and disappointment. But singing songs that come from cultures that have known the underside of life can round out our picture of discipleship. A song with words such as, "God is so good. God is so good. God is so good. He's so good to me!" is going to be understood differently in a suburban community than in an inner-city community. In a suburban community, we likely think about God's blessings to us materially: the gifts of our families, jobs and homes. But God's goodness also involves breaking free from addiction, getting out of prison, having a roof over our heads and being there for us when we go through trials.

We have three options regarding our approach to diversity in worship. First, we can require *uniformity*: the majority culture can say that "our one size has to fit all." Since the majority rules, the minorities can be forced to assimilate into the majority culture. Second, we can have *bedlam*, in which we break into tribes and groups. Each of the groups can get a representative vote and a certain percentage of the worship time can be devoted to each style. Third, we can forge a *worship style that uniquely reflects the particular people that the church is called to reach.* This third option, I believe, ought to be the goal of every church. This option will require tons of prayer from the church's leadership and from the church's worship teams. Inclusive love is never easy!

THE BODY OF CHRIST

Paul says in Romans 12:4-5, "For just as each of us has one body with many members, and these members do not all have the same function, so in Christ we, though many, form one body, and each member belongs to all the others."

What is the church? The church is not a building with a steeple on top and a cemetery out back. That building may house the church, but the metaphor the apostle Paul uses often to describe the church is a body. If you want to teach your children to understand the church properly, don't tell them to put their fingers together and say, "Here is the church. Here is the steeple. Look inside and see all the people!" According to Paul's thinking, you should tell your child to stand in front of a mirror and look at her or his body. See: you have a head, arms, fingers, a trunk, legs, feet and toes. Your body is a picture of the church. We are one body, but we have many parts. We are one church, but we are made up of people of many different cultural backgrounds and gifts. We are not a church of just noses and arms; we all need each other, in all our intercultural diversity, to be the church that God intends us to be!

5

What Is Our Concern?

MERCY . . .

Jeanine and Tom (not their real names) are a Haitian couple who came to our church a few years ago. They came to the United States legally from Haiti and for many years lived in New York City, where both of them worked at various jobs. While in New York, Jeanine and Tom had three children. By no means were they well off, but they were able to provide for their family and were grateful to live in the United States.

In order to legally remain in the United States, Jeanine needed to have her visa renewed. She paid an attorney five thousand dollars to handle her visa renewal application and then heard nothing from the attorney for a year. Jeanine and Tom had friends in Columbus and decided that it would be wise for their family to move to a less expensive place than New York. So Jeanine and Tom packed up their three children and their few belongings and moved to Ohio. While in Ohio, they scraped together two thousand dollars, which constituted the last of their savings, to pay an Ohio attorney to look into Jeanine's visa application. They discovered that their New York attorney had done absolutely nothing on Jeanine's case other than to cash her check.

One day, while the three children were in school and Tom was at work, Jeanine was arrested by officials of the Immigration and Natural-ization Service (INS) and deported back to Port-au-Prince. To make a bad situation even worse, after Jeanine was deported, the major earthquake hit Haiti, killing over 300,000 people and injuring countless others. Tom and his children didn't hear from Jeanine for months and didn't know whether she was alive or dead. When they were finally able to get in touch with her, they discovered that she had been severely injured in the earthquake. Because of current American law, Jeanine has virtually no chance of being reunited with her family again.[1] Tom recently showed up at our congregation's free legal clinic, desperately asking for help.

What is a Christian's responsibility to a family like this? What would you do? What would your church do?

Here's another true story. The Mbutu family—Mike, Nancy (not their real names) and their six children—are refugees from the Republic of the Congo who recently relocated to the Columbus area. Mike had been tortured severely in his home country and had many medical issues that limited his ability to work and to provide for his family. Nancy was pregnant and could not afford any prenatal care. Mike spoke no English, and the family had no ability to connect with social service agencies. The Mbutu family lived in a cramped, two-bedroom apartment in our city. Mike had stacks of documents to sort through in order to determine the family's current social service supports and needs. Not knowing what to do, he came to our church for help.

What is the Christian responsibility to people like Mike and Nancy? What would you do to help them? What would your church do?

WHAT IS MERCY?

Jesus told his followers, "Be merciful, just as your Father is merciful" (Luke 6:36). What does it mean to be merciful? "Mercy" is a translation of the Hebrew word *rahamim*, which is derived from the same root as *rehem*, meaning "womb." It communicates the deep feeling of a mother toward the child of her womb.

In describing this Hebrew word *rahamim*, a friend told me about the miscarriage of his baby. His wife was five months into her pregnancy when their son died. One evening after the miscarriage, my friend came home and found his wife sitting on their bed, weeping. He put his arm around her and tried to comfort her. Not knowing what to say, my friend said to his wife, "It will be okay, honey. We can have another child." She pushed him away and screamed, "I don't want another baby! I wanted this baby! This was my baby!" Mercy is the internal and even visceral response of a mother for the child of her womb.

Theologian Karl Barth describes *mercy* with the phrase, "the personal God has a heart."[2] One Greek word in the New Testament that is translated "have pity" or "feel sympathy" is *splanchnizomia*. It derives from the word *splanchna*, which means "the inward parts" or "entrails," especially the heart, lungs, liver, spleen and kidneys. It is used to describe the feeling that Jesus had at the sight of profound human suffering and need. Mercy is a visceral feeling of pity.

In general, we don't get deep feelings of mercy toward *issues*. Feelings are evoked by *people in need*. The abstract problem of teen drug abuse doesn't evoke feelings of mercy. But when your son, the child of your womb, falls in with a bad crowd and begins to take drugs, your heart goes out to him. The abstract problem of teen pregnancy doesn't evoke feelings of mercy. But when fifteen-year-old Dawn, whom you've watched being shuttled between foster homes and her family during her childhood, shows up at church with her baby and proudly exclaims, "Look, I'm a mama!" it is not hard to feel mercy.

But mercy in the Bible is more than feelings. Let's consider some of the attributes of mercy.

MERCY IS COMPASSION IN ACTION

Mercy is more than feelings, and it is also more than talk. It is easy to be deceived that we are fulfilling Jesus' command to be merciful as our heavenly Father is merciful because we have talked about the plight of the poor. It is not mercy to simply do a Bible study about "the poor" for ten weeks. Nor is it mercy to talk about the sources of poverty, to share statistics on homelessness in one's community or to compare American poverty with global poverty and suggest that the American poor are really doing quite well, relatively speaking. It is not mercy to consider the effects of the welfare system on the poor or to discuss how people may be misusing food stamps. Discussion, debate, argument or filling the air with piles of words until we all get hoarse is not mercy.

So what is mercy? The best biblical picture of mercy is the figure of the good Samaritan in Jesus' parable in Luke 10. We read that the Samaritan *took pity* and then *acted decisively* to help the wounded traveler on the roadside. It was his action that demonstrated mercy. Jesus concludes this parable by asking, "'Which of these three do you think was a neighbor to the man who fell into the hands of robbers?' The expert in the law replied, *'The one who had mercy on him.'* Jesus told him, *'Go and do likewise'*" (Luke 10:36-37).

MERCY IS MUNDANE ACTION

Mercy is not only compassion in action; mercy is often *mundane action*. We are awed by special talents—the amazing capacity to play an instrument or sing or preach or play professional sports. We are dazzled by great spiritual gifting—by someone's ability to teach or prophesy or lead a movement. But in Matthew 25, Jesus describes the people who are going to inherit the kingdom. He suggests that people will inherit the kingdom because they did six things: "For I was hungry and *you gave me something to eat,* I was thirsty and *you gave me something to drink,* I was a stranger and *you invited me in,* I needed clothes and *you clothed me,* I was sick and *you looked after me,* I was in prison and *you came to visit me*" (Matthew 25:35-36).[3]

Notice what Jesus didn't say. He didn't say, "The basis upon which I'm going to judge the reality of your faith is whether you raised someone from the dead at least one time." Nor does he ask whether you prophesied in church or whether God ever used you to heal a terrible disease. And notice that the activities in Jesus' list are accessible to virtually everyone in the world. You don't need special training to feed someone who is hungry; you don't need a seminary degree to give your lunch away.

It is all very mundane and very simple. If you see someone who is hungry, give them your lunch. No training is required! You don't need to be a millionaire to go to a McDonald's to buy a couple of hamburgers for a hungry man who is standing on the street corner. And you don't need dazzling spiritual gifts to sit in a hospital room with someone who is sick. Just about anyone of any age can visit with an elderly, sick relative in a nursing home. One can be three years old and visit a great-grandmother.

Consider the various activities that mothers and fathers do to take care of their children: they feed the hungry, clothe the naked and sit with the sick. Showing mercy is what moms and dads do all the time. They are mundane acts. Jesus simply teaches that *we should extend these mundane acts of mercy to people outside of our families.*

Over the past twenty years, there has been a great politicization of the family. It has become commonplace for some groups to label themselves as "pro-family" and to label other groups as "anti-family." But here is an interesting thought regarding mercy. What if Jesus didn't want the pro-family crowd to be pro-*just-our-own*-families? What if Jesus wanted pro-family people to include *other people's families* in our sphere of concern? What if the mundane things I do for my family—providing shelter, food, clean water and access to health care when my family members are sick—I tried to do for other families as well?

Historically, Christian churches have practiced what have been called the "seven corporal works of mercy."[4] They have fed the hungry, given drink to the thirsty, clothed the naked, sheltered the homeless, visited the sick and prisoners, ransomed captives and buried the dead. Showing mercy to those both outside of one's family *and* outside of one's church has been the practice of the church throughout history.

MERCY IS GIVING PEOPLE WHAT THEY DON'T DESERVE

God doesn't give us what we deserve but what we *don't* deserve. God does not consume us in his wrath, but instead he consumes his wrath on himself by becoming our substitute, paying for our sins and giving us the gift of salvation. The world is an unmerciful place. "You've made your bed, now lie in it" is the world's motto. Mercy demonstrates that a new world order has broken in through Christ. Over and over again, Jesus, quoting the prophet Hosea, says, "Go and learn what this means: 'I desire mercy, not sacrifice'" (Hosea 6:6; Matthew 9:13). The kingdom of God is all about mercy.

Mother Teresa once told this story.

> At a seminary in Bangalore a nun once said to me, "Mother Teresa, you are spoiling the poor people by giving them things free. They are losing their human dignity."
>
> When everyone was quiet, I said calmly, "No one spoils as much as God himself. See the wonderful gifts he has given us freely. All of you here have no glasses, yet you can see. If God were to take money for your sight, what would happen? Continually we are breathing and living on oxygen that we do not pay for. What would happen if God were to say, 'If you work four hours, you will get sunshine for two hours?' How many of us would survive then?"
>
> Then I also told them, "There are many congregations that spoil the rich; *it is good to have one congregation in the name of the poor, to spoil the poor.*" There was a profound silence. Nobody said a word after that.[5]

Individuals and churches are often concerned that someone may be abusing their charity. Certainly, we want to not only love much but "love appropriately. You need to use your head and test your feelings so that your love is sincere and intelligent, not sentimental gush" (Philippians 1:9-11 *The Message*). For example, I rarely give a homeless man cash, because of the possibility that he may simply use it to buy drugs or alcohol. But I do occasionally ask if I can buy him a meal. We don't want to create huge disincentives for people in helping themselves or their own families. Nevertheless, the inclination of our hearts ought to be like Mother Teresa—and like God, who in mercy regularly gives people what they don't deserve.

MERCY INVOLVES RISK

If you are going to show mercy, you will put something at risk. You potentially will lose money, time, health or reputation. Giving people what they don't deserve will always be in tension with conventional wisdom. Mercy is not the ordinary counsel that most investment advisors will give you. It is the rare investment advisor who will say: "Of course you will want to risk half of all of your assets because that's what needs to be available to show mercy to others; let's set aside most of your pension for acts of mercy."

Mercy doesn't fit with what our families might expect. "You are in your fifties and you are going to bring into your home a foster child because she needs you? Are you crazy?" "You have three children and you're going to adopt a child from where? Where in the world is Namibia?"

The good Samaritan takes a risk simply by drawing near to the man who is lying on the roadside. What if it's all a setup? What if this "victim" is just pretending and has friends hiding in the bushes? I might get mugged if I stop to help this guy. Not only is there a physical risk to showing mercy; there is a risk to the Samaritan's reputation and even to his freedom. He could have thought, "I'm a Samaritan. If I take this beaten Jew to a Jewish town, they may accuse me of doing this. I may be arrested. I may be held responsible."[6]

It is impossible to show mercy without taking a risk. In other words, *mercy makes us vulnerable.* We become vulnerable to being taken advantage of and to being hurt. But isn't this risk-taking vulnerability precisely what Jesus modeled when he showed mercy to us?

MERCY DOESN'T REQUIRE A CROWD

What difference can one person make regarding injustice in this world? A few years ago Jim Hicks, a man in our church, woke up in the middle of the night with a sense that God was speaking to him. A few words formed in his mind: *thirst* and *pure water*. He felt like the Lord was speaking to him about starting an organization to fight injustice and bring health to people around the world. He wrote down these words—

thirst and *pure water*—and went back to sleep. The next day he began to do some research and learned about the world's water crisis. He learned that over one billion people in the world don't have access to clean water.

So Jim decided to do something about it, using what I call the "triple-A method" of making a difference in the world. First he became *aware* that there was a need. Then he *appealed* to God. And then he took *action*. He started a little organization called Thirst Relief. Working with some other folks, he built a filter for water that could be used anywhere in the world. In the last few years, they have learned to manufacture this type of filter at a very low cost, and they have given the filters to missionaries in different places of the world. Thirst Relief has brought clean water to twenty thousand people in the last few years.

MERCY TODAY

To end this chapter, let me tell you what happened to the Mbutu family, the Congolese refugees who came to our church for help. It became immediately apparent that many people in our church needed to partner together to "show mercy" to this family. Our Value Life Ministry, which is our pro-life ministry, supplied the family with grocery cards, baby supplies and diapers for three of their children. One of our pastors facilitated multiple group meetings with key leaders and the family to coordinate efforts to get the family stabilized and acclimated to life in central Ohio. The leadership of the family's small group adopted the family by providing meals, transportation, companionship, discipleship and childcare. They threw the family a huge baby shower and cared for the children when Nancy went into the hospital to deliver her baby. They even drove her to the hospital and remained with her. While Nancy was in labor, Mike suffered a seizure, a side effect of past torture that he had endured, and he ended up in intensive care. The group continued to love and care for this family as they recovered.

A church member has continued to assist Mike in working with a social worker on our church staff to access various social service assistance programs. Mike has learned English and now calls the social worker himself to provide family updates or requests for additional support. Mike has also earned a driver's permit and has learned to independently navigate the public bus system, which is not an easy task. He called us recently to inform us that he and his family moved to a bigger apartment with the help of their small group. The new residence is closer to a bus line, which will assist the family in becoming more self-sufficient. He also shared that his wife is now in ESL classes and is learning to speak English. Physically, Mike still struggles, but he repeatedly gives thanks for his brothers and sisters in Christ at the Vineyard.

We will continue to extend mercy to Mike, Nancy and everyone else lying by the side of the road whom we come across. We will feed them, give them shelter, care for them and love them as Christ loved us. Our responsibility does not end there, however. We will do everything in our power to bring about change not just in the individual but also in the system.

And what about Jeanine, the Haitian woman who was permanently separated from her family and deported to Haiti, having been cheated by her New York attorneys? Jeanine cannot be reunited with her husband and children by acts of mercy alone. The sick and broken American immigration system needs to be changed to bring this Haitian wife and mother back from Haiti. In Jeanine's case, our church needed to do justice: to advocate for sweeping immigration law changes that would provide an earned pathway to citizenship for Jeanine and millions like her.[7] Justice is the subject of the next chapter.

6

What Is Our Concern?

. . . AND JUSTICE

Robert Mugabe took over Zimbabwe following the collapse of the white-ruled government in 1980, and he held on to power for more than three decades. Initially, his own people and other African leaders hailed him as a great advocate for social justice and for peaceful transition to black rule. In fact, many considered Robert Mugabe to be similar to Nelson Mandela: not only a governmental leader but a moral and spiritual leader.

Unfortunately, Mugabe turned out to be nothing like Mandela. He drained the Zimbabwean treasury to purchase luxury items for himself and Grace, his former secretary who is now his wife and who is forty-one years his junior. Grace is infamous for her extravagant shopping sprees in Paris. Mugabe purchased new limousines while the citizens of his country literally starved to death. This dictator wrecked the country's economy so that the inflation rate in Zimbabwe at one point exceeded 11,000 percent! (In the United States, we get upset if the inflation rate goes above 4 percent.) In Zimbabwe, prices on goods changed twice daily. When the few wealthy men in the country played golf, they purchased their drinks at the beginning of the golf outing because by the time they got through playing eighteen holes, the price of the drinks had doubled. Mugabe surrounded himself with thousands of secret police who were feared throughout the country because of their brutal methods of torture and murder. In one particularly cold-hearted act, Mugabe sent his men out to bulldoze the shacks of 700,000 squatters scattered throughout the country. The campaign to knock down the squatter shacks was cruelly called "Take Out the Trash."

Mugabe amassed more and more land for himself. Using his secret police, he went to the farms of white landowners and seized the land for his own private possession. Then, out of the government treasury, he hired government workers to build roads to his newly seized farms and to work the farms for his own personal enrichment. Along with Mugabe's violence and suppression of all political and religious opposition, he abused power through the unjust taking for himself of property that belonged to others.

Frederick Douglass, the great American social reformer and leader of the abolitionist movement, said, "Where justice is denied, where poverty is enforced, where ignorance prevails, and where any one class is made to feel that society is an organized conspiracy to oppress, rob, and degrade them, neither persons, nor property will be safe."[1]

WHAT IS INJUSTICE?

When we say that something is unjust, what are we talking about? In one of the most moving books that I've read in recent years, *Good News About Injustice*, Gary Haugen, the president of International Justice Mission, writes, "Injustice occurs when power is misused to take from others what God has given them, namely, their life, dignity, liberty or the fruits of their love and labor."[2] In other words, injustice is fundamentally about an abuse of power.

World Vision, a Christian relief agency, introduced Haugen to a ten-year-old girl named Kanmani in India. From eight in the morning until six o'clock at night, six days a week, Kanmani sits in the same place on the floor at a factory that manufactures cigarettes. Her job is to close the ends of the cigarettes with a little knife. She is required to complete two thousand cigarettes a day; if she doesn't work fast enough, her overseer hits her over the head with a club. Her ten-hour work day is broken up by a single thirty-minute lunch period. At the end of a long work week, she receives her wages. And what does this girl earn for working ten hours a day, six days a week? She earns seventy-five cents. Kanmani has worked at this job for five years, since she was five years old.

Kanmani is a bonded laborer, which means she is forced to work to pay off a family debt. In a moment of economic crisis, her family borrowed fifty dollars. But to secure the loan, Kanmani's parents agreed to send her to work for the moneylender. By the terms of the agreement, the entire debt has to be paid off in a lump sum, but the family is never able to put fifty dollars together at one time. They need Kanmani's seventy-five cents a week to survive. All the while, the moneylender makes thousands of dollars off this little girl.

What is injustice? It is the abuse of power. God gives each of us power, but it is to be exercised in the way that God exercises power. God exercises power on behalf of the weak and to lift people up, heal people and reconcile marriages. God uses power to give and to bless, but the unjust use their power to take from the weak.

WHAT DOES THE LORD REQUIRE OF US?

Richard Stearns, in *The Hole in Our Gospel*, writes, "Being a Christian, or a follower of Jesus Christ, requires much more than just having a *personal* and transforming relationship with God. It also entails a *public* and transforming relationship with the world."[3]

In one of the most famous verses in the Bible, the prophet Micah tells us, "He has shown all you people what is good. And what does the LORD require of you? To act justly and to love mercy and to walk humbly with your God" (Micah 6:8 TNIV). Micah was the last of the four great eighth-century B.C. prophets. The other three were Amos, Hosea and Isaiah. Commentators have noted that in this one verse, Micah summarized the three great themes of the prophets Amos, Hosea and Isaiah. Amos urged Israel to do justice. Hosea spoke about loving mercy (better translated as "having steadfast love"). And Isaiah spoke about the importance of the quiet faith of a humble walk with God. Micah, being the last in the line of the prophets, underlined for the people of Israel what they had been hearing for a century: act justly, love mercy and walk humbly with God!

But how does "doing justice" add to what churches and Christians generally do in showing mercy?

The typical Christian church feeds hungry people either through its own food pantry or by working with other churches and nonprofits in giving food away to hungry people. Running soup kitchens, giving away Christmas dinners and donating money to feed the hungry are all common activities for churches and for individual Christians. It is the rare church that doesn't have a hospital visitation ministry or a visitation ministry to nursing homes and shut-ins. Likewise, it is common for Christians to be involved in prison ministry, to volunteer time at a homeless shelter, to help build houses with Habitat for Humanity and to give money to relief agencies for sheltering those who have been left homeless after a natural disaster. Many refugee resettlement agencies are run by Christians, and it is common for Christians to assist international students to feel at home while they study in our country. The world would be an infinitely harsher place without the abundance of Christian acts of mercy. So why must we be concerned with justice as well?

In recent years, some vocal people on the conservative right in America have severely critiqued doing justice. Glenn Beck, an American conservative radio talk show host and political commentator, said this to his listeners: "I beg you, look for the words 'social justice' or 'economic justice' on your church's website. If you find it, run as fast as you can. Social justice and economic justice, they are code words. Now, am I advising people to leave their church? . . . Yes, leave your church! Social justice and economic justice. They are code words. If you have a priest that is pushing social justice, go find another parish."[4] Beck went on to claim that "social justice" was the rallying cry of both the Nazis and the communists, because both wanted totalitarian government.

Beck is not the only critic of social justice. On her radio show, Sandy Rios critiqued Wheaton College, one of America's premier evangelical institutions, for embracing "anti-American" and "pro-Marxist" theories under the guise of social justice. The show focused on a Wheaton education department document that included phrases such as "social justice" and "becoming an agent of change." In a response, Wheaton College provost Stan Jones said that the Rios show quotes "significantly misrepresented how social justice is addressed at Wheaton College." He continued: "We equip our students to think carefully and biblically about issues of justice, and encourage them to commit to act justly through their lives as defined by a biblical worldview. . . . There is an enormous difference between recognizing as a justice issue of concern to God the tragic state of so many rural school systems and inner-city school systems that serve disproportionately minority constituencies, on the one hand, and a radical, naturalistically-driven call for a Marxist redistribution of wealth on the other."[5]

If God teaches us to act justly, then why is there such a negative reaction from people—especially from some who claim to be Christians—when we talk about justice? Obviously, talking about justice touches something deep in our hearts. Because there is much confusion around the word *justice*, and because some Christians are afraid to uphold the biblical command to "do justice," let's discuss exactly what justice is. What did God command us to do through the prophet Micah?

JUSTICE IS GIVING PEOPLE THEIR DUE

Christian philosopher Nicholas Wolterstorff said "Justice is present among persons, groups and institutions when their rights, their legitimate claims, are honored."[6]

But what is a person's due? Some people argue that justice only demands that procedures be fair. Thus, the fourteenth amendment to the United States Constitution requires states to give individuals "due process." Due process includes such things as having an impartial arbiter who makes the final decision, the right to adequate notice of a proceeding, the right to present evidence on one's own behalf and often the right to counsel. But are individuals due more than just, fair procedures in court or from our government? Does justice also require the just distribution of food, shelter, healthcare, money and goods and services necessary to sustain life?

According to the Old Testament prophets, "doing justice" includes more than providing fair courts and fair procedures for litigants. It certainly includes impartial judicial proceedings (see Exodus 23:1-3, 6-8 and Leviticus 19:15), but justice concerns economic justice as well. We read in Deuteronomy, "He [God] defends the cause of the fatherless and the widow, and loves the foreigner residing among you, *giving them food and clothing*" (Deuteronomy 10:18). And Isaiah condemns the injustice of his people, in which some selfishly grab everything for themselves and others are left with nothing. Thus, we read,

He [God] looked for justice, but saw bloodshed;
　　for righteousness, but heard cries of distress.

Woe to you who add house to house
　　and join field to field
till no space is left
　　and you live alone in the land. (Isaiah 5:7-8)

Providing people with the basic necessities to sustain life is rooted in the biblical principle that every person is made in God's image and likeness and is, therefore, endowed with inalienable dignity. This is true regardless of who we are, where we were born or what we have accomplished (Genesis 1:26-27). As the United States Conference of Catholic Bishops stated: "[In light of our creation] we are called to treat all people—especially those who are suffering—with respect, compassion, and justice."[7] Our private "ownership" of property is relative, because "the earth is the LORD's and everything in it, the world, and all who live in it" (Psalm 24:1). Because everything ultimately belongs to God and not to individuals, corporations or governments, God demands as an act of "justice" (as opposed to "charity") that every individual be given *access to the means of production*. So in ancient Israel, God gave every single family a plot of land so that every family could earn a living. According to the extraordinary principle of Jubilee, if a family lost its land because of the death of the father, negligence, physical handicap or some other cause, every fifty years the land was returned to its original owners or their descendants (Leviticus 25). In God's just economy, no family would be permanently denied access to the means of production.

How can it be just to take property from the wealthy—those who, in our economy, would be labeled the "most productive"—and give it back to the poor people who had lost it—and who, in our economy, would be labeled the "least productive"? God's justification is this: "The land must not be sold permanently, *because the land is mine* and you reside in my land as foreigners and strangers" (Leviticus 25:23).

How might the Jubilee principle apply to a modern economy? Today land is generally not the means of accessing the basic necessities of life such as food, clothing, clean water and shelter. Rather, a good education is one way of accessing resources. Likewise, having adequate healthcare is essential in giving people the opportunity to become productive. Might justice in the twenty-first century demand that individuals have the opportunity to receive basic healthcare and a solid, publicly supported education so that access to the means of production is maintained?[8]

JUSTICE IS NAMING THINGS CORRECTLY

Through the prophet Isaiah, God pronounced a woe on those who deliberately misname things.

> Woe to those who call evil good
>   and good evil,
> who put darkness for light
>   and light for darkness,

who put bitter for sweet
  and sweet for bitter. (Isaiah 5:20)

One of the characteristics of the totalitarian state ruled by Big Brother in George Orwell's novel 1984 was its regular mislabeling of things. Orwell's totalitarian empire had four ministries housed in huge pyramids. The ministry called the Ministry of Peace was responsible for conducting the country's ongoing wars. Its Ministry of Plenty rationed and controlled food and goods. The Ministry of Truth was the propaganda arm of the regime and controlled information and rewrote history. Finally, the Ministry of Love was responsible for identifying, arresting and torturing dissidents. The three slogans of the regime were: War Is Peace; Freedom Is Slavery; Ignorance Is Strength.[9]

Injustice is often perpetuated through the constant misuse of language. The Nazis put the slogan *"Arbeit Macht Frei"*—"Work Will Set You Free"—over the Auschwitz concentration camp. Even the term *concentration camp* rather than *death camp* was designed to cover up the truth. The Nazis talked about the "Final Solution" rather than the extermination of Jews. Their policy of "relocating Jews" was a cover-up for killing Jews.

We perpetrate injustice whenever we call things by the wrong names. It is injustice when we call all Muslims "terrorists," when we call the poor "lazy" and when we call those who grab a disproportionate share of wealth for themselves "successful" or "job creators." It is injustice when we call those who oppose war "un-American" or "unpatriotic," when we call pro-life people "anti-choice" and when we call environmentalists "tree-huggers." It is injustice when children born outside of wedlock are called "illegitimate." Whenever a government, corporation, political campaign, marketing company, church or individual engages in doublespeak, injustice is likely being covered up.

JUSTICE DEALS WITH ROOT CAUSES

When you feed hungry people, you are showing mercy. The search for justice begins when you ask *why* the hungry are hungry. The late Harvie

Conn, in distinguishing between charity and justice, asked, "What will the instrument of the church be in affecting . . . change? Not simply charity, but also justice. Charity is episodic, justice is ongoing. One brings consolation, the other correction. One aims at symptoms, the other at causes. One changes individuals, the other societies."[10]

Ron Sider has often distinguished between mercy (or charity) and justice by telling a story:

A group of devout Christians once lived in a small village at the foot of a mountain. A winding, slippery road with hairpin curves and steep precipices wound its way up one side of the mountain and down the other. There were no guardrails, and fatal accidents were frequent. The Christians in the village's three churches decided to act. They pooled their resources and purchased an ambulance so they could rush the injured to the hospital in the next town. Week after week, church volunteers gave faithfully, even sacrificially, of their time to operate the ambulance twenty-four hours a day. They saved many lives, although some victims remained crippled for life.

One day a visitor came to town. Puzzled, he asked why they did not close the road over the mountain and build a tunnel instead. Startled, the ambulance volunteers quickly pointed out that this approach, though technically possible, was not realistic or advisable. After all, the narrow mountain road had been there for a long time. Besides, the mayor would bitterly oppose the idea. (He owned a large restaurant and service station halfway up the mountain.)

The visitor was shocked that the mayor's economic interests mattered more to these Christians than the many human casualties. Somewhat hesitantly, he suggested that perhaps the churches ought to speak to the mayor. After all, he was an elder in the oldest church in town. Perhaps they should even elect a different mayor if he proved stubborn and unconcerned.

Now the Christians were shocked. With rising indignation and righteous conviction they informed the young radical that the church dare not become involved in politics. The church is called to preach the gospel and give a cup of cold water, they said. Its mission is not to dabble in worldly things like changing social and political structures.

Perplexed and bitter, the visitor left. As he wandered out of the village, one question churned in his muddled mind. Is it really more spiritual, he wondered, to operate ambulances that pick up the bloody victims of destructive social structures than to try to change the structures themselves?[11]

People need both mercy and justice. When we serve people by providing them with medical or dental or vision care at our two free medical clinics, those are acts of mercy. When we start to ask the "why" questions—as in "Why don't people have the ability to get medical care at a reasonable price in our country?" or "Why are there so many uninsured people?"—then we are dealing with issues of justice.

A pastor in a suburban community wrote to me and said, "Rich, you talk a lot about justice and racial diversity in your sermons. I've been listening to your messages for years. But our church is in a wealthy suburb outside of the city and, frankly, we don't have much racial diversity in our church. So we've decided to concentrate on age diversity. We want to have a mix of people of different ages in our church. Isn't age diversity sufficient?"

I wrote back to this young pastor and said:

Yes. I think that God does want age diversity in church. Young people need spiritual parents and spiritual grandparents. There is something wrong with the way the contemporary church has been organized according to age-specific groupings and age-specific churches. We need each other. Older people need the idealism, energy and innovation of the young. And young people need the wisdom, experience and counsel of the old. We need each other. Nevertheless, age diversity is not enough. We also need to be around people who are very different than us. The body of Christ should be a visible sign to the world of what the future kingdom of God is going to look like. People need to see evidence now of what it will look like when the Lord returns. That's what the church is meant to be. People should look at the church and say, "Okay, I get it! One day, the human race will be reconciled before the throne of God. I get it. Red and yellow, black and white, all are precious in his sight. Jesus loves the little children of the world. I get it. I see it in the church!"

So I pressed this young pastor, "How radical do you want to be in making your church an outpost of the kingdom of God? How far do you want to go?" I continued,

One thing you could do is begin to build a bridge of friendship with an inner-city pastor with whom you share common values. There are many churches in the city that would value a friendship with a suburban church. Many city churches are facing tough situations. Church members often have relatives in prison. Many churches often have a hard time fixing the furnace or the leaking roof of the church building. People in your church need the faith and vibrancy of the church in the city. Friendship with a city church could be exactly what your church needs and what an inner-city church needs.

I continued, "But if you want to be still more radical, you need to ask 'Why?'"

Why is your community 99.9 percent white? Asking this question may lead to the discovery of some very uncomfortable truths. For example, your community zoning requires three- to five-acre plots for home building. On the surface, requiring three- to five-acre plots may seem racially neutral, but these zoning laws exclude the poor, who are disproportionately brown and black. Do you want to lead your church to fight against the zoning commission? You also might want to explore your community's racial history. Have the banks historically loaned money to people of color? Did realtors steer African Americans away from your community? What can you do to push your community to create some lower-income housing?"

Asking the "why" questions force us to deal with how far we are willing to go to do justice.

JUSTICE DEALS WITH SYSTEMS

One of the least understood areas in the evangelical church is what theologians call *institutional sin*: sin that goes beyond any individual and that is bigger than any one person. A spider web is a great illustration of institutional sin. Institutional sin is systemic sin: sin that affects an entire system. Let me illustrate systemic sin by a true story from our church.

Jane (not her real name) was a member in our church. By all outward appearances, Jane's family was normal. They were a bright, middle-class, attractive family. But this family was anything but normal.

Jane's mother beat Jane severely when she was a child, and her father regularly gave her the silent treatment even though she did well in school while her two siblings used drugs, cut classes and stole from stores. "I always felt like an unwelcome guest in my family," Jane recalls. "No one really seemed to want me." She came home from college one holiday to find a "Sold" sign in front of her parents' home. It never occurred to her parents to mention to her that they had moved.

Only as an adult did Jane discover that there was a lot more to her family's history than she had realized. Her mother had had an affair with her dad's brother. As the web of lies began to unfold, Jane discovered that it was as a result of this affair that she was conceived, so the person she had thought was her uncle was actually her father. The whole family system was polluted and distorted by sin. A sick system distorted everything that it touched.

Especially when dealing with children who are having serious problems in school or with the law, therapists often insist on doing family therapy. "We don't believe that the child is the only patient here," they say. "We believe that the whole family is the patient. There is something wrong with the whole family system." In other words, an individual's behavior cannot be explained unless we look at the whole family unit. Doing justice often requires us to look at an entire system, not just the problems of an individual or a group.

A modern example of institutional sin would be apartheid in South Africa. If a white person grew up under apartheid, it didn't matter if he or she was a good person or a bad person. They were caught up in a sinful structure that distorted everything in their lives. I have friends from South Africa who have told me, "It is so distressing now to realize what we were taught as little children to believe about blacks by our parents and even our churches. It's painful to discover that we grew up in a society that was so radically unjust and that we simply took for granted." Apartheid was a spider web of sin involving the legal system, the army, landowners, big business, families and, sadly, churches, which offered a theological defense for the separation of races.[12]

JUSTICE WORKS FOR CHANGE

Back in 1968 the singing group Crosby, Stills and Nash sang what became an anthem for a generation. It is best known for its famous chorus: "We can change the world." The song was written in reference to the Democratic National Convention that was held in Chicago that year. The Vietnam War and civil rights were white-hot issues, and rioters gathered to protest the convention. Mayor Richard Daley told the police that they could use all necessary force in subduing the rioters, so the police literally beat thousands of young people into submission. It was in this context that Crosby, Stills and Nash sang, "Won't you please come to Chicago? No one else can take your place. We can change the world!"[13]

"We can change the world!" The children of the baby boomers who listened to this song flocked to Senator Barack Obama's presidential campaign in 2008, which had as its slogan, "Change we can believe in." And the crowds chanted throughout the campaign, "Yes, we can!" In other words, "Yes, we can change the world!"

But sinful systems resist change. Just because we determine that we're going to do justice and try to change a sinful system doesn't mean that the system is going to roll over and say, "Okay! We give up! You're right!" If a family has a secret—that Dad is an alcoholic, for example—and that secret is exposed, it doesn't mean that Dad will immediately admit his problem and go into rehab. If Mom had an affair with Dad's brother and that secret is exposed, it doesn't mean that the whole, sick family system will change. Family systems fight change and use every weapon to resist it: guilt, threats, appeals to loyalty and even violence. It's a sociological reality that systems generally change individuals far more than individuals change systems.

During the Montgomery bus boycott that launched the civil rights movement in 1954, a white woman named Juliette Morgan was a city librarian from a well-known family. She was involved in an interracial women's prayer group (which, incidentally, had to be hosted in a black church, because no white church would host an integrated gathering). She wrote a letter to the editor of a Montgomery newspaper in admiration of the boycotters. She said in her letter that the boycotters' willingness to suffer for great Christian democratic principles should inspire deep admiration among decent whites.

But sick systems resist change. Vocal opposition to the system of segregation was silenced. Morgan, the white librarian, was harassed. Stones were thrown through her windows at night. A cross was burned on her lawn, people insulted her as she walked down the street, and her neighbors shunned her. The massive rejection by everyone she knew, along with the isolation from her community, led Morgan to a complete breakdown. One night she took an overdose of sleeping pills and killed herself.

The change that Juliette Morgan wanted to see didn't happen for years, but it did come. In recognition of her great work, Montgomery has renamed the main branch of the library the Juliette Hampton Morgan Memorial Library.

When systems fight back—whether they are family systems, office systems or political systems—most people who fight for change give up. It is easy to become cynical and to begin to believe that change is impossible. It's easier to say, "Let's just let sleeping dogs lie." As Christians, we may be tempted to give up and say, "I will serve a *privatized* Jesus, who only cares about blessing me and who answers my prayer to get a good parking spot when I'm going to the movies." Or we may be tempted to say, "I'm going to believe in a *charitable* Jesus, who assists me and my church to perform individual acts of charity for people in need." But it's simply too hard to serve a *just* Jesus, who wants us to partner with him to change the world.

Changing sinful systems demands deep reserves of faith in Christ. Without deep roots in the worship of Christ, personal devotion to the calling of Christ and connection to the community of Christ, we will fall away. Jesus tells us what will happen to us when we confront sinful systems: "Others, like seed sown on rocky places, hear the word and at once receive it with joy. But since they have no root, they last only a short time. When trouble or persecution comes because of the word, they quickly fall away" (Mark 4:16-17). People who are not deeply rooted in Christ can never shake any system.

But change is possible! History is full of examples of change by people who worked in partnership with Christ. Just think about the extraordinary change for African Americans as a result of the civil rights movement, which largely sprang out of Christian churches in the South.[14] Southern life was segregated in every sphere, a system undergirded by state-sponsored terrorism in which the police, the courts and the government, together with the Ku Klux Klan, conspired to terrorize Southern blacks through lynchings, bombings and church burnings. Blacks were disenfranchised through literacy tests and poll taxes.

But today, less than six decades after the famous Montgomery bus boycott, there are over five hundred African American mayors now in the United States, including the mayors of some of our largest cities. Since 1870, when Senator Hiram Revels of Mississippi and Representative Joseph Rainey of South Carolina became the first African Americans to serve in Congress, a total of 132 African Americans have served as U.S. representatives or senators. Today, forty-four African Americans serve in Congress (eighteen from the former Confederacy, where for one hundred years there wasn't one). Two of our most recent secretaries of state have been African American, and of course, Barack Obama became the first African American president of the United States when he took office in 2009.

Changing the world and tearing down sick systems is possible through partnership with Christ.

JUSTICE DEMANDS ADVOCACY

As I mentioned earlier, in almost all churches, doing mercy comes naturally. Doing justice may be on the agenda for a small minority of churches, but most evangelical churches are not involved in advocacy.

Unjust social structures can only be changed by legislation. Laws can't make bad people good, and they won't give eternal life to people. But laws can restrain evil and promote the common good in society.

Dr. Martin Luther King Jr. understood both the benefits and the limitations of legislative actions. He wrote, "Morality cannot be legislated, but behavior can be regulated. Judicial decrees may not change the heart, but they can restrict the heartless. . . . Government action is not the whole answer to the present crisis, but it is an important partial answer. . . . The law cannot make an employer love an employee, but it can prevent him from refusing to hire me because of the color of my skin."[15]

So how should we now move forward? Borrowing from contemporary Roman Catholic teaching, which provides wise guidance for advocacy, I believe that churches should be:

- *Political but not partisan.* We should not tell people how to vote or for whom to vote, but we must not avoid advocating for certain "political" changes that are expressions of biblical justice.[16]

- *Principled but not ideological.* As Christians, everything we do in life should be driven by the principles taught by Jesus. However, our principles must not lead us to cease dealing with present realities. Just because we can't fix everything does not mean that we can't fix some things. We must do what we can, whenever we can, to help whomever we can.

- *Civil but not soft.* As modeled by Dr. King, we should courageously stand up against injustice everywhere, but we should do so with civility. Answering evil with evil is not an option for the followers of Jesus. The means by which we achieve the end is, in some ways, more important than the end itself.

- *Engaged but not used.* Engaging in the political arena always comes with its own set of challenges and temptations. As followers of Jesus, we should be fully engaged, but we must be wary of being used as a tool for political gain.[7]

THE BOTH-AND OF MERCY AND JUSTICE

Karen was a single mom with two children. Her years of personal poverty made her sensitive to the needs of people around her. One day Karen decided to start a program to feed homeless people in the city of Columbus. She and her two kids went to the day-old bakery outlet and bought several loaves of bread. Then they went to a grocery and got a big tub of peanut butter and made dozens of sandwiches. They wrapped the sandwiches in napkins "borrowed" from a local McDonald's, and then Karen and her two kids drove the streets of Columbus, handing out peanut-butter sandwiches to homeless men and women.

After a while, a few of Karen's friends asked her if they could join her in passing out sandwiches. One of her friends bought toiletries to pass out with the sandwiches. Another gave out wool caps and gloves. Pretty soon more than a dozen people accompanied Karen in showing mercy toward the homeless.

Eventually, Karen's ministry became part of Vineyard Columbus.

With her inspiration, we opened a food pantry. Then, next door to the pantry, we opened a free medical clinic. But we realized that providing food and medical care was not enough. Mercy needed to be married to justice, and so our urban ministry began assisting people in finding jobs, advocating for the homeless before government agencies and providing a range of services for immigrants. Today dozens of activities of mercy and justice can be traced to one woman and her two children who decided to hand out a few peanut-butter sandwiches to the poor. Many would see in her story a modern-day recreation of Jesus' multiplication of five loaves of bread and two fish.

Let me encourage you to pray this prayer to God: "Is there one area that you would have me assist in doing mercy or in fighting injustice— just one area?" Perhaps the Lord will speak to you about "adopting" some children through a relief agency and providing those children with education, food or housing. Perhaps he will speak to you about getting involved in an organization that deals with global sex trafficking. Perhaps God will prompt you to get involved in an organization that provides medical care for AIDS victims in sub-Saharan Africa. Or perhaps God will fill your heart with a fresh idea like he did with Karen.

William Penn, the English philosopher and founder of Pennsylvania, said, "I expect to pass through life but once. If therefore, there be any kindness I can show, or any good thing I can do to any fellow being, let me do it now, and not defer or neglect it, as I shall not pass this way again."[18]

How will you do justice in this world?

7

What Is Our Method?

PROCLAMATION . . .

Billy Graham is one of the most influential and well-known Christians alive today. He has counseled the past twelve American presidents. He has been on the cover of numerous national and international magazines, and for virtually every year since the 1950s, he has been on lists of the ten most admired people in America or the world. One magazine once ranked him second only to God for achievements in religion.

I once heard a joke about Billy Graham. One day, Billy was returning to Charlotte after a speaking engagement. When he got off the plane, a limousine was waiting to take him home. Seeing the limousine, Billy had an idea. He said to the driver, "You know, I am eighty-seven years old and I have never driven a limousine. Would you mind if I drove it for a while?"

The driver said, "Sure, why not? Go ahead!" So Billy got into the driver's seat and began to speed. He was doing seventy miles an hour in a fifty-five zone. As luck would have it, he went through a speed trap and caught the attention of a rookie state trooper. Billy pulled over, and the young trooper walked up to the driver's door. When he rolled down his window, the trooper immediately recognized him as Billy Graham. The trooper didn't say a word; instead, he got right back in his car to call his supervisor.

"I know we are supposed to enforce the law," he said to his supervisor. "But I also know that important people are given certain courtesies. I need to know what I should do, because I have stopped a very important person."

The supervisor asked, "Who is it? Is it the governor?" The trooper said, "No, he's way more important than that."

The supervisor asked, "Well then, is it the president?" The trooper said, "No, he's even more important than that."

Who could be more important than the president? The supervisor was now dying to know who this was and said, "Well then, just tell me! Who is it?"

The trooper answered, "I think it's Jesus, because he's got Billy Graham for a chauffeur!"

It is said that Billy Graham has preached the gospel in person to more people than any other person in history: over two hundred million people in 180 countries! According to the Billy Graham Evangelistic Association, more than 2.5 million people have stepped forward at his crusades to accept Jesus as their Savior. As of 2008, his lifetime audience, including radio and television broadcasts, topped 2.2 billion people!

SHARING OUR FAITH

One survey said that 95 percent of Christians have never led another person to Christ. Some people live and breathe evangelism, but the vast majority of Christians do not share their faith with others on a regular basis. In Matthew 28:18-20, we read Jesus' words that have been labeled the Great Commission. We have to talk about our faith, because this Great Commission—Jesus' call on the church to make disciples of all nations—is not merely a suggestion. It is not just a good idea or a recommendation. It is a command!

Former president Jimmy Carter, who is a Christian, said, "My faith demands—this is not optional—my faith demands that I do whatever I can, wherever I am, whenever I can, for as long as I can, with whatever I have, to try to make a difference."[1]

The biggest difference we as Christians can make in this world is to tell people about Jesus. We are called to make disciples of *all the nations.* Evangelism is the task of the whole church. And every single Christian, even if we're not Billy Graham, is called to live and die for this great cause. If we truly believe the things that we claim to believe as Christians, if we really do believe in this good news, then why don't we share it with others? Why do we shy away from evangelism?

One person told me, "For me, the hardest thing about evangelism is not having all the answers or being confident enough to say what I think." Another person said, "For me, the hardest thing about evangelism is overcoming my fear of sounding like an idiot and knowing how, what and when to start talking." Another person told me, "For me, the hardest thing about evangelism is thinking that I am responsible for whether or not the one I'm witnessing to accepts Jesus as his Lord and Savior."

Most people can relate to these responses, and we can probably add a bunch more to that list. We all agree with the need for people to be pointed to Christ; we just struggle with how to get it done. Many of us have tried sharing our faith with a classmate, a friend or a coworker, but it didn't go quite the way that we had hoped. So we say, "I'm obviously not gifted in evangelism. I'll leave evangelism to Billy Graham." But the gospel spread in the early church not primarily through gifted evangelists but through ordinary men and women, like you and me, who shared their faith.

HOW GOD DRAWS PEOPLE

There is only one way to come to God: through his Son, Jesus Christ. But there are a million ways to come to Christ. Let's consider a few of the ways that God draws people to Christ.[2]

Evangelism is not solely a human effort. Rather, evangelism is something that we human beings do in partnership with God. Part of the overwhelming reluctance that Christians have regarding sharing our faith is that we wrongly think that we are responsible to bring God to a godless person. That would be a pretty daunting task: to bring almighty God to another human being.

But what if we changed the paradigm altogether? What if our job was not to bring God to people and places where God was not? What if our job was to partner with God—to join with God concerning what God was already doing with a person and in a place?

The great founder of the Methodist church, John Wesley, used the term *prevenient grace* in asserting the wonderfully liberating doctrine that the Holy Spirit "goes before" the preaching of the gospel, readying individual hearts to hear and to respond. In other words, we don't bring God to anyone. The Holy Spirit operates everywhere to prepare and move people so that they may make a decision to follow Christ.

A great illustration of prevenient grace is found in Don Richardson's *Peace Child*.[3] In 1962 Don Richardson, along with his wife, Carol, and their seven-month-old baby, went to work among the Sawi tribe in what was then Dutch New Guinea. The Sawi were known to be cannibalistic headhunters. Don and his wife worked hard to learn the language and customs of the Sawi people, but they were frustrated that they couldn't get them to understand the story of Jesus or his death for their sins. They prayed that God would show them a way to convey the true message of Christianity in a form the people would understand.

God gave the Richardsons an unexpected opportunity. Another tribe attacked the tribe with whom the Richardsons were living. For weeks they fought with one another until the Sawi tribal chief decided to initiate peace. He did so by taking his own newborn son from the arms of his wife and giving him to the tribal chief of his enemy. The other tribe disappeared into the bush with the infant. The baby was gone, never to be returned to his grieving parents. The Richardsons asked what the ceremony meant. The tribal chief said: "I offered my son as the peace child for our tribes. As long as my son lives, there will be peace between our tribes. If he dies, war will resume. Anyone who kills a peace child will himself be killed."

Don Richardson realized that the chief was giving him the cultural key that would open this people to the truth about Jesus Christ. So Don gathered the tribal leaders together and told them the story of God's

Peace Child. Don spoke of the war that wages between the kingdom of this world and the kingdom of God. Don showed how our heavenly Father sent his Son, Jesus, to earth as his Peace Child to make peace between God and human beings.

The Sawi people understood the teaching of the incarnation of Christ and his atonement after Don explained it to them. Following this event, many villagers became Christians. From this experience, Don Richardson argued in his various writings that hidden among tribal cultures are usually some practices or understandings that he called "redemptive analogies." These analogies prepare the culture to hear and receive the gospel through their own customs, rituals, tribal myths, prophecies and even titles for God.[4]

Rather than thinking that I need to start the work of God in another person's life, I personally find it much less burdensome to ask myself, "What is God already doing in this person's life that I may contribute to?" When I assume that God is the Savior (which he is) and I also assume that God is up to something in every person's life (which he also is), then I have the exciting job of trying to trace over the lines that God is already drawing.

PERSONAL EVANGELISM

Stephen Van Dop, pastor of evangelism at our church, did a study for his seminary dissertation of why people came to Christ at our church. He literally spent hundreds of hours meeting with focus groups, which were made up of people who had come to Christ over the previous couple of years. He carefully recorded people's stories. After listening to the tapes, he discovered that one major theme emerged: people came to Christ at our church because of *life crises*.

Stephen then subdivided life crises into three types: intrapersonal, interpersonal and situational crises. *Intrapersonal crises* had to do with issues within an individual, such as addictions, depression, thoughts of suicide and troubling memories. This was the most reported category of crisis of the three identified, accounting for 63 percent of all reports of life crisis.

Interpersonal crises were those dealing with broken or severely strained relationships with spouses, children, friends or parents; 53 percent of the crises mentioned were in this category. Separation and divorce easily stood out as the most reported interpersonal crises, accounting for 63 percent of this subcategory. *Situational crises*—such as the loss of jobs or loved ones, a pregnancy out of wedlock, a legal matter or academic or athletic problems—accounted for 34 percent of the total crisis responses.[5]

So when we meet a person in crisis, we can assume that the person may have exhausted their own resources for humanly solving their own problems and that the Holy Spirit is at work preparing that person to receive the gospel. My dear friend Simon Ponsonby, who served as pastor of theology at St. Aldate's, Oxford, gave an excellent illustration of how the Holy Spirit's prevenient grace prepares a person for gospel reception. Philosophers have argued for centuries that certain innate qualities in individuals are pointers to God. According to Ponsonby:

- Auguste Comte said that an innate sense of *morality*, right and wrong, leads us to believe in an absolute moral referent who underwrites justice, whether in this life or the next.

- Søren Kierkegaard spoke of a universal sense of *anxiety*, whereby humankind is compelled to despair or driven to find rest in God.

- Karl Rahner and Richard Hooker suggested that *beauty* causes us to transcend our immediate context and touch the divine in awe and wonder.

- Rudolf Otto suggested that we have a profound sense of *spirituality*—*Mysterium Tremendum*—before the unknown God, which makes us religious.

- C. S. Lewis said that we are all filled with *appetency*—deep cravings that are unmet and unsatisfied with anything the world offers in material terms. This desire directs us toward God.

- Friedrich Schleiermacher spoke of a universal feeling of *dependency* upon a superior being, who is God.[6]

What if we listened to people long enough that we were able to discover their own innate desires—whether for beauty, justice, satisfaction or morality—and helped them to make an explicit link between these desires and Christ? What if we partnered with what God is already doing inside an individual? Perhaps God is creating a longing for the Moral One (Comte), the Rest-Giving One (Kierkegaard), the Beautiful One (Rahner), the Awesome One (Otto), the Satisfying One (Lewis) or the One Upon Whom We Are Dependent (Schleiermacher). What if our job was simply to help people find what they've always been looking for instead of trying to create an appetite for God where none previously existed? In other words, what if the burden of seeing someone get saved rested more heavily on God than on us, and our job was simply to proclaim and demonstrate the gospel as God gives us opportunity?

PROCLAMATION EVANGELISM

The gospel is a message that needs to be announced. Luke records that Jesus took upon himself the role of the anointed preacher of the gospel when he stood up in a synagogue in his hometown of Nazareth and read from the prophet Isaiah:

> The Spirit of the Lord is on me,
>   because he has anointed me
>   to proclaim good news to the poor. (Luke 4:18)[7]

Proclamation is the essential means by which God communicates the gospel message to an unsaved world. The apostle Paul puts it this way: "For there is no difference between Jew and Gentile—the same Lord is Lord of all and richly blesses all who call on him, for, 'Everyone who calls on the name of the Lord will be saved.' How, then, can they call on the one they have not believed in? And how can they believe in the one of whom they have not heard? And how can they hear without someone preaching to them? And how can anyone preach unless they are sent? As it is written: 'How beautiful are the feet of those who bring good news!'" (Romans 10:12-15).

Paul's logic is found in these five steps.

- To be saved, one must call upon the Lord.
- To call on the Lord, one must believe.
- To believe, one must hear.
- To hear, one must be preached to.
- To preach, one must be sent.

The fourth step—to hear, one must be preached to—is the one with which we are presently concerned. The gospel message must be clearly preached if people are to hear, believe, call upon the Lord and be saved. Yet sadly, in many churches, members assume that if people are attending church, they don't have to hear the gospel. And individuals in most churches are not trained to verbally communicate the gospel.

A few years ago I was invited to deliver the plenary sessions for our state's chapter of the National Council of Churches (NCC), which is an ecumenical partnership of many mainline Christian denominations in the United States. When the NCC leaders approached me to speak at their annual event, I was curious about why they wanted me to come. "I'm an evangelical," I said. "I've never attended one of your events. Why do you want me to deliver the plenary talks?"

The head of the group replied, "Well, Rich, your church is growing and many of our churches are shrinking. We thought you might give us some advice about how to make our churches grow."

I replied, "I don't know the secret of church growth. But if I come to speak at this NCC event, I'm going to talk about evangelism."

The leader responded, "It's funny that you should mention the 'e' word. The leaders of our local denomination were just commenting about how uncomfortable many of our members are with the 'e' word." Evangelism is so threatening for some that they can't even mention the word!

So I spoke about evangelism. At one of my sessions, I asked the 250 pastors in attendance, "How many of you have presented the gospel message at your churches in the past year in such a fashion that people there knew that you were expecting an immediate response of some kind? In other words, how many of you, within your denominational tradition, spoke to your church in such a fashion that people knew that you were asking them to personally appropriate Christ for themselves, then and there?"

I asked for a show of hands. In a room of 250 pastors, only ten responded that in the last year they had asked for a personal response to the gospel. Less than one out of twenty pastors at this gathering had invited people to call upon the Lord in order to be saved even one time in the past year!

I said, "Beloved friends, I believe this is the reason why your churches are not growing. You must regularly invite people to personally appropriate for themselves the saving benefits of the life, death and resurrection of our Lord Jesus Christ!"

BECOMING GOOD MESSENGERS

When we consider evangelism, it's important to realize that we are *messengers*. To be a good messenger, six things matter.

Love matters. To become good messengers, we must be compelled by love. Paul could say that his "heart's desire and prayer to God for the Israelites is that they may be saved" (Romans 10:1) and that he would willingly experience God's eternal damnation if only his brethren would receive Christ (Romans 9:3) because he was motivated by love. His evangelism was compelled by love.

Do you love the people outside of your church, or is your love reserved for friends seated in church next to you? To put it more strongly: have you developed an aversion to nonbelievers? Do you go to great lengths to avoid the exact people that Jesus came to save? Have you been so turned off by someone's sin that it became hard to see that person as someone Jesus came to seek and save?

Maybe it's their sexual orientation. Maybe it's the fact that they are living with someone who is not their spouse. Maybe they have a baby born out of wedlock or had an abortion. Maybe it's their immigration

status, or how they spend their money or how much they drink or
smoke. God's challenge to us is, "Will you still love them? Will you still
share the good news with them?" There is no way that we can be the
good news of Jesus if we're not compelled by love. We don't have to like
the sin, but we must love the sinner. Love matters.

Prayer matters. If you want to share your faith with others, the first
person you must talk to is not your coworker or your neighbor or your
roommate. The first person to talk to is God. Evangelism begins with
prayer. As Christians, we know that prayer is important, but isn't prayer
often our last resort? We say, "I've tried everything else that I can think
of. I've argued. I've nagged. I've manipulated. And since none of that
worked, I guess the only thing left to do now is pray!"

If you look back at history, the difference between Christians who
made a huge impact for the kingdom and those who did not can often
be traced to the power of prayer. Prayer is where it all begins!

Many of us are Christians because someone prayed for us. Do you
regularly pray for people who are far from God? Prayer matters.

Proximity matters. Even the most incredible evangelist among us
will be utterly ineffective in reaching people for Christ unless she gets
near the people who are living far from God. We must be mindful of
this, because the sad fact is that the average Christian will, over time,
grow more and more isolated from the very people that she or he is
called to reach. For many of us, the longer that we are Christians, the
harder we must work to be near nonbelievers. In this sense, the youngest
Christians among us are the ones who are best positioned to reach nonbelievers. For those of us who have been Christians for a long time (to
cite Becky Pippert's memorable book title), we must get "out of the
saltshaker and into the world!"[8]

If proximity matters, then most of us can have the most impact for
Christ in two places: where we live and where we work. From Monday
through Friday, most of us spend a third of our day at work. We spend
a third of the day at home sleeping, and during the other third we
commute, eat, do chores, entertain ourselves and take care of personal

business. We often spend evenings and weekends in our neighborhoods.

Some of us pray, "God, if you would just send me, I will share the good news with everyone I meet." God may be saying, "Open your eyes and look around you. I have already sent you to where I want you to share about me." Take a coworker out to lunch. Invite a neighbor over for dinner (or at the very least, get to know your neighbors' names). Knowing who your neighbors are is a minimal first step to praying for them. Ask a roommate if there is anything that you can pray for. Start viewing your neighborhood and your work as your primary mission fields. Proximity matters.

Your story matters. One of the greatest pieces of evidence for the truth of the gospel is your own story. There is something incredibly powerful about sharing how you came to Jesus and how your life changed because of Jesus. There is a great example of this in John 9, in which Jesus heals a blind man. This man had no theological or evangelism training, but he did one thing right: he testified about what Jesus had done in his life. In response to the Pharisees' questions about Jesus, the formerly blind man said: "Whether he is a sinner or not, I don't know. One thing I do know. I was blind but now I see!" (John 9:25).

"I was a drug addict, but Jesus set me free." "I used to be addicted to porn, but Jesus healed me." "I used to live life for myself, for money and for my satisfaction, but Jesus is using me to love others." "I was the last person in the world who would have volunteered my Saturdays to work in a juvenile detention facility or at a food pantry. I do this not because I'm such a great person, but because of what Jesus did in my life." "My marriage used to be in shambles, but Jesus has brought new life for us." There is tremendous power in our stories.

So what is your story? How did you come to Jesus? How has your life changed because of Jesus? What are you willing to do now that you never were willing to do before? If you have never shared your story with anyone and you feel a little nervous about doing it, start by sharing your story with a few Christian friends. Then, as God gives you courage, share your story at your work, at school and with your neighbors. Your story matters.

Invitation matters. John 4 tells a great story about Jesus' interaction with a woman at the well. The woman is so moved by this interaction that she "went back to the town and said to the people, 'Come, see a man who told me everything I ever did. Could this be the Messiah?' They came out of the town and made their way toward him" (John 4:28-30).

After encountering Jesus, this woman invited everyone to Jesus, saying, "Come and see!" Because of her invitation, many people in her town were saved. "Come and see": those are three powerful words. Invite someone to your church this week. Invite someone to an outreach event or to watch you or a family member get baptized. Invite someone to your small group or to join you in a service project: whether a person is Christian or not, they can pack a bag of groceries, clean up a local park or help paint a playground. Invitation absolutely matters.

Faithfulness matters. As we step out to share our faith with others, we will experience opposition and rejection, and we may think that nothing is happening. Maybe you have prayed for a family member or a friend for years, and you feel discouraged because it doesn't seem like anything is happening. Maybe you have reached out at work and in your neighborhood to share your faith with others, and you feel like nothing is happening. Keep going! Don't give up! Just because we can't see something with our eyes does not mean that God is doing nothing in a person's heart. God calls us to sow generously, liberally and faithfully, and God promises we will reap. Faithfulness matters.

When Billy Graham was in his eighties, he said, "My mind tells me I ought to get out there and go, but I just can't do it. But I'll preach until there is no breath left in my body. I was called by God, and until God tells me to retire, I cannot. Whatever strength I have, whatever time God lets me have, is going to be dedicated to doing the work of an evangelist, as long as I live."[9]

Love matters. Prayer matters. Proximity matters. Your story matters. Invitation matters. And faithfulness matters. Each of us is called to do the work of an evangelist!

8

What Is Our Method?

...AND DEMONSTRATION

During his first career, our executive pastor, Craig Heselton, was a chemical engineer and plant manager of a local pharmaceutical company. While Craig served in that capacity, he had an incredible experience. Craig found out that the wife of the company's research director had been diagnosed with cervical cancer. He offered to pray for her, but since neither Bill nor Lilly believed in God or miraculous healing, they declined Craig's offer. It wasn't long after this that Lilly had surgery and began receiving chemotherapy. Unfortunately, the chemotherapy didn't work, and she was given about a one in seven chance of surviving.

Feeling hopeless and desperate, and having nowhere else to turn, they decided to take Craig up on his offer of prayer ("After all, it can't hurt, right?"). Prior to praying for her, he had the opportunity to share the gospel with her. Craig explained to Lilly that the only reason our prayers for healing work is because of what Christ had done in dying for our sins. She accepted Christ, which was the first miracle! And then Craig prayed for a second miracle: the healing of her cancer. At her next doctor's visit, she was told that her tumor was significantly smaller. They prayed some more over the next several months, and she was eventually declared cancer free by her doctors!

Despite having experienced his wife's miraculous healing, Bill did not immediately become a Christian. He was, however, willing to accompany her to our church. They began attending our services, and he said he felt God's presence for the first time in his life. After listening to the messages over the course of six months, Bill also gave his life to Christ.

If you consider yourself to be a follower of Christ, what means did God use to draw you toward his Son? Was there an event or a series of events that got your attention? Did God use your parents, a friend, your spouse or a pastor to explain the gospel message to you? Did you read something that finally answered your questions? Did you have a supernatural experience that made you aware that God exists and that he cares about you?

There is only one way to God—through his Son, Jesus Christ—but there are a million ways to come to Christ. The apostle Paul summarized his life's mission this way: "I have become all things to all people so that by all possible means I might save some" (1 Corinthians 9:22).

WHY DOES THE CHURCH EXIST?

Many people treat church as if it were a religious country club. Members join the church the way they join their country clubs: by paying their membership fees: tithes. By becoming members, they are entitled to club privileges: the receipt of religious goods and services. One woman who labored under this false image of the church emailed me. She wrote to complain that we have parking spaces for "first-time visitors" closest to the door, while long-time attenders are forced to park farthest away.

Somehow, despite the fact that this woman had attended our church for a number of months and even had gone through our newcomers' class, she evidently forgot—or simply did not understand—our church's vision statement, which is posted in huge letters in our main lobby: "Our church exists not for itself, but for Christ and for the world." Or as the former Anglican archbishop William Temple put it,

"The church is the only cooperative society in the world which exists for the benefit of its nonmembers."[1]

Why does the church exist? To serve God and to bring good news to the world through word and deed!

WHAT IS THE GOSPEL?

The gospel is nothing short of good news for all creation. Christopher J. H. Wright, who is the international director of the Langham Partnership, explains the gospel (according to the apostle Paul) this way:

> The God of Israel, who is the only true and living God, has been faithful to his covenant promise, originally made to Abraham and then amplified and testified all through the Law and the Prophets (Romans 3:21). In and through Messiah, Jesus of Nazareth, God has decisively acted to deal with the problems of human sin and division (Genesis 3 and 11). Through the death and resurrection of Jesus, according to the Scriptures, God has borne our sin and defeated its consequences—enmity and death. And in Christ's exaltation to God's right hand (the place of government), the reign of God is now active in the world, so that we now live under the kingship of Christ, not of Caesar. Jesus, the Messiah of Israel, is Lord, God, and Savior of the world. So turn from your futile idols to the living God who alone can save you, repent of your sins and believe in Jesus.[2]

This is a wonderfully full definition of the gospel. It tells us that the gospel message reaches back thousands of years in the past, to the covenant promises of God, and deals comprehensively with all of our problems—namely, sin and division. To Wright's wonderful explanation I might add the following: to those who repent and believe, God promises the gift of the Holy Spirit, who will live in you, transform you to be like his Son and enable you to influence this world for Christ through word and deed. In the company of God's people, the church, you will be sent out to live a purpose-filled life of proclamation and demonstration of the gospel. One day Christ will return to remove the curse that presently rests on the universe and bring redemption and renewal to God's whole creation.

DO SOMETHING!

This enormous message, reaching back in time to creation and reaching forward to the new creation, could easily paralyze us by its scope and depth. How can we, being so small and frail, possibly contribute to the transformation of the entire universe?

My friend David Parker is the senior pastor of the Desert Vineyard in Lancaster, California. When he became the pastor of that church, it was (to put it kindly) a religious country club for members who sought ever more exotic religious experiences. As the church's new pastor, David prayed for months for God to give him wisdom regarding how to turn the church away from itself and toward the world. He prayed and prayed, "God, show me how our church can reach the city. What form should our evangelism take? How can we best bear witness to Christ in our community?"

After about nine months of praying, David says he finally felt the Holy Spirit speak to him: "David, *do something!*" Just do something! Start somewhere! So over the next few years, David led his church to do many things. But the main thing David regularly did was to insist that every activity of the church contain an outward focus. Whether in small groups or Sunday morning worship, recovery groups or Bible classes, the church did everything keeping at least one eye on people who do not yet know Christ.

Mother Teresa's Missionaries of Charity runs orphanages, AIDS hospices and charity centers across the world. The organization cares for refugees, the blind, the disabled, the aged, alcoholics, the poor, the homeless and victims of floods, epidemics and famine. The scope of the work done by the Missionaries of Charity is truly daunting. But as Mother Teresa put it, if she hadn't picked up the first person, who had been found nearly dead on the street, many years ago, the more than

77,500 others would never have been picked up off the streets.

The scope of the gospel is big enough to meet the scope of the universe's need. But God doesn't ask you and me to do everything. Just *do something!*

And we must do more than speak! Jesus' ministry was always one of *show and tell.* In other words, Jesus' methodology was always Both-And. Or as John Stott put it, Jesus modeled both the Great Commission of proclamation and the Great Commandment of love and service, meeting people's spiritual and physical needs alike. Proclamation and demonstration are partners.[3]

We read many verses in the Gospels such as this: "Jesus went throughout Galilee, teaching in their synagogues, proclaiming the good news of the kingdom, and healing every disease and sickness among the people" (Matthew 4:23). Everywhere Jesus went, he always proclaimed and demonstrated the inbreaking of the kingdom of God. This Both-And ministry of proclamation and demonstration was transferred to his apostles. So we read, "He appointed twelve that they might be with him and that he might send them out *to preach and to have authority to drive out demons*" (Mark 3:14-15).

Of course, the demonstration of the gospel is not just through healing, deliverance or prophecy. Jesus tells us when his Father's children do good deeds, this also announces the inbreaking of God's kingdom. So we read, "In the same way, let your light shine before others, that they may see your good deeds and glorify your Father in heaven" (Matthew 5:16). Often our "good deeds" are shown in unspectacular ways—for example, using normal church activities and directing them outwardly toward those who do not yet know Christ.

Let's look at several different methods of evangelistic demonstration: programmatic, prophetic, power, presence and prayer.

PROGRAMMATIC EVANGELISM

God calls individuals and churches to be active in bearing witness. Part of success in bearing witness is having an intentional strategy for reaching seekers. That intentional strategy could involve the Alpha program.[4] It could involve women's breakfasts or Christmas teas. It doesn't matter what intentional strategy you use. As David Parker learned, what's important is that you *do something!*

A number of years ago a woman on our church staff decided to host swing-dance classes. The swing-dance class attracted about thirty-five people to their monthly meetings. But a few years ago, it hit a tipping point and the dance class grew from thirty-five to one hundred people, then two hundred people, and then three hundred people. It didn't involve great prophetic discernment for us to say, "God is building a wave through this dance class. It is our responsibility to surf the wave." So two of our pastors started small groups based on Rick Warren's best-selling book *The Purpose Driven Life* with a couple of hundred people who came out for swing dancing. Many of the people who got involved in those groups were completely unchurched, and a number of them came to Christ as a result.

The lesson is this: look for places of surprising success in your church or fellowship group. Where is there outsized blessing? For example, is your church's teen ministry disproportionately large relative to the size of your church? Is a particular women's group wildly popular? You can assume that unusual success in ministry is due to God's Spirit. That's the time to put together an intentional plan for evangelism through a particular program.

PROPHETIC EVANGELISM

The apostle Paul speaks about the impact of a word of prophecy on an unbeliever who comes into a church service when he notes, "But if an unbeliever or an inquirer comes in while everyone is prophesying, they are convicted of sin and are brought under judgment by all, as the secrets of their hearts are laid bare. So they will fall down and worship God, exclaiming, 'God is really among you!'" (1 Corinthians 14:24-25).

As unbelievers listen to prophecy, they may experience profound conviction as the secrets of their hearts and even their past sins are exposed. It was through Jesus' prophetic words that the Samaritan woman's barriers to the gospel were broken down. "[Jesus] told her, 'Go, call your husband and come back.' 'I have no husband,' she replied. Jesus said to her, 'You are right when you say you have no husband. The fact is, you have had five husbands, and the man you now have is not your husband. What you have just said is quite true'" (John 4:16-18).

The woman responded, "Sir, I can see that you are a prophet" (John 4:19). The impact of Jesus' prophetic insight was a massive revival that broke out among the Samaritans. "Many of the Samaritans from that town believed in him because of the woman's testimony, 'He told me everything I ever did.' So when the Samaritans came to him, they urged him to stay with them, and he stayed two days. And because of his words many more became believers" (John 4:39-41).

Disclosing secrets through prophecy, which brings conviction and opens the door to gospel proclamation, was a regular occurrence in the ministry of Charles Spurgeon. Many consider Spurgeon to be the greatest preacher in the English-speaking world of the nineteenth century. The following incident is taken from Spurgeon's autobiography.

> While preaching in the hall, on one occasion, I deliberately pointed to a man in the midst of the crowd, and said, "There is a man sitting there, who is a shoemaker; he keeps his shop open on Sundays, it was open last Sabbath morning, he took ninepence, and there was fourpence profit out of it; his soul is sold to Satan for fourpence!" A city missionary when going his rounds, met with this man, and seeing that he was reading one of my sermons, he asked the question, "Do you know Mr. Spurgeon?" "Yes," replied the man, "I have every reason to know him, I have been to hear him; and, under his preaching, by God's grace I have become a new creature in Christ Jesus. Shall I tell you how it happened? I went to the Music Hall, and took my seat in the middle of the place; Mr. Spurgeon looked at me as if he knew me, and in a sermon he pointed to me, and told the congregation that I was

a shoemaker, and that I kept my shop open on Sundays; and I did sir. I should not have minded that; but he also said that I took ninepence the Sunday before, and that there was fourpence profit out of it. I did take ninepence that day, and fourpence was just the profit; but how he should know that, I could not tell. Then it struck me that it was God who had spoken to my soul through him, so I shut up my shop the next Sunday. At first, I was afraid to go again to hear him, lest he should tell the people more about me; but afterwards I went, and the Lord met with me, and saved my soul."

Spurgeon then added this comment:

I have known many instances in which the thoughts of men have been revealed [to me] from the pulpit. I have sometimes seen persons nudge their neighbours with their elbow, because they had got a smart hit, and they have been heard to say, when they were going out, "The preacher told us just what we said to one another when we went in at the door."[5]

I love the little phrase "a smart hit" to describe the words of prophecy on a hearer. I believe that very often, pastors and other communicators of the gospel—including those who wouldn't call themselves charismatic—experience the phenomenon of prophecy without knowing what label to put on their experience.

I also believe that the apostle Paul was not only referring to past sin when he spoke of the secrets of the heart being laid bare through prophecy. Sometimes the secrets could be secret hurts or secret wounds.

Several years ago I had coffee with a gay man, Tim. I tried to talk with Tim and engage him, but he was utterly walled off. Tim was particularly hostile to pastors. At a certain point in our conversation, he began talking with someone else. While he was distracted, I remember silently praying, "Lord, show me something about Tim that will reach under his defenses."

I immediately got a picture of Tim holding a burning coal in his hand. He was squeezing the burning coal so tightly that it actually burned through his hand. I received an impression from the Holy Spirit, which was, "The coal that is burning through Tim is unforgiveness toward his mother."

Tim and I talked for a while longer after I received this impression. Finally, I asked him, "May I share with you a picture that I felt the Lord gave me about you?"

He said, "Go ahead." As I described the burning coal and the impression I had regarding unforgiveness toward his mother, Tim put his head down and began to cry. He told me that he had personally received a very similar picture about his life not too long before. The prophetic impression I received significantly advanced Tim's receptivity toward the gospel.

When someone receives a prophecy concerning a secret in his or her life—whether a secret sin or a secret hurt or a secret prayer—God essentially announces to the person, "I am alive and I am interested in your life."

POWER EVANGELISM

John Wimber, the founder of the Vineyard movement, coined the term *power evangelism* to describe the presentation of the gospel that is preceded by and undergirded with a supernatural demonstration of God's power and presence.[6] The demonstration of God's power and presence could be the result of a healing or deliverance. (In Wimber's original definition, he would have included prophecy under *power evangelism*. For the sake of clarity, I am restricting the term to situations involving healing, a deliverance or a miracle.) In power evangelism, God uses a supernatural demonstration of his power to communicate to an individual that the kingdom of God has broken in through his Son, Jesus Christ, and that the message regarding Christ's life, death and resurrection must be believed.

A young woman in our church used to be an alcoholic. She was a brilliant attorney who walked around her law firm carrying a huge cup of diet soda mixed with vodka and sipping it all day long. A few summers ago, she decided to attend a summer camp that we held for young adults in our church. At one of the meetings, she felt God's presence and then went through a major deliverance. After the deliverance, she immediately quit drinking, and her heart was opened to receive the gospel. Today she is actively serving at our church and ministering to our young adults.

A few years ago, I had the opportunity to pray for a Muslim woman in central Asia whose daughter was thought to be barren. This barrenness caused a huge crisis in her daughter's marriage. Not long afterward, she received the news that her daughter had become pregnant. The mother (now a grandmother) with whom I had prayed embraced Jesus. One of the pastors who worked for years in central Asia said this: "We serve a living God. If we invite God to work in the life of a Muslim friend, Muslims encounter Jesus in contexts like that."

PRESENCE EVANGELISM

A more common form of evangelism is the demonstration of the gospel's impact through the transformed life of a Christian. Christians "need to look like what they're talking about," John Poulton has written. "It is *people* who communicate primarily, not words or ideas. . . . what communicates now is basically personal authenticity."[7] John Stott, the great English evangelical leader and pastor, helped me to understand the impact of the transformed lives of Christians upon nonbelievers when he said:

> God's purpose is that the good news of Jesus Christ is set forth visually as well as verbally. [As it says in] 1 John 4:12, "No one has ever seen God; but if we love one another, God lives in us and his love is made complete in us." God is invisible. Nobody has ever seen him. . . . [The invisibility] of God is a great problem for faith. . . . How, then, has God solved the problem of his own invisibility?

First and foremost he has done so by sending his Son into the world. . . . To this people tend to reply: "That is truly wonderful, but it happened nearly 2,000 years ago. Is there no way in which the invisible God makes himself visible *today*?" Yes, there is. The invisible God, . . . who once made himself visible in Christ, now makes himself visible in Christians, if we love one another.[8]

According to Jesus, seeing Christians love each other and love other people is one of the major ways that the gospel would be spread. On the night before Jesus went to the cross, he said this to his followers at the Last Supper, "A new command I give you: Love one another. As I have loved you, so you must love one another. By this everyone will know that you are my disciples, if you love one another" (John 13:34-35).

There are, of course, multiple ways that God's love can shine through Christians. For example, at the height of the second great epidemic, around A.D. 260, Dionysius, bishop of Alexandria, wrote a lengthy tribute to the heroic nursing efforts of local Christians, many of whom lost their lives while caring for others.

Most of our brother Christians showed unbounded love and loyalty, never sparing themselves and thinking only of one another. Heedless of danger, they took charge of the sick, attending to their every need and ministering to them in Christ, and with them departed this life serenely happy; for they were infected by others with the disease, drawing on themselves the sickness of their neighbors and cheerfully accepting their pains. Many in nursing and curing others, transferred their death to themselves and died in their stead. . . . [But] the heathen behaved in the very opposite way. At the first onset of the disease, they pushed the sufferers away and fled from their dearest, throwing them into the roads before they were dead and treated unburied corpses as dirt, hoping thereby to avert the spread of the contagion of the fatal disease; but do what they might, they found it difficult to escape.[9]

It was this response of love from the early Christians, compared to the self-centeredness of nonbelievers, that arrested the attention of the Roman emperor. A century later the emperor Julian launched a campaign to institute pagan charities in an effort to match those run by Christians. Julian complained in a letter to the high priest of Galatia in A.D. 362 that the pagans needed to equal the virtues of Christians, for recent Christian growth was caused by their "moral character, even if pretended" and by their "benevolence to strangers and care for the graves of the dead."[10]

Julian also wrote this to another priest: "I think that when the poor happened to be neglected and overlooked by the [pagan] priests, the impious Galileans observed this and devoted themselves to benevolence. . . . The impious Galileans support not only their poor, but ours as well, everyone can see that our people lack aid from us."[11]

Deeds of love that demonstrate the transforming power of the gospel do not always need to be heroic or dramatic. My friend Steve Sjogren coined the term *servant evangelism*, which he defines as, "Demonstrating the kindness of God by offering to do some act of humble service with no strings attached."[12] The church that Sjogren founded, Vineyard Community Church of Cincinnati, has been a model to churches across the globe of arresting the attention of one's community through simple acts of kindness. These acts of kindness have been as varied as giving away sodas in the local park, offering free car washes, helping to bag groceries, cleaning toilets at small stores in town and raking leaves for neighbors.

PRAYER EVANGELISM

Prayer evangelism concerns the power of answered prayer in the life of nonbelievers—answers that cause them to seriously consider the claims of the gospel. I have discovered that God is incredibly generous, and he often reveals himself by answering the prayers of nonbelievers who ask him. In so doing, he reveals his love and the reality of his existence.

For example, I have a friend who is a scientist and who did his postdoctoral work in chemistry at Ohio State University. When his girl-friend brought him to our church, he was a thoroughgoing atheist. He told me that he had only been in a church building once or twice before in his life. At the time we met, Eric was in his early thirties. We became friends and we often talked about the existence of God. One day I said to him, "Eric, have you ever considered praying and seeing if God will answer your prayers?"

He said he couldn't remember praying since he was a little boy. I said to him, "Eric, let me present you with a challenge. If you get in a jam where there is no way to humanly maneuver or manage your way out, ask God for help. I do not believe that God is going to write his name in the sky to prove himself to you; nor do I believe that God is going to give you a billion dollars. But if you get into a jam where there is no way out, pray and say to God, 'Will you help me get out of this situation?'"

Eric called me less than a week later and said, "Rich, you will never believe what happened. I was arrested for speeding two days ago. Now I'm the kind of guy who is never able to talk my way out of a speeding ticket. I don't know if it's my face, or what, but not only can't I talk my way out of a ticket, I'm the sort of person the police throw against the car and say, 'Spread 'em.' So the police officer took my license and registration and went back to his car to check me out. I thought to myself: *Well, Rich said if I'm ever in a jam, I should pray to God. So I guess this is a good test case.* So I prayed, *God, if you are there, will you get me out of this?*"

Eric said that shortly after his prayer, the police officer got out of his car and came over to him and said, "You know, I'm feeling pretty nice today. So I'm going to let you off with a warning. This is your lucky day." And then he let him go.

Eric said he sat in his car, gripping the steering wheel and thinking to himself, "I am in touch with the supernatural!" That encounter with the God who answers prayer opened Eric up to the claims of the gospel, and he became a Christian shortly after that experience.

DOING BOTH-AND EVANGELISM

Russ is a physician who attends our church. He heard me mention an incredible book titled *The Hole in Our Gospel* by Richard Stearns, president of World Vision. So Russ picked up a copy of the book in our bookstore. In this book, Stearns explains that the American gospel is shaped like a donut. We're good at proclamation but poor at demonstration, especially to those who are experiencing extreme poverty around the world. Russ said he was "destroyed" as he read Richard's book. He decided to not just feel bad, however, but to do something!

With some physician friends, Russ began traveling to the Central African Republic to perform surgeries on women who have suffered terribly because of problematic pregnancies. Russ told me about a woman named Rachel, who was discovered in a hallway lying in a pool of fresh blood from her placenta. Care would have been unavailable to her apart from Russ and his team, and their presence saved Rachel and her baby. Through Russ and his team, many people like Rachel have discovered eternal life through Jesus Christ.

But you don't need to be a physician and travel to the Central African Republic to marry proclamation with demonstration! Remember Karen, the single mom who with her two children handed out peanut-butter sandwiches to homeless people in our city? Karen also regularly shared the gospel with homeless men and women. She had the joy of seeing several people come to know the Savior.

As followers of Jesus, we are called to proclaim the gospel and to demonstrate the reality of this gospel through power and love. What's important is not necessarily what we do, but that we all *do something*!

9

What Is Our Ethic?

PERSONAL...

Robert Putnam and David Campbell's book *American Grace: How Religion Divides and Unites Us* is an extensive study of the religious landscape in America from 1950 until 2010.[1] The authors note that church attendance was the highest in the 1950s, which could be called the most religious decade on record for the United States. Then in 1960, things changed drastically, and we saw the most precipitous drop in religious adherence ever. This drastic change was prompted in large part by the political liberation movement and the sexual revolution.

During the 1960s, many churches became more politically liberal than much of America. But in recent decades, much of the church has become more politically conservative than much of the country. So what should the church be? More conservative or more progressive than the surrounding culture?

BE HOLY

When it comes to the discussion of ethics, the word that the Bible uses is *holy* or *holiness*. What exactly does it mean to "be holy"?

In Hebrew, *qadosh* (holy) means "different" or "distinctive."[2] God calls someone or something holy when they are set apart for a distinctive and godly purpose. In the Old Testament, the people of Israel were called to be holy—to be distinctive and different from the rest of the world, which worshiped other gods. That's why God says to them, "You are to be holy to me because I, the LORD, am holy, and I *have set you apart from the nations to be my own*" (Leviticus 20:26).

God calls his people to be a distinctive people because he is a distinctive God. He doesn't fit within any of our categories: Republican, Democrat, conservative, liberal, socialist or capitalist. We are called to be a holy people to demonstrate to the world that the God we worship is a holy God.

To be holy means to be *wholly other*. It means being out of step with surrounding culture. Sometimes we are called to be more conservative than the surrounding culture; other times we are called to be more progressive than the world around us.

ISRAELITES AND THE HOLINESS CODE

How did the Israelites live out God's call to holiness? In Leviticus 19:2, God commands the Israelites, "Be holy because I, the LORD your God, am holy." And in the rest of the chapter, God gives very specific instructions in what is known as the *holiness code*. One might imagine this code to be instructions on various religious practices and responsibilities, but only a few of them are religious in nature. The holiness code is amazingly practical and social in nature, addressing topics like generosity in agriculture (Leviticus 19:9-10), integrity in the legal system (Leviticus 19:12-15), sexual integrity (Leviticus 19:20-22, 29) and racial equality (Leviticus 19:33-34). God's command to "be holy" was both personal *and* social. It was Both-And.

In many ways, Sodom is an illustration of what our fallen world looks like. "Sodom" is used in the Bible to represent our world at its very worst. The prophet Isaiah condemns Jerusalem by likening it to Sodom and Gomorrah, and the objects of condemnation were bloodshed, corruption and injustice (Isaiah 1:9-23). Ezekiel also portrays Judah as a Sodom, with the objects of condemnation being pride, affluence and their ill treatment of those who were in need (Ezekiel 16:49).

Today we often think that the people of Sodom were judged because of their sexual immorality. Certainly immorality was one cause of God's judgment, but it is clear from both Isaiah and Ezekiel that judgment came not just because of immorality. Rather, we see immorality coupled with injustice. Sodom's sin was not just sexual sin; it was just as much about how its residents failed to come to the aid of those in need.

To be holy is to be sometimes morally traditional, sometimes socially progressive and sometimes fitting into neither box. To be holy is to be like Jesus, who won't fit neatly into any humanly constructed category. To be holy is about both personal ethics *and* social ethics. It is Both-And.

WHY HOLD TO THE TRADITIONAL CHURCH TEACHING ABOUT SEX?

C. S. Lewis, the great Christian apologist and author, set out the traditional Christian understanding of sex in *Mere Christianity* when he said, "There is no getting away from it; the Christian rule is, 'Either marriage, with complete faithfulness to your partner, or else total abstinence.'"[3]

At a conference in Chicago that I attended, N. T. Wright, the great New Testament scholar, noted that the early church was known for two things: they believed in the resurrection, and they didn't sleep around. Both are tied to the Christian view of the body. The body—not just the soul, as in Greek philosophy—is the arena of God's redemptive activity.

The Christian church is often criticized for only caring about sexual ethics. Well, that is not completely true, but it is also not completely false. There is a good reason why sex is such a big deal for Christians. It's because sex is a big deal for God!

C. S. Lewis accurately summed up the Bible's basic rule concerning sex. The only proper context for sex is between a man and a woman in marriage. Everything else is forbidden. And this offends every single one of us. Gay people are offended and may ask, "Why can't we enjoy sex outside of heterosexual marriage?" Single people are offended and may ask, "Why can't we enjoy sex even though we're not married?" Married people are offended and may ask, "Why must I only have sex with this one other human being for the rest of my life and have to swear off every other person?" No one likes the biblical standard.

Sex as an economic exchange. I heard pastor and author Tim Keller some years ago refer to what sociologists call the *commodification of relationships*. Sociologists for the last thirty years have said that in the West social relationships are increasingly being reduced to economic relationships. We approach relationships as consumers going to a vendor. We stay in the relationship as long as the product comes to us at a cost that we consider acceptable.

Throughout history, people's closest relationships with their friends, neighbors, families, children and spouses were commitment-based relationships. In a commitment-based relationship, you stay even if your needs are not being met. Every culture has said that your life is richer if you multiply commitment-based relationships. And everyone (until our generation) believed that a life filled with economic-exchange relationships is lonely and barren.

But in the last thirty years in America, more and more of our relationships have become economic-exchange relationships rather than commitment-based relationships. We now approach every relationship as consumers. As long as our needs are being met and the price is not too high, we will stay in this marriage. As long as our needs are being met and the price is not too high, we will stay in this church. Otherwise, we're moving on.

And so we also have what might be called the *commodification of sex*. Sex becomes another economic exchange, another way for us to meet our needs at as low a cost as possible.

Sex as a covenant commitment. The Bible, however, never puts sex in the context of an economic exchange. The Bible always puts sex in the context of commitment and covenant. Here is one passage from Proverbs that illustrates this point:

Drink water from your own cistern,
  running water from your own well.
Should your springs overflow in the streets,
  your streams of water in the public squares?
Let them be yours alone,
  never to be shared with strangers.
May your fountain be blessed,
  and may you rejoice in the wife of your youth.
A loving doe, a graceful deer—
  may her breasts satisfy you always,
  may you ever be intoxicated with her love.
Why, my son, be intoxicated with another man's wife?
Why embrace the bosom of a wayward woman?
    (Proverbs 5:15-20)

This text is all about sex within the context of total commitment. The Bible teaches that you should never give your body to someone else unless you are willing to give them your entire self in total commitment. And you should never receive sex without receiving this whole other person. You can't simply select out sex like a product on a shelf. You must put sex in the context of whole-person commitment.

What does this mean? It means you need to be married to have sex. If you're not married, you aren't sharing your whole self. If you are not married, you are not sharing with another person all of your money and all of your space and time. If you are not married, you are not receiving this whole other person, along with all of this person's problems—debts, family problems, pain and flaws. If you have not sworn total commitment to this other person, and if you have not received total commitment from this other person, then you are treating sex like a commodity, as just an economic exchange. You are saying, "I want the product. I want the pleasure. But I don't want all of you! And if the price gets too high—if you become too demanding or have too many problems—then I'll purchase this product elsewhere. See you later!"

God says sex is more than a product to be bought as long as the price is low enough. Our culture disciples single adults to believe that sex is nothing other than two physical bodies coming together for a great time. Joanna Hyatt, program director of Reality Check, a sexual and relational health education program in Los Angeles that promotes sexual integrity, said this:

> [If] sex is really just physical and not emotional, mental, or spiritual, why are we seeing higher rates of depression among those who are sexually active? Sex is not just about two bodies coming together for a rollicking good time. Sex is about an entire person—their past, their insecurities, their expectations, their hopes, their mind, their soul—coming together with another complete person and becoming physically and emotionally vulnerable. . . . [S]cientific research into the hormone oxytocin is reinforcing this belief. Oxytocin functions as a bonding agent. And it is released in the brain during intimate moments—and in especially high levels during sexual intercourse. . . . If you're having sex outside of marriage, you're still forming that bond. Studies have shown if you have multiple physical relationships that then break up, you damage your ability to form a long-term commitment. You train your brain to only do short-term. Most people who have sex outside of marriage, but still want to have a solid successful marriage someday, are making it that much harder for themselves."[4]

In other words, disobeying God makes it harder for you to bond with your spouse later. Rather than having a low view of sex, God values sex very highly. God values the deep, lifelong covenant and biological bond that can exist between a husband and wife who follow his plan for sex.

THE CASE OF HOMOSEXUALITY

We must admit at the front end that a discussion about homosexuality is very complex. First of all, there is a great deal of confusion about the meaning of homosexuality. Are we talking about self-identification, in which a person simply checks a box: *gay, heterosexual* or *bisexual?* Are we talking about sexual behavior, in which a person actually practices gay sex? Are we talking about attraction or sexual feelings toward someone of the same sex?

Homosexual *orientation,* or feelings of attraction to someone of the same sex, can be distinguished from homosexual *identity,* or a person's self-identification as gay. And then there is homosexual *behavior,* in which one decides to act on one's impulses by being physically intimate with someone of the same sex. The second and third are clearly choices: we have a choice regarding *how we self-identify* and also *how we respond to our impulses.* But we may, in fact, have very little choice regarding the first: our feelings of attraction.

Wesley Hill began his book, *Washed and Waiting: Reflections on Christian Faithfulness and Homosexuality,* this way:

> By the time I started high school, two things became clear to me. One was that I was a Christian. My parents had raised me to be a believer in Jesus, and as I moved toward independence from my family, I knew that I wanted to remain one—that I wanted to trust, love, and obey Christ, who had been crucified and raised from the dead "for us and for our salvation," as the Creed puts it. The second was that I was gay. For as long as I could remember, I had been drawn, even as a child, to other males in some vaguely confusing way, and after puberty, I had come to realize that I had a steady, strong, unremitting, exclusive sexual attraction to persons of the same sex.[5]

Hill notes, "There was nothing, it felt, chosen or intentional about my being gay. It seemed more like noticing the blueness of my eyes than deciding I would take up skiing. It was never an option—'Do you want to be gay? Yes, I do, please.' It was a gradual coming to terms, not a conscious resolution."[6]

THE CHRISTIAN APPROACH TO HOMOSEXUALITY

There is also much confusion about the Christian approach to homosexuality. Dennis Hollinger, president and distinguished professor of Christian ethics at Gordon-Conwell Theological Seminary, helpfully distinguishes between three things that Christians often stir together: Christian ethics, Christian pastoral care and a Christian approach to public policy.[7]

When we're talking about Christian ethics, we are talking about these things: God's ideal, God's will and God's intention for our sexuality. If we are talking about Christian pastoral care, we are talking about how we relate to people who have fallen short of God's ideal. Even if we agree on what God's ideal is regarding our human sexuality and on a pastoral approach regarding how we're going to relate to people who fall short of the ideal, when it comes to a Christian approach to public policy, we still have to decide our approach in a pluralistic society that doesn't necessarily agree with a Christian view of sexuality. As Christians relate to politics, we can't simply say, "Well, this is what it says in the Bible." We can't demand that everyone—Christian and non-Christian alike, people who know Jesus and people who don't—follow this. Public policy gets into practical concerns about what is enforceable, what is possible, what will harm the spread of the gospel and what is wise.

And there is confusion about the underlying causes of homosexuality. Popular media has generally coalesced around the idea that homosexuality is biologically based, so there are regular articles about differences in the brains of gays and straights. There are headlines touting "The Gay Gene" or "The Gay Brain." There are theories about hormonal levels in the womb. There is vigorous debate regarding causation even in the gay community. Older gays are committed to finding a genetic or biological cause for homosexuality. Some younger gays following a more postmodern approach would say that same-sex relationships are something that they choose as opposed to something that is forced on them by their "essential nature." But many gay people find themselves feeling attracted to persons of the same sex, seemingly without a choice. (Indeed, some say that being gay is contrary to what they would have chosen.)

The bottom line, according to William Byne and Bruce Parsons, psychiatrists at Columbia University, concerning the present state of research on the origins of homosexuality is this: "Recent studies postulate biological factors as the primary basis for sexual orientation. However, there is no conclusive evidence at present to substantiate a biological theory, just as there is no compelling evidence to support any singular psycho-social explanation. Homosexuality appears to be a pluriform phenomenon."[8]

In other words, sexual attraction appears to have multiple causes. Our sexuality is not simple, and it is not straightforward.

WHAT'S WRONG WITH SEX WITHIN A COMMITTED GAY RELATIONSHIP?

I noted earlier that a biblical approach to sex says that it must be practiced in the context of covenantal commitment. But what if a gay couple says that they are in a committed relationship? Isn't that biblical?

Sex, the Bible teaches, was given as a pointer to God.

The LORD God said, "It is not good for the man to be alone. I will make a helper suitable for him." Now the LORD God had formed out of the ground all the wild animals and all the birds in the sky. He brought them to the man to see what he would name them; and whatever the man called each living creature, that was its name. So the man gave names to all the livestock, the birds in the sky and all the wild animals. But for Adam no suitable helper was found. So the LORD God caused the man to fall into a deep sleep; and while he was sleeping, he took one of the man's ribs and then closed up the place with flesh. Then the LORD God made a woman from the rib he had taken out of the man, and he brought her to the man. The man said,

"This is now bone of my bones
    and flesh of my flesh;
she shall be called 'woman,'
    for she was taken out of man."

That is why a man leaves his father and mother and is united to his wife, and they become one flesh. Adam and his wife were both naked, and they felt no shame. (Genesis 2:18-25)

The scene is the Garden of Eden, and Adam is alone. So God makes Adam a helper—more literally, "a counterpart." God makes a woman to stand alongside of the man—not over the man or under the man but alongside the man, equal to and yet different from him. This equality and complementarity points to the mystery we Christians find in the Trinity: three persons of equal worth and dignity, yet differentiated. God the Father is not God the Son. And God the Son is not God the Spirit. Equality *and* difference.

And there is this extraordinary coming together we read in Genesis 2:24, "That is why a man leaves his father and mother and is united to his wife, and they become one flesh."

This union of the man and woman suggests that sex is designed to pull us out of ourselves to join us with another. Sexual intercourse is an act of self-giving, sacrificial love for the person who is different from us: our complement and our counterpart. And this relationship is exclusive. We're joined to this other person. It is permanent, and it is marked by faithfulness. All of these things point to our own relationship with Christ.

The apostle Paul picks up on this creation account in Genesis 2 in Ephesians 5:31-32, where he writes, "'For this reason a man will leave his father and mother and be united to his wife, and the two will become one flesh.' This is a profound mystery—but I am talking about Christ and the church." So the marriage relationship points to this exclusive, loving, sacrificial and self-giving holy union that a Christian believer can have with Jesus. Sex and sexuality, when it is right, points to the triune God and the relationship that exists between members of the Trinity. Sex, when it is right, also points to a believer's relationship with Jesus Christ: exclusive, faithful, self-giving, self-sacrificial and holy.

In the New Testament, probably the most important text forbidding the practice of gay sex is found in Romans 1:21-27:

> For although they knew God, they neither glorified him as God nor gave thanks to him, but their thinking became futile and their foolish hearts were darkened. Although they claimed to be wise, they became fools and exchanged the glory of the immortal God for images made to look like a mortal human being and birds and animals and reptiles. Therefore God gave them over in the sinful desires of their hearts to sexual impurity for the degrading of their bodies with one another. They exchanged the truth about God for a lie, and worshiped and served created things rather than the Creator—who is forever praised. Amen. Because of this, God gave them over to shameful lusts. Even their women exchanged natural sexual relations for unnatural ones. In the same way the men also abandoned natural relations with women and were inflamed with lust for one another. Men committed shameful acts with other men, and received in themselves the due penalty for their error.

The apostle Paul is illustrating one of the many tragic consequences of rebelling against God. He asserts that when we move away from God, we turn God's creation order on its head. We exchange God's creation order for our own upside-down order. When we human beings turn our backs on God, we end up worshiping the creation. Instead of a man and woman coming together in an exclusive, faithful, lifelong union, we turn God's created purpose of sexuality on its head. We try to find our completion and our fulfillment not in our counterpart, our complementary other, but in someone who is just like us, a person of our own gender.[9]

Gay marriage, of course, is no longer an abstraction. It is a legal reality in many states and in a growing number of countries. So how should Christians relate to a growing number of gay friends, neighbors and family members who are getting married or who are in long-term committed relationships?

PASTORAL CARE TOWARD GAYS AND FELLOW STRUGGLERS

What happens when we don't live up to God's ideal in some area of life—whether it is God's ideal regarding money, marriage, the use of alcohol, our emotions or our sexual lives and homosexual practice? How should the church approach someone who has sinned sexually? When we fall short of God's ideal of either total fidelity within lifelong heterosexual marriage or complete abstinence, how should the church approach us?

The apostle Paul's great moral analysis of the entire human race is this: "for all have sinned and fall short of the glory of God" (Romans 3:23). In this text, Paul is echoing the prophet Isaiah who said, "We all, like sheep, have gone astray, each of us has turned to our own way" (Isaiah 53:6). And if you say, "That doesn't describe me!" the Bible speaks to that attitude as well. The apostle John says, "If we claim to be without sin, we deceive ourselves and the truth is not in us" (1 John 1:8).

Let's take the case of someone who is practicing gay sex and who now comes to church. We have many gay people and gay couples who attend the church that I pastor. How should they be pastored? Pastoral theology is not just a method; it's also a *tone*. When dealing with real humans beings with all their complexities and ambiguities, pastoral theology speaks with a tone of humility and something less than 100 percent certainty concerning all things. Often, it's not what we pastors or leaders say that is so off-putting. It is our tone, which is sometimes haughty, absolutist and severe. Let's look at a few things that the church should offer.

The church should offer love. The apostle Paul offers what I believe to be the very best strategy for relating to anyone, but especially for relating to people who have fallen short of God's ideal. It is Paul's strategic advice for all human relationships and for all situations. He says "Love never fails" (1 Corinthians 13:8). So when we talk about how we should relate to those who are sexually broken, the first thing we should do is offer love. You might say, "I don't know how to relate to my Muslim neighbor or my Jewish coworker." Paul says, "Have you tried love?" Love never fails!

That's what my friend Marlene did with me in college. I was a Jewish atheist. Marlene came from a little town in Ohio and had never met a Jewish person until a few days before she met me, when she met her Jewish roommate. I was the second Jewish person that Marlene had ever met. And trust me: Marlene was no expert in answering the questions of a Jewish atheist from New York. But she loved me. She was exceptionally kind, and she accepted me unconditionally. Love is always a great strategy when you don't know what to do toward another person.

Some Christians might honestly say, "I just find aspects of gay sex really upsetting. I'm turned off when a man acts effeminately or when a woman is overly butch or when people march down the street in a gay pride parade. How can I love someone when they do things that I find really upsetting?" C. S. Lewis wrote something that just nailed me to the wall. How do you love someone whose actions or behaviors you find really unacceptable, or worse than unacceptable, actions you find revolting? Lewis wrote, "There is someone that I love even though I don't approve of what he does. There is someone I accept, though some of his thoughts and actions revolt me. There is someone I forgive, though he hurts the people I love the most. That person is me."[10]

You and I have plenty of practice loving someone who disgusts us at times. We've lived with that person all our lives, and we're still able to function! We all do plenty of things that we don't like, but we still manage to love ourselves. Somehow we manage to accept ourselves without approving of everything we do. We do it all the time. So how about treating the rest of the world with as much love and acceptance as we have toward ourselves?

The church should offer grace. How should we relate to someone who has fallen short of God's ideal? Followers of Jesus should be better than anyone in offering grace because we have given our lives to the God of second, third, fifteenth, and three hundredth chances. The Christian faith is designed for moral failures. The Bible is the story of moral failures and the God who shows grace to these moral failures. Starting with Adam and Eve and going on to Abraham, Sarah, Isaac, Rebekah, Jacob, Moses, Aaron, Gideon, Samson, King David, the apostle Peter and the apostle Paul: the Bible tells us about folks who have blown it and received the grace of God. We don't clean ourselves up to come to God or to come to church. The story of the Bible is that we come to God and to the church as we are. *Then* the Lord cleans us up.

Some in the church have missed this most basic notion of showing grace. We think that our job is to be the moral police of the world. We feel obligated to let everyone know our moral standards so there are no misunderstandings regarding where we stand. But this is wrong-headed! The leading edge of a Christian's relationship with anyone is not where we differ morally. The first thing that people ought to encounter is not our view of abortion or sex or greed. The first thing that they ought to experience when they meet us is the offer of friendship and grace.

The church should offer community. In addition to love and grace, the church should offer community. In the Garden of Eden, there was one thing that God said was not good. Seven times in Genesis 1, God saw something he created and he called it good. There was just one thing in that perfect garden that God saw wasn't good: "The LORD God said, 'It is not good for the man to be alone'" (Genesis 2:18).

Marriage is one way that the Lord heals the aloneness of men and women, the "not good" of being by ourselves in this world. But it is not the only way. Sadly, "family-oriented" churches sometimes so exalt marriage as the be-all and end-all of the Christian life that we communicate that there is no other way to heal aloneness. We need to remember Jesus, our model for perfect humanity, was not married. The apostle Paul, the primary interpreter of the meaning of Christ's coming, was not married, at least when he wrote his letters. Marriage is not the ultimate. It is a good gift, but it is confined to this world. There will be no marriage in God's coming kingdom (Matthew 22:30).

But there *will* be community. According to Jesus, our primary bond is our connection with other Christians who enjoy fellowship with God through our Lord Jesus Christ. If there is one thing that needs to be the center of any church's approach to healing whatever ails us, it is friendship and community. A young lady in my church recently shared with me that she is seriously thinking about leaving her partner because of what God is doing in her life. However, this has been a very difficult decision for her because she knows it will result in her being shunned by her gay community, which has been her only family for the last decade. She actually tried to leave her gay community once before, only to return later because she could not find another group that offered what they did. So it is absolutely vital that our churches offer genuine community where this young lady and others like her will find a true family.

The church cannot offer marriage to everyone, but we can offer friendship. We can offer community to everyone. We all need people we can spend our lives with, folks we can hang out with, friends we can laugh with and cry with, friends we can grieve with and pray with and debate with. Gays need friends! Straights need friends! Churches ought to be better at connecting people to friends than any other group on earth.

The church should offer the forgiveness of sins. This is the case for both the heterosexual sinner and the homosexual sinner. Joanna Hyatt of Reality Check in Los Angeles says,

> I absolutely think we should encourage "renewed abstinence." You cannot talk about sex within the Christian community without also mentioning God's grace. If we're serious about people growing in their faith, we have to help them see this issue will stand in the way of their relationship with God, but doesn't have to keep them from God. We need abstinence as a way to make a stand, to commit again of living a life of purity in body,

heart, and mind. There may be consequences you'll have to deal
with from past decisions, but those decisions do not define who
you will be going forward, or the nature of your relationships.[11]

In other words, churches must reject the one-strike-and-you're-out
rule for us sexual sinners. Many Christians feel that they are "damaged
goods," since they are no longer virgins and have engaged in either
heterosexual or homosexual sex. But right on the heels of texts that
condemn sexual activity outside of marriage come incredible promises
of God's grace and mercy—grace and mercy bought with the price of
God's own self-sacrifice. Paul wrote to the Christians in Corinth: "Or
do you not know that wrongdoers will not inherit the kingdom of God?
Do not be deceived: Neither the sexually immoral nor idolaters nor
adulterers nor men who have sex with men nor thieves nor the greedy
nor drunkards nor slanderers nor swindlers will inherit the kingdom of
God" (1 Corinthians 6:9-10). But immediately after this, as the apostle
Paul often does when stating those things that God condemns, he issues
a statement of God's grace and mercy toward sinners: "And that is what
some of you *were*. But you were washed, you were sanctified, you were
justified in the name of the Lord Jesus Christ and by the Spirit of our
God" (1 Corinthians 6:11).

The church should offer a call to self-denial as the key to living a
full life. Jesus said: "Whoever wants to be my disciple must deny themselves and take up their cross and follow me. For whoever wants to save
their life will lose it, but whoever loses their life for me and for the
gospel will save it. What good is it for someone to gain the whole world,
yet forfeit their soul? Or what can anyone give in exchange for their
soul?" (Mark 8:34-37).

A call to self-denial is issued to every person on earth. Every one of
us has to continually deny our impulses if we want to follow Jesus and
experience his friendship in our lives. If you are a single person, heterosexual or gay, you are called to abstinence. If you are a married person,
you are called to lifelong fidelity to one person in sickness and in health

until death. All followers of Jesus must continually say no to themselves and to their appetites, prejudices, sinful desires and rebellion. This is not cruelty. You say no to yourself and to your sin so that you can say yes to God. Saying yes to God, means you say to God, "I will stop pushing you away. I will give you permission to do whatever you want to do in my life!" When you say "Yes, Lord!" that's when you experience abundant life.

Wesley Hill, a gay Christian who is committed to lifelong celibacy, wrote to an older single friend to ask, "How can I go on living with this frustration?" In other words, why not throw in the towel and enter into a committed, loving and sexual relationship with another man? His friend wrote him back saying:

> Many, many people are (and have been) in the same boat [as you]. I am 41 years old, a virgin, and one who has NEVER experienced physical intimacy with a woman or a man. Do I long for it? Sure. But God's grace is fully sufficient to accomplish his purposes in me. Furthermore, I suggest that living with unfulfilled desires is not the exception of the human experience, but the rule. Even most of those who are married are as Thoreau once said, "living lives of quiet regret." Maybe they married the wrong person or have the pain of suffering within marriage, or feel trapped in their situations, and are unable to fulfill a high sense of calling. The list of unfulfilled desires goes on and on. But . . . the gospel does not necessarily promise a rescue plan out of the pain of living with homosexual desires. Instead, it is a message about God's strange working in and through that pain—God's "alchemy of re-demption" as Philip Yancey calls it. "My power is made perfect in—not in the absence of, but in the midst of—weakness," the Lord said to Paul (2 Corinthians 12:9).[12]

In other words, most people in this world live with significant degrees of unmet needs. Forty-five percent of the people in the church that I pastor are single adults. Many (though not all) would like to be married. Statistically speaking, it is likely that a significant percentage of these single heterosexual adults will never find a marriage partner. And many of the people in our church who are in heterosexual marriages find their marriages to be very challenging. But self-fulfillment is not God's ultimate goal for our lives: Christlikeness is! And Christlikeness most often comes about through pain and waiting.

It is imperative for the church to offer gays love, grace, community, hope for change, forgiveness of sins and a call to self-denial. But if we are to be faithful to Scripture and to the Christian church's universal understanding of Scripture, the church simply cannot and must not offer affirmation for behavior the Bible labels as sin. Thus the church, if it is to be faithful, should not ordain someone (or recognize someone as a leader in the church) who is committed to having sex outside of heterosexual marriage. In other words, we should not ordain a person or recognize someone as a church leader who is involved in an extramarital, premarital or same-sex sexual relationship, and we must discipline those leaders who violate Scripture in these ways. Neither should the church participate in a same-sex marriage ceremony.[13]

A REAL-LIFE STORY

There is a guy in our church who I will call Dave. He was raised in a large Roman Catholic family, and his dad was absent a lot while he was growing up. Dave went to a Catholic seminary, where he was molested by a teacher. Dave went to speak to the rector of the Catholic seminary, not knowing that the rector was himself a pedophile. The rector decided to head Dave off at the pass by calling his parents and saying that he had real concerns about Dave—that Dave was delusional and that he was making up stories and that he had seen some other real problems in Dave's life. Sadly, Dave's parents believed the rector. When Dave came home with the story of the abuse that he was suffering, they did not believe him.

This led to a major crisis in his life, during which Dave began cruising the parks and going to gay bars to meet men. He had a four-year relationship with a guy until one day he discovered that this man had been unfaithful in their relationship from the beginning. It wasn't long after this relationship ended that Dave was diagnosed with HIV.

Around this time, a former college roommate and his wife moved to Columbus and reentered Dave's life. Together, they started attending our church. The first Sunday that he was here, someone made an announcement about Project Compassion, which was our ministry to folks who have HIV/AIDS. Dave couldn't believe that a church would so openly minister to people who, in his past experience, the church just disregarded. That night when Dave got home, he cried uncontrollably for hours as he began to reconnect with God again. A couple of weeks later he gave his life to Christ, and so did his college roommate.

The story doesn't end there. Dave got involved in a men's group here in the church—not a group focused on homosexuality but just a group of guys who got together to help each other live authentic Christian lives in this world. These men had no experience with gay men, but Dave found that they were really honest about their own brokenness. Many of them were struggling with their own sexuality and issues from their pasts. The more they opened up, the more Dave felt free to open up about his life. And in this environment of friendship, acceptance and love, these men helped each other to walk out of their brokenness. Dave says now, "I've left the homosexual lifestyle entirely behind. That's not who I am anymore."

For several years, Dave has led a ministry in our church to men and women who are struggling with homosexuality and with homosexual desire and temptation. He calls the ministry Gideon's Call. Several of Dave's friends who he knew from his days of going to bars to meet men have come to Jesus through this ministry and the power of Dave's testimony.

I've heard dozens of stories like this one. There are Daves all around us who desperately need to experience the love and grace and friendship and healing that can only be found in the community of God's people.

SHOULD THE CHURCH ENGAGE IN THE FIGHT OVER SAME-SEX MARRIAGE?

The tide of public opinion regarding gay marriage is shifting rapidly across America. At the time of this book's writing, the United States Supreme Court has just struck down key provisions of the Defense of Marriage Act (DOMA) by a 5-4 vote, ruling that married same-sex couples were entitled to federal benefits. The Supreme Court also cleared the way for same-sex marriage in our nation's most populous state, California. There are now thirteen states that allow same-sex marriage. The Defense Department chose to join with many cities and states in celebrating June as Gay Pride Month. The California state legislature passed a first-of-its-kind ban on reparative therapy, which is therapy intended to heal same-sex attraction. And Robert Spitzer, considered by some to be a father of modern psychiatry, apologized for his prior support of reparative therapy. Exodus International, the nation's largest ex-gay ministry, just closed their doors and their CEO offered an apology to the gay community for the hurt their ministry has caused so many people.

Sincere Christians will differ on whether Christian churches should be involved in attempting to legislate against same-sex marriage. Some Christians believe that marriage ought not to be a state issue in the first place. Marriage, in their opinion, is a church rite. They say things like "We must not confuse church rites with civil rights. So let civil society do whatever it wishes concerning its definition of marriage; we in the church will have our own standards for performing 'Christian marriage.'"

I think this position is naïve. As Abraham Lincoln said in his House Divided speech, "I believe this government cannot endure, permanently, half slave and half free. I do not expect the Union to be dissolved—I do not expect the house to fall—but I do expect it will cease to be divided. It will become all one thing or all the other."[14] Regarding affirming homosexual sex as the moral equivalent of heterosexual sex, we will, I believe, become "all one thing or all the other." The larger society will not long tolerate churches that dissent from a consensus view of what contributes to the common good. As the consensus moves toward acceptance of same-sex marriage, churches will experience pressure to fall into line. For example, Illinois canceled its contract with Catholic Charities over the church agency's refusal to place adoptive children with same-sex couples. New York recently did the same. And depending on court decisions, it may soon become illegal for churches in California to engage in healing prayer for gay and lesbian teens who wish to change their sexual orientation.

On the other hand, I believe that the church generally should confine itself to the teaching of Scripture and the demonstration of Scripture through love and good deeds. History and wisdom would suggest that in most situations, we ought to leave it to individual Christians to fight for or against particular pieces of legislation. I am particularly concerned when advocacy for or against legislation might create a major obstacle to an individual's embrace of the Savior.

While I would not suggest this to be an absolute rule, in the case of same-sex marriage, I currently believe that it is the role of churches to teach their members God's plan for marriage—one man and one woman who live together in a lifelong covenant before God. The church should then encourage individual Christians to work through the democratic processes, as their consciences dictate, concerning whether to vote for or against a particular piece of legislation. Christians should be as invested in civil society as anyone else, bringing their own moral perspectives to bear on decisions. But churches should be very reserved about supporting or opposing specific pieces of legislation.

Let's come back to the question we asked at the beginning of the chapter: Should the church be more conservative or more progressive than the surrounding culture? The answer is not as simple as we sometimes make it out to be. How we live out our holiness is very much tied to what we see around us in the world. To live out of sync with the world means that we must constantly rethink and reevaluate our perspectives as the world changes. We must never lose sight of the Holy One who is calling us to live in holiness, *both* personal and social.

10

What Is Our Ethic?

. . . AND SOCIAL

One. Twenty-five. Fifty-one.

These numbers are not signals being called by a quarterback in the huddle. They're not my birthday. This is not a secret code. *One* is precisely the number of texts in the entire Bible that appear to directly prohibit a woman from preaching or being a senior pastor.[1] *Twenty-five* is the number of interpretive difficulties that Bible scholars have run into in attempting to interpret that text.[2] *Fifty-one* is the percentage of the human race that has had the door slammed in their faces in pursuing a calling to preach or to lead a congregation.

In my New York Jewish family, I simply assumed that a woman could do virtually anything a man could do. The women I knew were strong and competent and were leaders in my high school class. So I grew up in an environment in which women were free to be and to do anything that their gifts and talents permitted them to be and do. In my Inter-Varsity Christian Fellowship college group, women were permitted to lead without restriction because of gender.

My wife, Marlene, and I moved to Columbus in the late 1970s for me to attend law school. We joined a little church that was the predecessor of Vineyard Columbus. That church came under the teaching of an ecumenical community from Ann Arbor, Michigan, called The Word of God Community. The Word of God Community had a very traditional perspective regarding appropriate roles for men and women. In fact, they taught that men should not even change their babies' diapers because that is a woman's role! None of us in Columbus ever went that far. But they taught that women could not be ordained as pastors in a church and that they could never even preach to a mixed assembly of men and women.

In the early 1990s, I began to reject this traditional teaching as a result of several things. First of all, there was a growing body of excellent biblical scholarship that challenged the traditional reading of texts such as 1 Timothy 2.[3]

The second thing that changed my views from the traditionalism that our church was taught in the 1980s was the incoherence of church practice when it came to women. Everywhere I looked, I found churches saying one thing and doing something else. Their actions were based, supposedly, on one biblical text: 1 Timothy 2. Some churches would permit women to "share" from the Bible for an hour, but forbid women from "teaching." Or women could teach so long as they were "under the covering of their husbands" (whatever that meant). Or women could preach and lead on the mission field in Africa or Latin America, but they couldn't do those things here at home. This last practice, in essence, is saying that those people on the mission field are like children, not fully adult or fully human.

In one particular denomination, a very prominent woman was permitted to preach from the floor of the convention hall, but she wasn't permitted to stand on the stage. Another denomination even permits women to preach from the pulpit on the right side of the stage but never from the pulpit on the left. One seminary prepares women to teach but never to be ordained as pastors. Another denomination permits women to be senior pastors but never bishops.

One evangelical theologian has written a massive tome that lists thirty-five different kinds of teaching, from teaching Bible or theology in a seminary to singing hymns in a congregation. This particular theologian would, according to his reading of Scripture, forbid women from teaching men in a college fellowship group but would allow women to teach men in a high school fellowship group. He would permit a woman to be the director of an adult Sunday school program, but not allow her to serve as the permanent leader of a coed home fellowship group.[4]

Now if you can keep all of these different rules straight in your mind, you are doing better than I am. The most likely conclusion to draw from such differing and incoherent rules is that churches set the standard for permissible roles for women based on subjective feelings of comfort rather than a clear word from God.

The thing that really pushed me toward a progressive view of women's roles in the church was the realization that the door to church leadership was being slammed in the face of 51 percent of the human race, without regard to gifting or calling. This prohibition was based on one single biblical text—and one that was being inaccurately read.

DETERMINING GENDER ROLES IN THE CHURCH

A woman named Rita wrote to me and said that from the moment she came to Christ, she believed she was called to ministry. The day after she received Christ, she led someone else to Jesus. She went to a seminary and was trained, but the church she joined would not permit women to be pastors. They strung her along for years allowing her to teach in youth ministry, to be an administrator and to work with other women. They even gave her a ministry license, but they refused to give her the title of *pastor*. She is a licensed minister of the gospel—but not a pastor.

The new pastor of Rita's church says that he might permit women to have the title of pastor, but he is still deciding on that. She's been waiting for the past year for him to make a decision. My heart breaks for women like Rita: women who are rejected from church leadership not because of any character defect or want of gifting but simply on the basis of gender.

How should we approach the subject of women in Christian ministry and women as senior pastors? Let me suggest four rules for determining women's appropriate roles in the church.

Creation and redemption. First, women's roles should be determined by starting with creation and redemption. When we discuss Christian theology, ethics or practice, it is important to pay attention to which texts we choose as we begin to form our views. Our beginning point often determines our ending point. For example, if we are thinking about the person of Christ and whether, as deity, he is coequal with the Father, where do we begin? Do we begin with a text like Mark 13:32, which reads, "But about that day or hour no one knows, not even the angels in heaven, nor the Son, but only the Father"? This text could be read to suggest that the Son is less than the Father. Or should we begin with a text like John 1:1, which says, "In the beginning was the Word, and the Word was with God, and the Word was God"? Orthodox theologians throughout Christian history have started with John 1:1 and interpreted texts like Mark 13:32 in light of John 1:1, not the other way around.

So if one's starting point in Scripture determines one's ending point, it matters where we start when figuring out what roles are open to women in the church. Do we begin with the most restrictive text in the Bible and interpret everything in light of that seeming restriction? Or do we begin with texts that suggest the equality of men and women in creation and redemption? The restrictive texts reflect the complexities of a fallen world and may be a reflection of what *is*, but they do not necessarily reflect God's intent for what *should be*. Creation and redemption should overrule the fall.

I would suggest that the conversation about appropriate roles for women in the church would be furthered by starting with Genesis 1, the fundamental creation text: "Then God said, 'Let us make mankind in our image, in our likeness, so that they may rule over the fish in the sea and the birds in the sky, over the livestock and all the wild animals, and over all the creatures that move along the ground.' So God created mankind in his own image, in the image of God he created them; *male and female he created them"* (Genesis 1:26-27).

Equality between the genders is established in creation, and it is confirmed in redemption. "So in Christ Jesus you are all children of God through faith, for all of you who were baptized into Christ have clothed yourselves with Christ. There is neither Jew nor Gentile, neither slave nor free, nor is there male and female, for you are all one in Christ Jesus" (Galatians 3:26-28).

So in approaching the subject of gender roles, one of the fundamental questions is: what is our starting point in Scripture?

Spiritual giftedness. A second way to approach the subject of women's roles in the church is by spiritual giftedness. My understanding of appropriate roles in the church is based primarily on my conviction that spiritual giftedness determines one's role in the body. The church movement that I belong to has been shaped by our experience of the Holy Spirit. Our experience is that the Holy Spirit is nondiscriminatory among us. For example, we read,

> Even on my servants, both men and women,
>   I will pour out my Spirit in those days,
>   and they will prophesy. (Acts 2:18)

This text is fundamental to the worldwide Pentecostal, charismatic and empowered evangelical streams of the church. It is also a good example of why evangelicals need the perspective of the charismatic emphasis on giftedness. Pentecostals and charismatics have tended to be more affirming of women in ministry than evangelicals largely because of their understanding of the Spirit and gifts.

When we study Paul's teaching about spiritual gifts, we see that gifts are not given due to human merit, ethnic origin, social status or gender. Spiritual gifts are simply the result of the will of the sovereign Holy Spirit, as well as the grace of the risen Christ.[5] There is no text that limits the endowment of leadership or teaching gifts simply to men.

Thus, as I consider whether a role in the church ought to be open to a person, my first question is, "Has the Holy Spirit sovereignly given that person gifts for that role?" If I see teaching gifts or leadership gifts in a woman, I find myself in the position of the apostle Peter, who, when he was challenged by the Jerusalem church because he had eaten with Gentiles, said, "So if God gave them the same gift he gave us who believed in the Lord Jesus Christ, who was I to think that I could stand in God's way?" (Acts 11:17). I never want to find myself opposing what God is doing in the life of another person. If God has given a woman gifts to teach or to lead, then who am I to stand in God's way?

The kingdom of God. Third, women's roles should be determined with an eye to the coming kingdom of God. The central message of Jesus was the inbreaking of the kingdom of God. This means that through the coming of Christ, God's reign was breaking into this world. Christ introduced into this world the age to come, in which God will reign unopposed. In the future age every other ruler, dominion and authority that stands in opposition to almighty God will ultimately be destroyed. Because Christ introduced that future age in his first coming, we get to taste something of the ultimate purpose of God right now.

So when we wrestle with theological, ethical and practical problems in the church, we must ask: What is God's *ultimate purpose?* And to find God's ultimate purpose, we must ask: What will the future kingdom of God be like? What will the world be like when Christ returns and sets up his kingdom here on earth?

The Lord taught us to pray in the Lord's Prayer, "Your kingdom come, your will be done, on earth as it is in heaven" (Matthew 6:10). What are we praying for in that petition? We're praying, "God, bring your reign into this world now just as it will be when Jesus returns and sets up his eternal kingdom." "Bring your reign into this world now in such a way that my mother's cancer is healed." "God, bring your reign into the world in such a way that my friend decides not to leave her marriage but instead to be reconciled." "God, bring your reign into the world in such a way that hungry people are fed, thirsty people are given clean water and children are loved and protected and not sold into prostitution."

By focusing on the coming kingdom, abolitionists during the nineteenth century argued that slavery does not reflect God's ultimate purpose for this world. They understood that there is a trajectory to Scripture. It points ahead of itself toward God's ultimate reign, and in the ultimate reign of God, there will be no slavery. Likewise, when the ultimate reign of God comes, men will not rule over women.

Promoting the gospel. Fourth, women's roles in the church should be determined by asking: What role will promote the gospel? In 1 Corinthians 9:19-23, the apostle Paul offers us his *modus operandi*:

> Though I am free and belong to no one, I have made myself a slave to everyone, to win as many as possible. To the Jews I became like a Jew, to win the Jews. To those under the law I became like one under the law (though I myself am not under the law), so as to win those under the law. To those not having the law I became like one not having the law (though I am not free from God's law but am under Christ's law), so as to win those not having the law. To the weak I became weak, to win the weak. I have become all things to all people so that by all possible means I might save some. I do all this for the sake of the gospel, that I may share in its blessings.

According to Ben Witherington, professor of New Testament at Asbury Theological Seminary, "[Paul] accommodates his style of living, not his theological or ethical principles, to whomever he is with *so as better to win that person to Christ*."[6] The apostle Paul is expounding a principle of missionary accommodation and flexibility.

Such accommodation is, of course, limited by the ethics of Christ. As D. A. Carson, research professor of New Testament at Trinity Evangelical Divinity School, points out, it is difficult to conceive of Paul saying, for instance, "For the adulterer I became as an adulterer in order that I might win the adulterer," or "To the idol worshiper I became an idol worshiper in order that I might win the idol worshiper."[7] Likewise, Paul's willingness to accommodate is limited by the gospel itself. In other words, Paul wishes to win people by all means *to the Christian gospel.* Where he feels that the gospel itself is being compromised, Paul is radically inflexible.[8]

Some suggest that this argument—the flexible accommodation to contemporary sensibilities in order to promote the gospel—opens the door to the possibility of the church ordaining gays or lesbians. But as William Webb points out in *Slaves, Women & Homosexuals,* "Just because some things in Scripture are cultural, that does not mean that everything in Scripture is cultural."[9]

The Bible draws a bright line of distinction between moral prohibitions, on the one hand, and rules pertaining to cultural and social relationships, on the other. When the Bible calls something sin, it is sin for everyone, everywhere and for all time. Adultery, premarital sex and homosexual sex will always remain sin no matter how frequent or popular their practice becomes. But ordaining a woman is never called sin in the Bible. Its appropriateness is rooted in pragmatic concerns regarding the gospel's promotion.

How did Paul's flexibility and willingness to accommodate non-Christian sensibilities work itself out regarding men's and women's roles? The biblical world was thoroughly male dominated and hierarchical. Commands in the Bible about men's and women's appropriate roles ought not to be detached from the world to which those commands were addressed. But the ultimate concern of the apostle Paul and other biblical writers concerning appropriate social roles is *the promotion or hindrance of the gospel.*

We see this explicitly stated in the pastoral epistles. For example, in 1 Timothy and throughout Titus, there is a concern that Christians should live in a manner that promotes the gospel and presents the best possible face to the first-century world. Throughout the pastoral epistles, the apostle Paul displays an overriding missional concern. The motive clauses used to promote certain kinds of behavior (especially regarding social relations) point strongly in this direction: "to give the enemy no opportunity for slander" (1 Timothy 5:14); "so that God's name and our teaching may not be slandered" (1 Timothy 6:1); "so that no one will malign the word of God" (Titus 2:5); "so that those who oppose you may be ashamed because they have nothing bad to say about us" (Titus 2:8); "so that in every way they will make the teaching about God our Savior attractive" (Titus 2:10).

Regarding women's roles and 1 Timothy 2 specifically, the apostle Paul argues that for the sake of the church's reputation in the Greco-Roman world of the first century, women must not cease to model the ideals of submissiveness and silence when the church gathers. David deSilva states, "Wherever non-Christians might observe Christians, the impression must be made that Christians embody traditional social and domestic values rather than overturning them. . . . [The instruction regarding women's behavior] and the theological rationales are driven by the larger agenda of building bridges between the Christian culture and the larger society that will, in turn, assist the church to win the battles that it deems essential."[10]

Likewise, Christian leaders are summoned to instruct slaves to model the qualities of obedience and respect toward their masters (1 Timothy 6:1-2; Titus 2:9-10). Considering these passages, deSilva writes, "By such conduct they [Christian slaves] will clarify that Christianity is not a revolutionary movement that breeds revolt and threatens the fundamental bedrock of the Greco-Roman economy—namely, slave labor. Older women are enjoined to teach the younger women how to embody the Greco-Roman ideal of the 'virtuous wife,' which combines submissiveness to the husband, modesty in dress and demeanor, silence ('invisibility') in public and competent diligence in the management of domestic concerns."[11]

Virtually all of the commands found in Paul's writings concerning women's roles are written in the context of limiting feminine freedom in order not to hinder others from accepting the gospel. To cite another example, the apostle commands women to wear a head covering and to wear long hair (1 Corinthians 11:5-6). Why? Because according to the social customs of the day, short hair and the absence of a head covering would interfere with the promotion of the gospel. The apostle wants women's worship practice not to involve any appearance that would be considered shameful or disgraceful to the larger Greco-Roman world.

In sum, the apostle enjoins Christians to engage in winsome behavior that will provide the witness of a virtuous life (according to the standards of that culture) and will contribute to the positive value of the Christian gospel.

A contemporary application of the apostle Paul's approach to the social order might be counsel to Christians living in China. The great fear of the Chinese government is that Christians may, because of their prior loyalties to Christ and each other, subvert the state's authority. Thus we might, along with the apostle Paul, advise Chinese Christians to show support for the government by praying for their leaders, being dependable, hard-working employees and not participating in revolutionary activities. In other words, we might urge them to be model citizens, to the extent to which this does not conflict with scriptural commands or prohibitions. All of this counsel would be part of an overriding missional agenda designed to promote the Christian movement and to further the gospel.

A contemporary application of the apostle Paul's specific counsel to women might be for Christian women to limit their Christian freedom in a rural Pakistani village by being veiled in public, showing no public affection to their husbands and refraining from publicly communicating with men who are not family members. On the other hand, Paul's limitations on women would not keep women in most American or Western European communities from serving in any ministry role, since the reputation of the Christian church would not be damaged by such service. Indeed, in twenty-first-century America and throughout the Western world, the reputation of the church and the gospel itself would be severely injured by discriminating against women simply based on their gender. Imagine attempting to explain to a Boston or New York or Amsterdam audience why a gifted, godly and qualified woman could not lead a coed small group or preach or pastor a church. You had better bring police protection!

The basic biblical rule, then, is this: *live out your freedom in Christ in a way that is neither culturally offensive nor unstrategic to the spread of the gospel.* Paul said there is neither Jew nor Greek, yet he was willing to become like either to win Jews and Greeks (Galatians 3:28; 1 Corinthians 9:19-22). He desired no offense to either Jews or Greeks, that they may be saved (1 Corinthians 10:32-33). He also affirmed that there is neither slave nor free, but he encouraged slaves to be subject to their masters so that the gospel could be spread (Ephesians 6:5-8; Colossians 3:22-25). This pragmatic principle should not suggest that Paul or the other biblical writers simply advocated submission to the status quo, however morally offensive the status quo is. But he could be enormously flexible in different cultural settings.

Paul promoted gender equality. He had coworkers who were women, and he let women teach men in different contexts (Romans 16:3; Acts 18:25-26). He often mentioned that women were of great value to him in spreading the gospel (Philippians 4:2-3). And women apparently exercised leadership in some of Paul's churches.[12] Indeed, Paul mentions Junia as "outstanding among the apostles" (Romans 16:7).

Thus, there is no biblical prohibition against women teaching or leading in the church. All roles are open, including those of senior pastor and elder, and they are entirely dependent on gifting and calling by God. But the role that a woman chooses depends on the culture in which she lives and whether her exercise of leadership or teaching would *promote or hinder the gospel.* Challenging the status quo involves a discerning inquiry into whether one's actions will ultimately hurt or help the gospel's spread.

Florence Nightingale, above all else, wanted to serve God in Christian ministry and in Christian leadership. But the door was slammed in her face. She said, "I would have given her [the church] my head, my hand, my heart. She would not have them. She did not know what to do with them. She told me to go back and do crochet in my mother's drawing-room; or, if I were tired of that, to marry and look well as the head of my husband's table. You may go to the Sunday

School, if you like it, she said. But she gave me no training even for that. She gave me neither work to do for her, nor education for it."[13]

I will not reject any woman who wants to give herself in service to the church. In our church, we have appointed women as pastors, church planters, church council members and Sunday morning preachers. I want to make a heartfelt appeal to pastors: do not allow women in your congregation to spend years second-guessing themselves, wondering whether they are full of pride and selfish ambition because they feel called to leadership or preaching. If you believe that the Bible does not prohibit women from leading or preaching, then *boldly say so.* Bless women in your congregations. Affirm their gifts. Actively work to promote women in various roles. In your messages, use women as examples of leaders. In other words, don't just wait for a courageous woman to emerge. Look around the congregation for women who can be promoted. In so doing, you will be following the path of your Lord, about whom Dorothy Sayers wrote, "Perhaps it was no wonder that women were first at the Cradle and last at the Cross. They had never known a man like this man. There never has been such another."[14] Two millennia is enough time for women to meet other men who are like that Man.

ABORTION: THE MARRIAGE OF SOCIAL PROGRESSIVISM AND MORAL TRADITIONALISM

Another hot-button topic today is abortion. Abortion is an opportunity for Christians to be morally traditional in a socially progressive way. Abortion is usually framed as *either* pro-women *or* pro-child, *either* socially progressive *or* morally traditional. But why not *both*? Why can't we be *both* pro-women *and* pro-child?

Young people today are decidedly more conservative than their parents and grandparents on one social issue. Which one? The answer, according to Harvard professor Robert Putnam, is abortion.[15]

In *American Grace: How Religion Divides and Unites Us*, Robert Putnam and David Campbell cite extensive survey results that show that young adults are more liberal than their elders concerning almost every social issue. For example, young adults are more permissive regarding gay marriage, premarital sex and marijuana use than are older generations. But post-boomers are significantly less pro-choice than their boomer parents. According to Putnam and Campbell, abortion is a stunning outlier for young adults. There is particularly strong disapproval for abortion for social or economic reasons, such as a woman who is married and doesn't want another child, a couple who feel that they can't afford more children or an unmarried woman who does not want to marry the father of the baby.

What accounts for this unexpected conservative shift in opinion on abortion? Putnam and Campbell suggest a few possibilities. Because young adults have grown up in a world of widely available contraceptives, pregnancy is generally seen as a failure to take responsibility for one's choices. In many cases, young adults feel that abortion amounts to an unwillingness to accept the consequences for one's own choices rather than a so-called tragic moral dilemma. "Taking responsibility for one's behavior" has great potential as a message for increasing the valuing of life among young adults.

A second reason that young adults are more willing to restrict the availability of abortion has to do with changing technology and the impact of ultrasound technology. When a mother can bring home a 3D video image of her baby, it is increasingly implausible to refer to a child in utero as "part of a woman's body" or "tissue." Even the impersonal "fetus" doesn't do justice to what a woman sees on her ultrasound.

Where are doors open for policy change with regard to abortion? While young adults are not in favor of prohibiting all abortions, there are a number of extremely viable legal restrictions of current abortion laws. These restrictions would include such things as the required offering of pre-abortion ultrasounds, mandatory informed consent forms, waiting periods and fetal pain counseling. Moreover, there is a huge opening for state and federal support for pregnancy clinics, which provide both pre- and post-birth assistance to mothers.

Of course this is just the morally traditional side of our approach to abortion. Where does social progressivism come into the abortion debate?

Diane Bauman, the head of our congregation's Value Life Ministry (our pro-life ministry), recently met with some of the leaders of a local hospital. The hospital leaders found out about our Value Life Ministry and were amazed that we would help people who were not members of our church who were in the category of at-risk pregnancies. They kept asking questions like, "What if they are Muslim; would you help them?" Diane responded, "Of course we would!" "What if they had a baby and are not married; would you still help them?" "Yes, we will still help them!" "Well, what if they had an abortion before?" Diane replied, "Absolutely, yes!" One of the social workers was in tears after hearing about our willingness to help anyone in need. She said to Diane, "Your church does more than the government to help women who are already inclined to not terminate their pregnancies but don't know how they can have a baby and survive."

The goal of our Value Life Ministry, like many pregnancy centers in the United States, is simply to help women who may be vulnerable to considering abortion. If women need nursery items like diapers or formula, we help with that. If they don't have their GED credential, we help with that. If they need to take ESL (English as a Second Language) classes or need social services, housing or job training, we help with those things. Ultimately, we want to share Christ with them, but first we help a woman believe that she can have her baby and still have a meaningful life.

Recently, a local Christian pastor asked Diane, "How do you know that someone is not going to take advantage of you when you give out baby clothes, diapers and formula for free? How can you be absolutely certain that the person really needs baby clothes or furniture or help with housing?"

Diane responded, "What if they are taking advantage of us? Why does that matter? The Lord will deal with that. Our job is to be generous. After all, Jesus doesn't ask if we are morally worthy before helping

us." Our Value Life Ministry is utterly nondiscriminatory in its generosity. We want to help anyone and everyone in need regardless of their
circumstance, ethnicity or religion. Abortion is a place in which we
have learned to be *both* morally traditional *and* socially progressive.

Maria (not her real name) was five months pregnant with her fourth
child. Her husband, who did not want to have another child, was vio-
lently coercing her to have an abortion. It was during this time that an
area pregnancy center referred Maria to our church's Value Life Ministry. After meeting with Diane, Maria decided that a MotherHeart
mentor—a woman in our church who mentors someone with an un-
planned pregnancy—would be a good plan for her. The mentor realized this was a serious situation and that Maria's life and the life of her
baby were in danger. The mentor helped Maria find safe housing so
that she would be protected from her abusive husband, and people
filled Maria's new apartment with furniture, clothes, food and other
things she needed for her baby. Due to her past abuse, Maria experienced complications with the delivery. But thanks to the support of
people who faithfully came alongside her, Maria gave birth to a healthy
baby boy. She and her other children are doing well today.

The ethic that drives the Both-And Christian must go deeper than
simply choosing a conservative or progressive view of life. Conserva-
tives will opt for traditional roles for women and for severe restrictions
on the right to abortion. Progressives will opt for nontraditional roles for
women and unrestricted access to abortion. But the biblical attitude
toward social roles, abortion and sexual practices—indeed, toward all of
life—simply does not fit into any of the normal political categories: red
state or blue state, Democrat or Republican, conservative or progressive.

Those of us who are Christians are called to derive our fundamental identity not from contemporary politics but from the gospel.
The church should not be the "Republican Party on its knees," nor
should it ever walk in lockstep with the Democratic Party. Holiness
demands that the church live in a distinctive way from the world personally *and* socially.

11

What Is Our Expectation?

ALREADY . . .

After spending time with Peter, James and John on the moutain, Jesus encountered a huge crowd of people as he was making his way down. The air was thick with excitement and anticipation as people gathered to see this man who they heard had performed amazing miracles and who even claimed to be the Son of God

As Jesus made his way through this crowd, one particular man caught his eye. There was a look of pain and desperation on the man's face. Jesus noticed that he had brought his son with him. With tears in his eyes, the man told Jesus that there was something wrong with his son: "Jesus, my son, my son whom I love, he needs help! He can't speak. He has seizures all the time. And sometimes he stiffens like a stone. I've searched everywhere to find someone who can help him, but no one has been able to do anything for him. I have nowhere else to turn. Jesus, if you can do anything, take pity on us and help us!"

Jesus was moved with compassion for this father and his son, and he said, "Everything is possible for one who believes." In response, the father said to Jesus, "I do believe; help me overcome my unbelief!" (Mark 9:23-24).

I think that these are some of the most honest and powerful words ever spoken. Something resonates in my heart when I read these words. They are a prayer and a confession rolled into one. They are hope and pain intertwined. They are love and fear holding hands. "I do believe; help me overcome my unbelief!"

WHEN YOU DOUBT GOD'S POWER

I can't imagine what went through this father's mind. Here he was, face to face with Jesus. He had heard all the wonderful stories about him—how he healed a blind man, cured a leper, showed compassion to prostitutes and tax collectors and seemed to be so different than anybody he'd ever known. This father wanted desperately to believe that all these stories about Jesus were true, but he just couldn't get over the fact that some of them seemed like fairy tales. They seemed too good to be true!

The father was wrestling with two fears. On the one hand, he was afraid that Jesus wouldn't be able to heal his son. On the other hand, he was afraid that Jesus *would* heal his son. If Jesus did this, then it raised many other questions: *What if this Jesus really is who he says he is? What if everything that I've been hearing about him is actually true? Can he be the Messiah? Because if Jesus could heal my son, then everything changes! It changes how I think about my life, and how I should relate to God and how I think about the way this world works. And that is terrifying!*

If we were honest with ourselves, we would all probably say that we have, at some point in our lives, experienced something of what this father experienced. We've been afraid that God can't heal but also afraid that he can. It's easier to explain a God who doesn't interfere with our lives; in fact, a God like that is easy to rationalize away. We might say, "God used to do miracles in the past, but he doesn't work that way anymore! He only did that in the Bible because the people in those days weren't as smart or as advanced as we are today." We may even say, "God loves us, but that's really about all that he can do now!" But what happens to us when this God who isn't supposed to work miracles today surprises us with one? How do we explain that away? And what does that mean for our life?

EXPERIENCING GOD'S POWER

My friend Mike suffered from epilepsy for over twenty years. His condition was so bad that he had three grand mal seizures and hundreds of petit mal seizures every week. Due to the severe nature of his epilepsy, he had to take over sixty pills a day. One day, a few Christians gathered to pray for Mike. During this prayer time, Mike felt something like a tornado going through his body, and he knew right away that God had done something inside him. He knew that he was completely and miraculously healed at that instant. Since that day, he has never had another grand mal seizure again![1]

A few years after Mike was healed, he said to his neurologist, "Let me tell you what happened to me." Mike shared the experience he had when people prayed for him. After he shared his story, he asked the doctor, "What do you think about that?" In a condescending tone, the doctor replied, "Oh, Mike, it wasn't the prayer. It's all just a coincidence. Your medication just began to take effect."

Mike had been taking sixty pills a day for over twenty years without any noticeable change in his condition. But the doctor claimed that suddenly, at the precise moment that Mike received prayer, the medicine finally took effect? I love how one person responded when someone told him that answers to prayers are just coincidences. "That may be so," he said. "But all I know is that when I pray, coincidences happen, and when I don't pray, they don't!"[2]

YOUR GOSPEL IS TOO SMALL!

One of the great tragedies among Christians today is that our gospel has become too small. The gospel is the amazing good news that the crucified and resurrected Jesus is Lord of the world and that he invites us, in every dimension of our lives, to be personally transformed. Then Jesus says to those who are transformed by him, "Come join me, and let's change the world together!" This is the gospel! Sadly, the church has sometimes reduced this amazing message of personal and global transformation to a form of fire insurance: "Accept Jesus and when you die, you won't go to hell." For too many of us today, the gospel is just too small. We've settled for the "too much not yet" of the kingdom of God in our lives.

You don't have to look very hard in the Bible to see the people touched, transformed and healed by God. Here is one story.

Some time later, Jesus went up to Jerusalem for one of the Jewish festivals. Now there is in Jerusalem near the Sheep Gate a pool, which in Aramaic is called Bethesda and which is surrounded by five covered colonnades. Here a great number of disabled people used to lie—the blind, the lame, the paralyzed. One who was there had been an invalid for thirty-eight years. When Jesus saw him lying there and learned that he had been in this condition for a long time, he asked him, "Do you want to get well?" "Sir," the invalid replied, "I have no one to help me into the pool when the water is stirred. While I am trying to get in, someone else goes down ahead of me." Then Jesus said to him, "Get up! Pick up your mat and walk." At once the man was cured; he picked up his mat and walked. The day on which this took place was a Sabbath, and so the Jewish leaders said to the man who had been healed, "It is the Sabbath; the law forbids you to carry your mat." (John 5:1-10)

The Jews had a word for what the world would be like when the Messiah came: *shalom. Shalom* can be translated into such English words as "completeness," "soundness," "peace," "well-being," "health," "prosperity" and "salvation." *Shalom* is not just an inward, private relationship that we have with God. *Shalom* is peace where there has been war and violence and economic justice where there has been poverty. *Shalom* is the breaking down of racial barriers and the experience of God's love and righteousness. *Shalom* means total well-being in every aspect of your life: your health, finances, marriage, kids, relationships with extended family and neighbors, your flock, job, crops, herds and vines. *Shalom* means blessing and well-being not only in your relationships with other people but also in your relationship with God. Shalom touches your worship, your prayer, your sense of intimacy with God and your ability to hear God. Shalom touches your past through forgiveness, your present through the provision of spiritual power and your future by giving you hope. *Shalom* is both spiritual *and* material.

The word *shalom* is used today as a greeting in Israel. It has become a substitute for the word "goodbye" or "hello," but it really means health and prosperity in every realm of life. *Shalom* is what the Messiah was supposed to bring into the world. We read this prophecy of the messianic age in Isaiah 35:4-6:

> say to those with fearful hearts,
>   "Be strong, do not fear;
> your God will come,
>   he will come with vengeance;
> with divine retribution
>   he will come to save you."
>
> Then will the eyes of the blind be opened
>   and the ears of the deaf unstopped.
> Then will the lame leap like a deer,
>   and the mute tongue shout for joy.
> Water will gush forth in the wilderness
>   and streams in the desert.

Revelation 21:4 says that "He will wipe every tear" at the end, in the age to come. The Messiah is the one who brings heaven to earth and who makes all things new. The New Testament teaches that what the Jews were looking forward to in the future broke into the present. Heaven came to earth in Jesus! And part of this foretaste of future heaven was Jesus' ministry of supernatural healing and reconciliation. *Shalom*—wholeness, completeness, health and well-being—came to the world in Christ.

The New Testament teaches us that the ministry of healing was not confined to Jesus alone; "Jesus called his twelve disciples to him and gave them authority to drive out impure spirits and to heal every disease and sickness" (Matthew 10:1). And we know from Acts that Jesus' followers regularly prayed for the sick and saw many divine healings in Jesus' name.

Healing—emotional, spiritual, physical and relational—is the birthright and mark of the Christian church. Divine healing is not a bizarre practice confined to backwoods groups in Arkansas or storefront churches in Chicago. Healing is part and parcel of the Christian message. We cannot speak of authentic Christianity without including a message about healing.

In light of this, why are sick and hurting people not flooding into churches? Consider prostitutes: people who have sex with complete strangers for money, who often get sexually transmitted diseases and who are regularly abused by their pimps. Why don't sick and hurting prostitutes flood into Christian churches saying, "Help me"? Why don't cancer patients, drug addicts and alcoholics stream into churches saying, "I need help"? Obviously, prostitutes and addicts don't believe that churches will welcome them or help them. The same is true for the sick. Not many people who are sick would have as their first thought, "I need to go to a Christian church because they will pray for me and I will get well."

OBSTACLES TO EXPERIENCING GOD'S POWER

What are the obstacles to the Christian church experiencing God's divine power through the healing of addictions, illnesses and damaged emotions? Let's look at a few barriers when it comes to our trust in God's healing power.

We have a limited worldview. My wife, Marlene, leaves her reading glasses all over the house. (I think she has about eight pairs.) One of her pairs of reading glasses looks exactly like my prescription pair. One day I put her glasses on by mistake, and they completely distorted my vision of the entire room. Worldview is like wearing a pair of glasses. Put on different glasses, and you have a different way of looking at the world. God is the only one who sees the world as it is. The rest of us see the world through our prejudices, our education, our political affiliations, our family upbringing, our culture and our expectations, among other things.

In the 1940s, two researchers did an interesting experiment regarding people's ability to perceive unexpected facts. The researchers presented their subjects with a series of playing cards and asked the subjects to identify the cards. The problem was that the cards weren't normal. The cards were deliberately made unusual or anomalous in some way: red spades, for example, or black hearts. When a subject was asked to identify a single card that was a normal card, they almost always responded correctly. But when the subjects were shown an unusual card, they almost always still saw normal playing cards. In other words, the subjects fit the unusual cards into the categories of "what must have been there," based on their prior experience of playing cards. Only when the researchers increased the exposure time to the cards, flipping through them more slowly, did the subjects hesitate and become aware that they were seeing something out of the ordinary. Even then they struggled with how to identify them. It was only when the researchers went from flipping the cards every two seconds to flipping them every five or ten seconds that the subjects began to experience those "Aha!" moments and realize that they were looking at unusual cards.

What was fascinating was that some people were never able to perceive something out of the ordinary. It didn't matter how slowly the researchers turned the cards; they remained stuck in their old frames of reference. They couldn't make the mental changes necessary to identify a red spade or a black heart.

Today, our post-Enlightenment worldview teaches that healing doesn't come through Jesus or through prayer. We believe that if someone is to be healed, such healing will come through doctors, therapists, psychologists or medicine. The Bible, in which we find God's perspective on reality, teaches that the skills that doctors and therapists have, as well as the availability of medicine, are all gifts from God. But the Bible also teaches that God often heals apart from doctors and modern medicine. If we claim that the Bible is the lens through which we see reality, why do we not spend even 10 percent of our time and energy going to Jesus for healing? In the twenty-first century, our naturalistic worldview precludes the possibility of divine healing as a real option for healing our illnesses.

We give up too soon. In John 5, Jesus came to the pool of Bethesda, where there were a number of sick people. One particular person had been an invalid for thirty-eight years. When Jesus saw him lying there and learned that he had been in this condition for such a long time, he asked him, "Do you want to get well?" (John 5:6). Can you imagine being chronically ill for thirty-eight years? It's easy to understand how someone in that situation could become disillusioned and say, "If Jesus hasn't healed me by now, he never will!"

It is simply impossible for us to fully comprehend the ways of God. Someone may sit in a church for a decade and listen to five hundred sermons. But during the 501st sermon, something happens. For some reason, as she listens that day the penny drops, and for the first time the individual says, "Yes. I see now that my need is Jesus Christ." That day, having heard that 501st sermon, the person gives her life to Christ. Who can explain the ways of God? Who can explain why the light suddenly goes on when it hadn't before?

How many of us have sat in church for years and heard about Jesus fifty, one hundred, maybe even one thousand times, but it had no impact at all. And then suddenly, the light goes on and we finally get it. Why that day? Why at that moment and not the week before? One of the problems we have with the miraculous is that we sometimes give up too soon. Sometimes, because the miracle is delayed, we believe it has been denied.

There isn't a technique in praying for the sick. Praying for the sick is not magic! But there is something about listening to people who are long-time practitioners of divine healing that will boost your faith and confidence that you are included in God's plan for bringing *shalom* into this world. I guarantee you that if you pray for someone and they get well, you will be hooked forever. Our problem is that we've never seen God use us, so we don't believe he will. But if just one time you had a friend or a child or a loved one who was really sick and got better after you prayed for them, you will want to pray for every sick person you see! Being an instrument of almighty God: what could be better than that?

We want to look good. Another obstacle to healing is our desire to always look good. "Well, what if I pray for a sick person and they don't get well? God is going to look bad." You don't have to worry about God. God can take care of himself. In fact, maybe we are less concerned that God might look bad and more concerned that *we* might look bad. We have to be willing to put ourselves on the line—to risk not always looking good or being in control—in order to see God do something beyond us. The only way to get a hit is to take lots of swings at the ball. We must be willing to say, "It didn't work before, but I'm going to try again! I'm going to take a risk!"

INTIMACY IS WHERE IT BEGINS

What is the secret behind the divine healing that we see evidenced in the New Testament Gospels of Matthew, Mark and Luke? Divine healing is often the result of simple faith or the compassionate heart of Jesus or his power and authority. But in the Gospel of John, the underlying source of divine healing ultimately boils down to one thing: intimacy with God. Jesus says this in John 5:19-20: "Jesus gave them this answer: 'Very truly I tell you, the Son can do nothing by himself; he can do only what he sees his Father doing, because whatever the Father does the Son also does. For the Father loves the Son and shows him all he does. Yes, and he will show him even greater works than these, so that you will be amazed.'"

John's Gospel is all about intimacy with God. If you want to see divine healing, you've got to spend time with Jesus. You've got to open up your heart and listen to what the Spirit is saying. You've got to put yourself at God's disposal and ask, "God, what do you want to do through me? How should I meet this need? How do you want me to pray? How do you want me to act?" And then go do it!

Kathy, a woman in our church, wrote me a long letter about her experience.

Rich, let me begin by telling you a little about myself. Before I became ill, I was very active. I worked for the post office, walking several miles a day, worked out six days a week, lifted weights, swam and biked. I was very strong physically. But emotionally I was a wreck and spiritually I was dead.

I had to stop working due to arthritis in my feet. Very soon after leaving my job, I started having more and more medical problems. My immune system was very weak, causing constant infections. Damage to my joints, nerves and tendons was a constant source of surgery. I had over thirty surgeries in a period of eleven years. I went to every pain clinic around. I tried every experimental treatment available, and nothing helped. My pain was tremendous and never left me.

Even my family questioned if I was truly ill. I saw an endocrinologist who diagnosed me with accelerated degenerative metabolic bone disease and osteoporosis, which cause severe bone loss. My activity level at this point was practically nonexistent. I couldn't even do things like hold a cup of coffee or read a book.

I was in my living room crying. I was at my wits' end when I heard a voice telling me to call an old friend whom I hadn't spoken to for quite some time. I called him and we had a long conversation. Evidently not long enough, because when I hung up I heard the voice say to me again, "Call him back." I thought the voice was drug induced. In the second conversation, my friend told me about the Vineyard. I asked him if he went there and he said no, but that it would be a good church for me.

I came to the church and accepted Christ two weeks later and was baptized. After my baptism, many things took place. I was cleansed from my sins. I became a new creation. I no longer had a twenty-year smoking addiction. Soon after my baptism, I started to do volunteer work at the church even though my pain was increasing. But so was my love for life and Jesus. He became my constant source of strength and hope.

During a weekend service at our church, I was healed of my bone disease. The pastor called people up front to receive prayer. I heard a voice, the same voice I heard the year earlier telling me to call my friend. The voice I now knew to be the voice of the Lord. He told me to go up front. I was at that time a "back of the church" kind of person. I was shy and nervous. There were lots of people up front, and I froze in my seat. But the voice, much firmer this time, said with a gentle shove, "Go forward now."

I went up front to receive prayer, but no one came forward to pray for me. I felt totally exposed and wanted desperately to return to my seat. I prayed, "Father, I am here and no one is praying for me." At that point, God replied, "You don't need anyone else."

I began to cry and said, "Yes Lord, all I need is you." Just then a young girl asked if she could pray for me. I felt warm. I felt like I was being bathed in a bright light. My feet and shins began to burn and tingle. I felt like I was going to fall. Heat washed over me until my whole body felt like it was on fire. I was completely surrounded by love.

I find it impossible to describe exactly what God's presence feels like. When I left church, I felt like I had been on Novocain in my whole body. I was numb and tingly for the next two weeks.

I went back to the doctor soon after the experience, and she immediately saw a difference in me because I was standing straight up for the first time in three years. As I told her everything, she struggled to take down every word. She did blood work, bone scans and all the regular tests. Two weeks later she called to tell me what I already knew. My test results were normal.

However, I wasn't home to receive the message. I had gone to

Florida as I had done the year before, with one exception. The year before, I went in a wheelchair. This year I climbed the stairs to a lighthouse three times. It's now been over two years since my healing, and I still cry every time I go for a walk. I thank Jesus every day for my healing, for drawing me to him so he could love me and save me. I did receive a healing miracle from Jesus that night.

But I also received something better than a physical healing. I received all that was behind it. Jesus gave me an open heart, eyes to see, ears to hear him. He has totally transformed me. Thank you Jesus![3]

DO YOU TRUST ME?

Marlene and I like to watch movies on our date nights. We like different kinds of movies. I like action movies; she likes romantic comedies. So we watch romantic comedies. But once in a while—not very often—we find a movie that we both like. It usually involves a romantic relationship but is also action packed, so we both get a little bit of what we like.

In these movies, the guy and gal are inevitably being chased by the bad guys for some reason. They're jumping out of cars or blowing up trains. But no matter how hard they try to run away, these bad guys chase them down and corner them on the roof of a skyscraper. It always looks like there's no way out. And when that happens, you know something cool is about to happen. So here they are, hiding in the corner of the roof while dramatic music plays in the background, when all of a sudden the guy has an epiphany. He thinks of a way out! Of course, in these movies, the guy never explains what his plan is. He simply holds his hand out to the woman and asks, "Do you trust me?" And here's the moment of truth: she has to decide whether she will risk her life with this guy or stay where she is. Of course, in the movies, she always chooses to trust.

The moment she puts her hand into his hand—the moment she decides to jump off the roof with this man—their relationship changes forever. You cannot step out in faith and not be changed by that experience. And that's what faith does in our relationship with God.

"I do believe; help me overcome my unbelief!" Hearing these honest words uttered by the father, these words of love and fear, Jesus responds by healing his son and freeing him from oppression. Something powerful happens when our desperation meets the compassion of Jesus.

What are you desperate for today? Do you need to experience God's power in your marriage? Do you need to experience God's healing power in your body because of an illness? Do you need to experience God's power in your job situation? Do you need to experience God's power in your wayward child, who seems so far away? Whatever your situation or circumstance, God is holding his hand out to you and asking, "Do you trust me?"

What Is Our Expectation?

...AND NOT YET

Have you ever been severely tested in life? A couple in our church, Casey and Dana (not their real names), experienced a terrible tragedy not long after they got married. Dana shared this story.

> After we got married, we had planned to wait for five years before starting a family, but our "surprise" baby came after just a year of marriage. Life was exciting! We were in love, we were about to become parents and we were looking forward to serving as missionaries.
>
> Our son, Jeremy, was born on January 20. He was beautiful, and we took countless pictures the first hour after he was born. But our joy was cut short when his doctor told us that Jeremy did not seem to be getting enough oxygen, possibly as the result of a heart or lung problem. After a night of testing, we were told that the tests indicated the problem was with his heart. He was immediately transferred to a larger hospital. For the next ten days, we were on a roller coaster.
>
> Jeremy had good days followed by bad days. His oxygen levels improved, then dropped. Then he had a lung hemorrhage. Nurses who were used to seeing tiny premature babies had as-

sured us that Jeremy was a big, strong baby and would be fine. But then the blow came.

Further testing showed that Jeremy's veins were not connected properly. Instead of running from his lungs to his heart, Jeremy's veins went from his lungs to his liver. Jeremy had to be transferred to a third hospital, where he could undergo open-heart surgery. Though only offering a 50 percent survival rate, this surgery was Jeremy's only chance.

It was at this third hospital that I "heard" a thought in my mind that was loud and overwhelming. The thought was, "Just curse God, and this will all be over." Was I overwhelmed and exhausted? Perhaps, but I never felt that was the origin of this thought. I felt this was a direct spiritual attack, and I immediately said, "I will not curse the Lord my God. I will praise him," and I began worshiping the Lord in song and prayer. I prayed the Lord would protect Jeremy's little life and heal him, and I poured out my love and worship to the Lord.

On Super Bowl Sunday, Jeremy was wheeled out of the neonatal intensive care unit and into the operating room. He was on a tiny tray-like bed, hooked up to monitors and IVs. The image of the medical team wheeling him through the double doors is embedded in my mind. When those doors closed behind them, I somehow knew that would be the last time I would see him. Though the doctors were able to sew Jeremy's veins into the proper location, his little heart stopped beating during the surgery, never to start again. After eleven short days, our Jeremy was gone!

As grieving parents, we held each other and cried. We hadn't asked for this child, but after coming to accept him as God's gift, we had longed for him. We felt like little children who got up on Christmas morning to open a beautiful gift, only to find that it was smashed and broken beyond repair. We honestly asked God for meaning. Why did he allow this to happen?[1]

IF GOD IS SO GOOD

Why? This is the ache that resonates in our hearts when we come face to face with pain, evil, suffering or death. "If God is so good, then why did he let Jeremy die?" "Why did something so bad happen to someone so good?" "Why didn't God intervene?" "Why bother praying if God doesn't answer prayers?" "Why is there so much pain and suffering in this world?" "Why doesn't God care?"

These desperate cries rise up from the depths of our souls. There is not a person alive who hasn't experienced pain and hurt in one form or another. Suffering is all around us. Just look at these statistics.

- Every day, nearly sixteen thousand children die from hunger-related causes. That amounts to one child every five seconds.[2]

- About 5.6 million (or 53 percent) of child deaths worldwide are related to malnutrition.[3]

- More than one billion (one in seven) people live on less than one dollar a day.[4]

- Approximately 143 million children in the developing world (one in thirteen) are orphans.[5]

- Two-thirds of all murders of children under the age of five are committed by a parent or another family member.[6]

- Every year 1.2 million children are sold into sexual slavery.[7]

- Twenty first-graders were murdered in Newtown, Connecticut, by a twenty-year-old who gunned them down with an assault rifle.[8]

Where is God in the midst of all this? What happened to all the wonderful promises about joy, peace, protection and prosperity? Is God really in control or not?

From time to time, various people in our church have shared testimonies of God's healing in their lives. But for every story of healing, there are ten stories in which the person is not healed. What do you say when someone is not healed? In a church that prays for the sick, as we do, and encourages people to believe God for miracles, what do you do when there is no miracle?

And it's not just in the area of physical healing that we experience disappointment and heartache. James tells us, "Consider it pure joy, my brothers and sisters, when you face trials of many kinds" (James 1:2). Difficulties come in a variety of ways, and there are different kinds of problems. Your trials may involve living with an unsaved spouse. Someone else's trial may be living with a rebellious child or an aging parent whose health is declining or who has Alzheimer's. For another person, the trial may be an addiction or having someone in the family who is addicted to alcohol, drugs or pornography. For yet another person, the trial may be a difficult marriage or loneliness and a desire to be married. Underemployment, not being able to provide for one's family, the inability to get pregnant, getting pregnant and miscarrying: these are all trials that millions of people undergo.

As a pastor, I have the heart-wrenching responsibility of performing funerals. One dear friend of mine died on my birthday. Many people for whom I have prayed in hospitals remain unhealed. I had to bury a young man who was blown up in Afghanistan by an explosive. This was the same young man whose adoption I had handled when I practiced law. I had personally taken him from the hospital as an infant and handed him to his adoptive parents. Twenty-one years later, I buried him to the sound of a Marine bugler and a twenty-one gun salute.

THE ALREADY AND THE NOT YET OF THE KINGDOM OF GOD

Before we continue with this discussion of pain and suffering, let's pause for a minute to consider what the Bible calls the *kingdom of God*. I believe that we cannot truly understand pain and suffering without understanding what the kingdom of God is.

We read in Mark 1:14-15, "After John was put in prison, Jesus went into Galilee, proclaiming the good news of God. 'The time has come,' he said. 'The kingdom of God has come near. Repent and believe the good news!'" The gospel—the good news that Jesus preached—was the message of the kingdom of God. He preached it when he began his ministry. He preached it throughout his ministry. And right before Jesus ascended into heaven, what do we find him talking about? The kingdom of God. "After his suffering, he showed himself to [these men] and gave many convincing proofs that he was alive. He appeared to them over a period of forty days and *spoke about the kingdom of God*" (Acts 1:3).

So what exactly is the kingdom of God, and why did Jesus talk about it so much? Simply put, the kingdom of God is the rule and reign of God. Like any king who reigns over a kingdom, God reigns over his creation. He calls the shots. God has a sovereign plan to save the cosmos, a plan that was dramatically inaugurated by Jesus when he came into our world two thousand years ago. Through Jesus, God came to live among us. Through Jesus, something of heaven has broken into earth. God's plan for the cosmos is now being implemented by his Spirit-empowered church. The fullness of the kingdom will not be realized, however, until Jesus comes back. We may taste the kingdom now, but we must wait for its fullness at Christ's second coming. This is what we mean by the *already and the not yet* of the kingdom: the kingdom is already here but not yet in its fullness. This is why when we pray for healing, not everyone gets healed. This is why we see relief from pain and suffering sometimes but not all the time. This is why we experience the good and the bad in our world. The kingdom that our hearts eagerly desire is indeed here among us but not in its totality.[9] And the great divide in our churches is often the result of people trying to hold on to the already or the not yet, to the exclusion of the other.

TOO MUCH ALREADY: THE PROSPERITY GOSPEL

A man by the name of George lost his job a few years ago when an Ohio tile factory shut down. George decided that this would be a great opportunity for him and his family to move out of Ohio, so they packed up and moved to a new city, where they started attending a new church. George attended a church that taught what has been called the *prosperity gospel.* It is the idea that Christian believers have a right to the blessings of wealth, health and happiness in this life and that we can obtain these blessings through positive confessions of faith and by faithfully giving tithes and offerings to the church. The prosperity gospel teaches that it is God's will that every one of his children financially prosper, be in perfect health and enjoy total happiness. Prosperity teaching is incredibly popular. Three of America's twelve largest churches teach the prosperity gospel, and most of America's best-known televangelists promote this message. Two-thirds of Pentecostals say that they believe that God promises wealth to the faithful.

George walked into the local Ford dealer located near that church and said, "God has showed me that he doesn't want me to be a run-of-the-mill person." He believed God wanted him to be the dealer's top salesman. George got the job, and he said, "It is a new day God has given me! I'm on my way to a six-figure income!" When he began working, George's sales commission helped George and his family with the rent for their new apartment. But George wasn't satisfied. Once that six-figure income that God had promised him rolled in, he intended to buy his dream house on twenty-five acres. "We're going to have a schoolhouse (his children are homeschooled). We want horses and ponies for the boys, so a horse barn. And a pond. And maybe some cattle. I'm dreaming big—because all of heaven is dreaming big." George finished his interview by saying, "Jesus died for our sins. That was the best gift God could give us. But we have something else. . . . Why would an awesome and mighty God want anything less for his children?"[10]

In reading stories about people like George, I understand why those who are suffering and those who are poor are attracted to prosperity teaching. The teaching contains a liberating word of hope. "Regardless of the hardships in your life, or your race, or your education, or your poverty, or your past mistakes, or your family background or your neighborhood: you can improve your lot in life! You don't have to be controlled by all the negative circumstances of life. You can be better than you are!" That's a liberating message, and many,

many people who have heard the prosperity teaching have been encouraged to hold on and hope. More than that, many have been inspired to work hard, to pursue holy lives free from addictive habits and to use the abilities and gifts God has given them to improve not only their own lives but the lives of their families and those in their communities. It is liberating to realize that you don't have to be controlled by your past or any of the limits that other people impose upon you.

A Pew Research Center survey recently found that 73 percent of all religious Latinos in the United States agree with the statement, "God will grant financial success to all believers who have enough faith."[11] But is this true? Will God grant financial success to every believer who has enough faith? Is that what God promises in the Bible?

I have no doubt that many of the teachers of the prosperity gospel are sincere Christians who love God, pray diligently and want to see Christ's kingdom spread throughout the world. Many prosperity-teaching churches are very generous. One such church gave one million dollars for hurricane relief after Hurricane Katrina to help people struggling in New Orleans. Not everything about the prosperity gospel is bad. It is absolutely the case that God is good and that he wishes to be good to his children. Indeed, God wishes to be good to all of creation. Here is what we read in Psalms:

> The LORD is gracious and compassionate,
>   slow to anger and rich in love.
> The LORD is good to all;
>   he has compassion on all he has made. . . .
> The LORD upholds all who fall
>   and lifts up all who are bowed down.
> The eyes of all look to you,
>   and you give them their food at the proper time.
> You open your hand
>   and satisfy the desires of every living thing.
>   (Psalm 145:8-9, 14-16)

We always want to affirm the goodness of God and his desire to be good to people. I love the expectant faith of believers regarding God's desire to answer our prayers. There is a lot that is really good about expecting to see God's activity in your life and in the world today.

But some things are clearly wrong about prosperity gospel teaching. Let me share just two items here.[12]

A *misinterpretation of Scripture*. The first problem that I find in prosperity teaching is that it misinterprets Scripture. Even though prosperity teachers quote from the Bible, the lens through which they read the Bible is the lens of the American dream: a big house, big car, nice clothes, great vacations, perfect health and a great career. But it is not enough to quote the Bible; we must try to figure out what the biblical writers intended. The issue is not what I want the Bible to say based on my prejudices but what the author intended.

Let's consider the most commonly quoted prosperity text: 3 John 1:2. This reads, "Beloved, I wish above all things that thou mayest prosper and be in health, even as thy soul prospereth" (3 John 1:2 KJV). Many of the prosperity teachers would say, "John writes that we *should* prosper and always be in health."

But this is not at all what the text actually says. First of all, the Greek word translated *prosper* in the King James Version actually means "to go well with someone." The actual verse reads, "Dear friend, I pray that you may enjoy good health and that all may go well with you, even as your soul is getting along well." This combination—that things go well and that the recipient would be in good health—was a standard form of greeting in the ancient world. It would be like someone today saying in a letter, "I pray that this letter finds you in good health and that things are going well with you."

To expand that to a promise that God wills material and financial prosperity for every Christian at all times in all places and under all circumstances, so long as we are faithful, is utterly foreign to what John is actually communicating here. As Gordon Fee wrote in his commentary, "John neither intended that, nor could his recipient Gaius have so understood it. We could learn from this text to pray for people that everything would go well for them. But what we could not get from this text is that God *wills* our financial prosperity. That is abusing the text and taking a particular warm greeting of the letter's author and making it the eternal will of God."[13] This passage simply does not say and does not mean what prosperity teachers suggest that it says.

The other most commonly misapplied text is John 10:10, which quotes Jesus as saying, "I am come that they might have life, and that they might have it more abundantly" (John 10:10 KJV). This verse likewise has been twisted and misused. "Abundant life," according to the prosperity teachers, means material abundance: a big house, expensive cars, nice clothes and exotic vacations. That's not what John 10:10 is referring to. "Life" is John's equivalent to the phrase "the kingdom of God" in the first three Gospels. When John writes about "life," he is talking about the life of the age to come. It is the life that God has in and of himself. It is the life of intimacy with God, a life of joy, a life of freedom from addiction, a life of holiness and a life of loving service to others and to God. Jesus is not promising in John 10:10 a great vacation or a beach house. He is talking about the kingdom of God, not the kingdom of America.

A mechanistic view of God. A second problem that I find with the prosperity teaching is that it offers a mechanistic view of God. Some people have labeled the prosperity teaching's God as "the vending machine God": you put your faith and your tithes in, and out pop material blessings. This perspective on God—that if you believe enough and tithe enough, good things will always happen to you—was the view that Job's friends had of God. After poor Job had lost everything, Job's "friend," Zophar, said this to him:

> Yet if you devote your heart to him
>   and stretch out your hands to him,
> if you put away the sin that is in your hand
>   and allow no evil to dwell in your tent,

then, free of fault, you will lift up your face;
   you will stand firm and without fear.
You will surely forget your trouble,
   recalling it only as waters gone by.
Life will be brighter than noonday,
   and darkness will become like morning. (Job 11:13-17)

Is this the way life works? Does every good and faithful person only experience happiness, health and wealth in this life? And if you're experiencing financial problems, unemployment, an unhealed illness or a broken heart, does that mean that you have done something wrong? Does it mean that you just didn't believe enough or that you haven't tithed enough? Is that what Jesus taught us? Is the gospel a quid pro quo: put in your faith and your tithes and God gives you back material blessings, health and happiness?

Certainly, many Proverbs tell us that *in general* hard work, wisdom and righteousness will result in blessing, including financial blessing. Life does teach us that laziness and a refusal to listen to counsel will often result in poverty. We see some general rules concerning how life often works out in the Bible. But by the time we get to the New Testament, we find a more nuanced perspective, and we see that the link between what we do and financial prosperity and health becomes more and more attenuated.

The New Testament contains numerous examples of people whose sufferings are not caused by something they did wrong or some sin in their lives. In John 9, Jesus and his disciples encounter a man who has been blind since birth. Seeing this blind man, the disciples ask Jesus a question that today's prosperity teacher might have asked: "Rabbi, who sinned, this man or his parents, that he was born blind?" Jesus answered, "Neither" (John 9:2-3). The lens through which the disciples see the world simply does not allow for someone to be blind without there being some good reason for it. They appear to believe that there is always a sin behind suffering, and there is always a blessing for the righteous. But Jesus teaches that God "causes his sun to rise on the evil and the good, and sends rain on the righteous and the unrighteous" (Matthew 5:45). The blessings and sufferings in life are not neatly distributed based on a person's merit, according to Jesus (Luke 13:1-5).

One of my heroes is Joni Eareckson Tada. In 1967, at seventeen years of age, Joni was injured in a diving accident that left her in a quadriplegic state with minimal use of her hands. Joni said that when she was first injured, she could not imagine living in a wheelchair, having other people feed her, dress her and bathe her. When she realized the extent of the paralysis, and that it would be permanent, she collapsed emotionally. She was despairing and suicidal. She said she would wrench her head back and forth on the pillow at night, hoping to break her neck and kill herself. But step by step, she was able to find God:

> Thankfully there were Christian friends who were praying for me and lifting me up in their intercessions in a committed and specific way, and it didn't take long for me to begin to melt under the pressure of their love. They would come into the hospital with their guitars, doughnuts, bags of pizza, and teen magazines and they just kept me connected to reality and that connection was so important.
>
>   I'd been a Christian before the accident and had been saved at a Young Life weekend retreat, but up until my accident I guess I thought I'd done God a great big favor by accepting Jesus as my savior. But after the accident it was a different story. This was a holy high exalted lifted up God that I had to deal with and I humbled myself before him needing him desperately which is something I still do. I still wake up in the morning some 45 years later as a quadriplegic and I get up in the morning desperately requiring God's grace. It was when I recognized my urgent need of God that the depression began to dissipate and hope began to blossom in my heart.[14]

UNENDING HOPE

All of us live with something (or many things) that we wish would change and which stubbornly do not. The "something" may be a pre-disposition to depression, unwanted same-sex attraction, physical pain, an unhappy marriage, a child who suffers from mental illness, an incurable disease, infertility, unsatisfying work, poverty, singleness not by choice but by circumstance, a loved one who rejects Christ or any of the innumerable other things that afflict people in this fallen world.

Mark Galli, senior managing editor of *Christianity Today*, recently said in an interview that he thinks the term *transformation* is overused in Christian circles.

I noticed how often that word comes up—our lives can be transformed, our churches can be transformed, our culture can be transformed. We imagine if we do everything right according to what the New Testament teaches us, that things will be completely changed. And if they aren't completely changed, I've either bet my life on something that's not true, or the Gospel itself is not true.

I just keep on coming back to Luther's truth that we are simultaneously justified and sinners [notice Luther's Both-And]. I keep on looking at my own life, and at church history, and I realize that when the Gospel talks about transformation, it can't possibly mean an actual, literal change in this life of a dramatic nature, except in a few instances. It must be primarily eschatological; it must be referring to the fact that we will in fact be changed. The essential thing to make change possible has occurred—Christ died and rose again. (And in this life we will see flashes of that, just like in Jesus' ministry there were moments when the Kingdom broke in and we see a miracle. And these moments tell us there is something better awaiting for us and God is gracious enough at times to allow a person or a church or a community to experience transformation at some level.)[15]

I probably believe that the kingdom is more "already" than Galli does, and I might put fewer things into the "not yet" than he would. Nevertheless, I think that he is on to something. Having pastored a church for over a quarter of a century, I have come to believe that in contemporary Christianity, we have almost entirely lost the view that the kingdom of God is not yet fully here. Almost no Christians I know—under the age of seventy, who are not dying or who have not recently lost a loved one—think much about eternity or talk much about our future hope. Yet without a discussion of our future hope, there is ultimately no satisfying answer for present suffering. Without such a discussion, there is ultimately no compelling reason to delay immediate gratification when the prospect of present-day payoff is slim or none.

Millions of people around the world can personally relate to the story of Casey and Dana that I shared at the beginning of this chapter. Living in between the already and the not yet means living in the midst of suffering while desperately holding onto hope. Sometimes it seems like there is nothing but suffering. But other times, we do see a glimpse of the already that enables us to hope again. Here is the rest of Casey and Dana's story:

> With time, we began to heal. That summer we were accepted as missionaries and began taking Bible and missions classes. Just over a year later, we had a healthy baby girl with a perfect little heart. She confirmed what the doctors had told us—Jeremy's condition was so rare we didn't need to worry about ever seeing it again. In fact, it was so rare, they said, the chances of it happening are as low as getting struck by lightning.
>
> But lightning does sometimes strike in the same place twice.
>
> When our third baby, Samuel, was born, his face was dark purple and he seemed weak and floppy. They took him into the nursery for testing and when we were allowed to enter the room an hour later, we saw his oxygen monitor, one just like Jeremy's with the same low reading. When asked if he had the same con-

dition, the doctor assured us, saying that "lightning doesn't strike in the same place twice."

From there it seemed we were in a slow-motion movie, playing a repeat of our first experience. Samuel was taken by ambulance to a larger hospital, the diagnosis was confirmed, the medical procedures explained and the surgery papers signed.

Not again, Lord! Until now, all we knew at the end of this journey was grief.

But God had a different ending to Samuel's story. When Samuel was two days old, the doctors sewed his pulmonary veins onto his tiny heart, and God chose to keep Samuel's heart beating. On his eleventh day, our first son, Jeremy, went home to be with God. But on Samuel's eleventh day, he came home with us![16]

During Advent every year, Christians are taught to wait and to anticipate the coming of the Messiah into the world. We become "Israel" as we sing: "O come, O come Emmanuel, and ransom captive Israel." Our Advent longing for the Messiah trains us to look forward to Jesus' coming again and forces us out of our present-day preoccupation. As the apostle Paul put it, "If only for this life we have hope in Christ, we are of all people most to be pitied" (1 Corinthians 15:19). It is the prospect of the coming King and his kingdom that gives us encouragement to keep going despite present suffering. We are a Both-And people: we have already "shared in the Holy Spirit" and "tasted the goodness of the word of God and the powers of the coming age" (Hebrews 6:4-5). Nevertheless, as the author of Hebrews also says, "But now we do not yet see all things subjected to him [Christ]. But we do see Him who was made for a little while lower than the angels, namely Jesus" (Hebrews 2:8-9 NASB).

13

What Is Our Calling?

RELEVANT PRACTICE . . .

The notion that God saves people by allowing them to hear the gospel message in their own language has fueled the modern Bible translation movement. In past centuries, great missionaries such as William Carey, Hudson Taylor, Henry Martyn, and Adoniram Judson served as Bible translators.

One of the greatest missionaries in history, Cameron Townsend, felt called to missionary service and went to Guatemala as a young adult in 1917. While he was there, he tried to sell Spanish Bibles to the native Cakchiquel Indians, who lived in a remote, rural area of Guatemala. Only a few Cakchiquel Indians could read or speak Spanish. One day Cameron Townsend was confronted by an Indian man who asked, "If your God is so smart, then why hasn't he learned the Cakchiquel language yet?"[1] Cameron Townsend was so convicted by that question that he spent the next thirteen years of his life translating the Bible into the Cakchiquel language. Based on this experience, Townsend started an organization in 1942 called the Wycliffe Bible Translators. Their mission is to provide the Scriptures in every known language on earth so that people can hear God speaking in their own language.[2]

Every great missionary contextualizes the gospel. But contextualization means more than speaking the language of the person with whom we are sharing the gospel. Contextualization involves entering the thought world, the feeling world and the cultural world of the people we are trying to reach. So, for example, contextualization involves the experience of an unchurched person who walks into a church and, for the first time in his life, finds he can relate to God. One of the greatest compliments I receive from unchurched people who visit our church is, "Today when I came to your church, I felt for the first time like I had come home!" What they mean is that they did not have to jump through seventy-two cultural hoops in order to hear God speaking to them. They did not have to be transported back in time to a prior century to relate to God. The message, the music, the dress and the issues addressed all serve to connect twenty-first-century people to Christ.

To recreate in our time and place the miracle of Pentecost so that people might hear God's voice in their own language: this is the ongoing task of the church. This includes communicating the gospel in the increasingly diverse dress of America and other Western nations' newest immigrants. It also includes recognizing that the language and thought forms of seniors and baby boomers are not necessarily the language of young adults. It includes the recognition that the language of married couples is not necessarily the language of singles, and that the language of men is not necessarily that of women. Not everyone is a church person. Not everyone speaks "Christianese." As Christians, we must continually ask ourselves the question: *Do we love people enough to try to speak to them about God in their own language?* Do we love teenagers enough to speak to them in such a way that they realize that God is not simply the "God of their fathers"? Do we love Muslims enough to enter their worlds in order to communicate the gospel in a way that makes sense to them? Do we love the irreligious, gay people or postmoderns sufficiently to even try to learn their language?

I believe that the question posed to Cameron Townsend nearly a century ago is the question that is still being asked of Christians today:

"If your God is so smart, how come he doesn't speak my language?"

When we speak about contextualization, it is important to note that it is not the same thing as relativism. Contextualization is *relevantism!* Contextualization doesn't mean that all truth is up for grabs. The truth is the truth, as we will discuss in the next chapter on orthodoxy. But the cultural methods we use to communicate the truth are up for grabs. And the particular themes that we focus on in our gospel preaching are tailored for the audience that we are seeking to reach.

How might the gospel we preach be made relevant to our particular audiences? I would break this huge question down into a series of smaller questions.

- What shape do the "powers" take in a particular culture?
- What global and local trends are affecting the culture?
- What makes the church attractive to this particular culture?

WHAT ARE THE "POWERS" IN THIS CULTURE?

The New Testament uses the Greek word *kosmos* in a wide variety of ways. *Kosmos* might mean "the universe" or "the center of human history" or "humankind as God's creation" or "the totality of human society and activity." But often, especially in books like the Gospel of John, the word *kosmos* means "people in their fallenness and alienation from God." It is this meaning that helps us to figure out how the gospel might be made relevant. By *kosmos* in this last sense, we're talking about the world's system, structures of thought and spirit of rebellious autonomy from God.

We need to understand that behind the "world" there is a spiritual energizing that the New Testament calls the "powers." New Testament scholar G. B. Caird demonstrated a half-century ago that some mention of the "powers" is found in every one of Paul's epistles except for Philemon.[3] We find the powers everywhere seeking to frustrate Paul's missionary work by blinding people to the gospel and their need for it. Paul writes, for example, about hollow and deceptive philosophies that have penetrated their culture (and ours) and have enslaved Jews and Gentiles alike by legalism, mysticism and esoteric superstition (Colossians 2:8, 16-23). The apostle Paul writes about the ruler of the kingdom of the air who is at work among the disobedient (Ephesians 2:2) and about the "rulers of this age" (1 Corinthians 2:6-8). Many scholars believe he was almost certainly not just talking about human powers but spiritual powers that crucified the Lord of glory. Powers and authorities seek to keep people separated from the love of God in Christ (Romans 8:38-39). And Christians, according to Paul, must contend with the powers of this dark world if they are to serve their generation (Ephesians 6:12).

Caird summarized the New Testament teaching on the powers by saying, "The concept of world powers reaches into every department of false theology. So much so that it cannot be dismissed as a survival of primitive superstition. . . . Paul is describing spiritual realities with which he and his missionary companions have personal acquaintance and with which he constantly had to contend."[4]

Powers incarnate themselves into the fabric of nations and institutions and political and cultural structures. As Arthur Glasser put it in *Announcing the Kingdom: The Story of God's Mission in the Bible*, no culture has escaped the demonic element.[5] All are, as the writer of 1 John puts it, "under the control of the evil one" (1 John 5:19).

We could look at obvious examples of demonically influenced societies: Germany under the Nazis, Cambodia under the reign of terror of Pol Pot and the Khmer Rouge, or Rwanda during the violence that resulted in some 800,000 people being murdered in just one hundred days. Instead, I want to point to a few less obvious examples of how the powers have incarnated themselves into certain social structures and nations and resisted the spread of the gospel.

I travel to Europe quite often to teach at various leadership conferences. During these trips, I've noticed that one of the ways that the powers have incarnated themselves in some European countries is by convincing people to call into question all exercises of leadership. All forms of leadership, no matter how generous or humble or filled with a servant heart, are viewed with extreme suspicion by the larger societies and by people in the churches. When pastors in these countries try to communicate the vision that God may have for their congregations, they are often seen as self-exalting and self-promoting. A social norm called the "tall poppy syndrome" governs the Nordic countries: the moment one poppy grows taller than the rest, the society cuts it off!

In Amsterdam, the Netherlands, along with a shared suspicion of leadership comes an extreme rationalism. Churches in the Netherlands must contend with a rationalism that debates and discusses and dissects every church activity to the nth degree and demands endless process. Church leaders in Amsterdam say that they must regularly wrestle with the belief of members that talking about something is the equivalent of doing something!

In Berlin, Germany, I talked with a pastor who said, "What I run up against over and over in trying to express the gospel is an extreme suspicion of any kind of metanarrative. Any larger truth is dismissed as dangerous, because the people here were so abused by the Nazi metanarrative and the communist metanarrative. When you come and say there is a larger universal story that God wants you to believe concerning his plan to save the world, it immediately registers huge cultural resistance."

The powers are always incarnating themselves to resist the kingdom of God. In what ways have the powers incarnated themselves in the United States? How have the powers woven themselves into the fabric of American society to resist the gospel? It's hard to see these powers at work in the society when you are living within its influence on a daily basis. But if you ask any Christian living outside of the United States, they can easily tell you what powers are at work in America.

Militarism. Consider, for example, the spirit of militarism and the way that American society has been shaped around the exporting of American military might. Few Christians in America consider it strange that the United States, with less than 5 percent of the world's population, has a military budget equal to that of the entire rest of the world combined. Few Christians in America consider it strange that the United States has been in an almost continuous war somewhere in the world for the past fifty years, or that, as a nation that celebrates our essential goodness, we are by far the world's largest arms exporter.

I must immediately distinguish between what I am calling *militarism* and the men and women who honorably offer military service. To serve in the military does not automatically mean that one loves war or supports the expansion of a nation's military budget to the harm of other national priorities such as education, housing or poverty relief. Indeed, almost all of the people I know who have served in the military hate war, because they and their comrades-in-arms have to actually fight and possibly die in the war. The large majority of former military men and women with whom I've spoken wish that our politicians were far less bellicose in their approach to the world and sought means other than war making to address international issues.

Militarism, on the other hand, is what former president and commander Dwight D. Eisenhower was referring to when he warned in his last major speech,

> This conjunction of an immense military establishment and a large arms industry is new in the American experience. The total influence—economic, political, even spiritual—is felt in every city, every State house, every office of the Federal government. We recognize the imperative need for this development. Yet we must not fail to comprehend its grave implications. Our toil, resources and livelihood are all involved; so is the very structure of our society. In the councils of government, we must guard against the acquisition of unwarranted influence, whether sought or unsought, by the military industrial complex. The potential for the disastrous rise of misplaced power exists and will persist.[6]

If you think that militarism isn't one way that the powers have incarnated themselves in our culture, just try calling into question one of America's wars to someone in conversation. See how it works out for you.

If you were stranded on a desert island with only your New Testament, and you read through the New Testament over and over again in an effort to answer this question, "What does God want followers of Jesus to be willing to suffer and die for?" what do you think your answer would be? The apostle Paul had no difficulty answering this question. He said: "And now, compelled by the Spirit, I am going to Jerusalem, not knowing what will happen to me there. I only know that in every city the Holy Spirit warns me that prison and hardships are facing me. However, I consider my life worth nothing to me; my only aim is to finish the race and complete the task the Lord Jesus has given me—*the task of testifying to the good news of God's grace*" (Acts 20:22-24).

But if I as a pastor plan to send a young couple from our church to preach the gospel in a country that is hostile toward Christians, I face questions like these: "Do you think this is wise?" "Isn't this foolish?" "Why are we not waiting?" "How can we send a young family, especially a young woman, into such a difficult place?" There is no celebration of the couple's courage, no joy that they are giving their lives to follow Jesus, no cheers from the church for being willing to leave all. Instead there are only questions and resistance from the church.

On the other hand, why does nearly every church in America (other than the Mennonites and a few historically pacifist denominations) have Christian parents lining up to send their sons and daughters off to fight for the American military? How did it become that fighting in a war is considered normal for Christian men and women, while sending missionaries to these same countries has been discouraged? Shooting a gun at a fellow human being is never called into question; indeed, it is cheered by some in our churches. But serve the Prince of Peace by going to Afghanistan with a Bible to plant a church? You hear, "Are you sure God is asking this of you? Why would any sane person put their life on the line just for the gospel?" How did this become *normal?*

Demonstrating the gospel's relevance in America would compel pastors and Christian leaders to communicate why sacrificing all for the gospel message is eminently sensible. This is why the spread of the gospel ought to have priority over every other good and valuable thing, including a nation's security.

Consumerism. Another obvious example of the way the powers incarnate themselves in American culture is consumerism. The shopping mall presents people with a "counterfeit gospel." James K. A. Smith makes this profound observation in *Desiring the Kingdom*:

> One might say that marketing is the mall's evangelism; television commercials, billboards, Internet pop-ups, and magazine advertisements are the mall's outreach. The rituals and practices of the mall and the market are tactile and visceral—they capture our imaginations through the senses of sight and sound, touch and taste, even smell. The hip, happy people that populate television commercials are the moving icons of the consumer gospel, illustrations of what the good life looks like: carefree and independent, clean and sexy, perky and perfect. We see the embodiments of this ideal again in the icon-like mannequins in the windows of the mall. The mall, you might say, mimics that oft-repeated evangelical axiom that says, "We may be the only Bible that people ever read"; that is the mall communicates its story not through tracts and didactic lectures but through visual embodiments of the happy life.[7]
>
> [To paraphrase Descartes] I shop (and shop and shop), therefore I am. If the icons of the ideal subtly impress upon us what's wrong and where we fail, then the market's liturgies are really an invitation to rectify the problem.[8]

Smith suggests that consumerism provides people with an all-encompassing "gospel" that parodies the Christian gospel. It tells us that there is something dreadfully wrong with us—not sin, as in the Christian gospel, but a lack of stuff. It offers a solution—not the life, death and resurrection of Christ, but a purchase. It gives us a communal experience—not through church, but through shopping in a mall. It provides images—not through worship, but through pictures and mannequins. It even evangelizes—not through the preached Word, but through modern marketing.

Like Revelation does with the Roman Empire, a contextually relevant gospel will "unmask the powers" by showing them in all their ugliness. Then we Christians can demonstrate why the Christian gospel—not warfare, and not the shopping mall—offers a true, soul-satisfying, compelling call for our love and our lives.

WHAT GLOBAL AND LOCAL TRENDS ARE AFFECTING THE CULTURE?

Those who wish to be relevant in sharing the gospel understand the changing context to which they are called. Someone once asked the great hockey player Wayne Gretzky what made him so great. He answered, "Most hockey players skate to where the puck is, but I skated to where the puck was going to be." The Bible refers to people like that in 1 Chronicles 12:32; this text describes men from Issachar "who understood the times and knew what Israel should do." What are the times in which we are living? Where is the puck going in our culture?

Growing isolation. The average American adult has only two significant relationships. The problem of isolation is particularly acute with men. One quarter of all men in the United States have no one to talk to about the most important things in their lives. The problem of being isolated and disconnected from each other has been noted by many students of American culture. In the inner city, one of the best predictors of whether a young adult is going to have a good full-time job when they grow up is whether they regularly go to church in their teen years. Church attendance is a better predictor than employment programs.[9]

Robert Putnam, a professor of public policy at Harvard, said in his groundbreaking book *Bowling Alone: The Collapse and Revival of American Community* that if a state wants to dramatically improve the performance of students in schools, one of the best things to do is get kids to go to church at least twice a month. He also noted that virtually every informal network of people who meet together for a common purpose, which increases what sociologists call *social capital* for their members, has experienced a radical drop of membership in recent years. Thus, the PTA, the League of Women Voters, the NAACP, Jewish women's groups, bowling leagues and virtually every other place of connection between human beings has been in decline for decades. According to Putnam, there are only two places where social capital is growing today in America: church small groups and recovery groups. Churches have a wonderful opportunity to reach out to our communities by offering small groups and recovery groups that are intentionally designed to be open to those who are disconnected from church. We are saved to be part of something larger than ourselves. That we are saved to be part of the body of Christ is incredibly relevant for people who are isolated and are hungry for authentic community and real relationships.

The rising tide of addictions. Many communities have experienced an epidemic of prescription drug abuse in the past decade. Marijuana abuse is on the increase. Because of the growing trend toward legalized gambling, and especially with the spread of slot machines, several million adults in the United States meet the criteria for "pathological gamblers." Millions more meet the criteria for being considered "problem gamblers," according to the National Council on Problem Gambling.

If you do a Google search of the word *porn* or *pornography*, how many hits do you think you might come up with? One million? Two million? Try nearly two hundred million! The Internet Filter Review places the number of pornographic websites as encompassing nearly five hundred million web pages. This represents nearly 12 percent of the total number of websites found on the Internet.

One of the most frequent biblical images of salvation is redemption, in which someone is set free from bondage (to sin, self and Satan). This message could not be more relevant to an addicted society. Recovery groups that specifically show people how to access Christ's power for freedom from addictive bondage, such as Saddleback's famous Celebrate Recovery, have become extraordinary bridges to reach people for Christ.[10]

Many churches (including the one I pastor) offer recovery groups just for people who want to be set free from sexual addictions. This ministry includes separate groups for men and women, as well as recovery groups for those who have been sexually abused. These and other recovery groups have been contextually relevant environments not only for healing but for coming into relationship with Christ.

The age wave. The percentage of persons over age sixty-five is increasing dramatically all across the developed world. In the United States, 12.5 percent of Americans were over sixty-five in the year 1997. That percentage is predicted to grow to 21 percent by 2040! Might discussion about finding significance through giving and service be relevant to an aging population that is reaching what has been called "post-career" (with the first stage being childhood and the second being career)? Groups and ministries that focus on the "third stage" of life would be a relevant bridge for connecting older people with Christ.[11]

The rise of fatherlessness. Another feature of our changing context is the massive rise of fatherlessness. In the United States, over 50 percent of children born to women under the age of thirty are born to unwed mothers. More than 40 percent of all children born in the United States are born out of wedlock, including more than 72 percent of all African American children. Wade Horn, former assistant secretary for children and families in the U.S. Department of Health and Human Services, said, "The most consequential social trend of our time is the dramatic increase in the number of children growing up in father-absent families. It is not just that kids are going to bed without their fathers tonight; 40 percent of children who don't live with their fathers haven't seen their father in the past year. And one-half [of children in father-absent homes] have never set foot in their father's home."[12]

What would it mean for a fatherless child to hear the gospel's offer of adoption into God's family? The gospel offer of adoption is not a legal transaction; it involves a new identity and a new intimacy with God our

Father that enables the believer to call God "Abba." And what would it mean for disconnected, fatherless children to be connected to a church family in which they could find grandpas and grandmas, moms and dads, aunts and uncles, and brothers and sisters?

Many churches like our church have Big Brother and Big Sister programs as well as single mothers' gatherings to support fatherless families. And with the growing number of grandparents raising their grand-children—five million in the United States as of 2010—support groups for grandparents and other nontraditional families makes Christian faith profoundly relevant to contemporary families.

The growth of diversity. We looked at issues of diversity in chapters three and four. Census data from 2011 show that for the first time in US history, a majority of births were from ethnic minorities. And shortly after the year 2040, America is predicted to become a minority-majority nation, in which about 28 percent of the population will be of Hispanic origin, nearly 15 percent will be black (including mixed race) and nearly 9 percent will be Asian (including mixed race). Suffice it to say, if any church or institution wishes to remain relevant in the twenty-first century, it must take account of growing diversity.

A change in religious context. According to *American Grace: How Religion Divides and Unites Us*, attendance at religious services has declined slowly but very perceptibly in the United States over the last forty years—from about 40 percent of citizens attending religious services each week in the 1970s to about 30 percent today.[13] Mainline Protestants have hemorrhaged members over the past forty years, and there have been major declines among Anglo participants in the Roman Catholic Church. Robert Putnam and David Campbell suggest that the only reason that the Catholic Church in America has not imploded is because Anglo participants are being rapidly replaced by Hispanic immigrants. Evangelicals, as a percentage of the US population, have slightly declined in the last twenty-five years: from about 28 percent of the population to 24 percent.

The most rapidly growing trend in religious identity, according to

Putnam and Campbell, is the growth of the *Nones*: people who do not identify with any particular religion. Nones have grown from about 7 percent of the US population to about 17 percent.[14] It is hard to know why this group has grown so rapidly. At least a part of the answer may be people's willingness to self-identify as "having no religion." In the past, people with no religious identity might not have been as willing to admit that. But certainly some of the growth of the Nones demonstrates a real shift in religious adherence. A church that demonstrates its relevance through acts of social justice and through demonstrations of spiritual power might build a bridge of gospel receptivity to the Nones in our society.

WHAT MAKES THE CHURCH ATTRACTIVE IN THIS CULTURE?

Armand Nicholi is a clinical professor of psychiatry at Harvard Medical School. For more than thirty-five years, he has taught a course on Sigmund Freud and C. S. Lewis at Harvard College. He wrote a wonderful book comparing Freud and Lewis titled *The Question of God: C. S. Lewis and Sigmund Freud Debate God, Love, Sex, and the Meaning of Life*.[15] According to Nicholi, both Freud and Lewis became atheists when they were young men. Both were extremely pessimistic. Lewis said that as he was growing up, he had a settled expectation that everything in life would turn out the way you hoped it wouldn't. He lost his mother early, and he had great unhappiness in school. He spent World War I living in a trench, seeing death all around him. But after his conversion, one of his friends with whom he had been friends for over forty years, said, "Jack [C. S. Lewis] was unusually cheerful and took an almost boyish delight in life. He was great fun, an extremely witty and amusing companion . . . considerate . . . more concerned with the welfare of his friends than with himself."[16]

On the other hand, Freud, who never experienced a conversion to Christ, continued to have an extremely pessimistic outlook his entire life. He continued to suffer extreme bouts of depression. He started to use cocaine in order to lift his moods. He even carried around two cyanide pills in case, at some point, he wanted to kill himself. When he was eighty years old, at the end of his life, Freud said, "My mood is bad, little pleases me, my self-criticism has grown much more acute. I would diagnose it as senile depression in anyone else."[17]

The gospel is personally relevant in that it promises its recipients the life of the age to come. "Eternal life" in the Gospel of John is not just living forever and ever; it is enjoying a share in God's own life. As a result of sharing in God's life, Jesus says, "I have told you this so that my joy may be in you and that your joy may be complete" (John 15:11). This was the joy that C. S. Lewis knew and that tragically Sigmund Freud never found. Finding joy is personally relevant in an increasingly pessimistic and depressed era!

Among the many other ways that the gospel that we preach is personally relevant (see chapter seven) is the believer's experience of God's *peace*. At the beginning of many of Paul's letters, we read greetings such as, "Grace and peace to you from God our Father and the Lord Jesus Christ" (Galatians 1:3). Grace is the cause of the gospel coming into our lives. God is the author of the gospel, and it comes to us by grace. But the effect of the gospel being received in our lives is *peace*. I love what Martin Luther said in his commentary on Galatians.

> He [Paul] wishes them heavenly peace, the kind of what Jesus spoke of when he said, "Peace I leave unto you: my peace I give unto you." Worldly peace provides quiet enjoyment of life and possessions. But in affliction, particularly in the hour of death, the grace and peace of the world will not deliver us. However, the grace and peace of God will. They make a person strong and courageous to bear and to overcome all difficulties, even death itself, because we have the victory of Christ's death and the assurance of the forgiveness of sins.[18]

In other words, the difference between receiving the gospel and not receiving the gospel is the presence of God's peace. Anyone can have peace in good times. When you have a job, a nice house, a large bank account and affirmation from your colleagues, peace comes easily. But who has peace even if they lose a job? Who has peace when their retirement account is shrinking? Where is peace found when we have no health insurance coverage, or when we receive a bad diagnosis, or when we go through a romantic breakup, or when we've been mistreated or when we lose a loved one? Jesus promises peace, but not as the world gives (John 14:27). Plainly stated, Jesus promises peace not based on happy circumstances but peace that comes as a result of Christ's life in us. Can anything be more personally relevant in a conflict-ridden, anxious world than a church that powerfully communicates the availability of peace?

To cite one more example, consider the promise of "the good life" offered by Western consumer culture. You can have a life worth living if you: have lost thirty (or more) pounds, have glowing skin, wear designer clothes, drink craft beer (preferably one you have made in your cool loft apartment), finished in the top ten in a triathlon, drive a sleek and well-engineered sports car and carry the right credit card (with a six-figure credit limit). But as anyone who has gone after even one of these goals will tell you, all human achievements are ephemeral and subject to the law of diminishing returns. The novelty of our new purchase or success wears off, and we quickly need a new experience or acquisition. It is concerning the way to "the good life" that we need to hear the words of the prophet Isaiah afresh:

A voice says, "Cry out."
    And I said, "What shall I cry?"
"All people are like grass,
    and all their faithfulness is like the flowers of the field.
The grass withers and the flowers fall,
    because the breath of the LORD blows on them.
    Surely the people are grass.
The grass withers and the flowers fall,
    but the word of our God endures forever." (Isaiah 40:6-8)

According to the prophet Isaiah, we need to be committed not only to being relevant. We also need to be committed to communicating the truthfulness and the eternality of the Word of God as the only foundation for the good life Jesus promised.

14

What Is Our Calling?

. . . AND ORTHODOX DOCTRINE

On Christmas Day 2009, a young Nigerian man boarded a jet with the intention of blowing it up. Why did he intend to kill hundreds of people he did not know? His cousin said that he had sent his father a text message from Yemen in which he declared that he had "found a new religion, the real Islam," and that he was never coming home again. A number of years before this incident, he had posted on the Internet, "I imagine how the great jihad will take place, how the Muslims will win . . . and rule the whole world, and establish the greatest empire once again!"[1]

George Weigel, a Roman Catholic scholar, said, "Ideas have consequences and bad ideas can have lethal consequences."[2] Weigel also wrote, "Ideas are not intellectuals' toys. Ideas have consequences, for good and for ill, in what even intellectuals call 'the real world.'"[3]

What we believe matters. Truth matters. Ideas matter. The so-called war on global terrorism is not going to be won by military force alone. It has to be fought in the realm of truth and ideas and beliefs in the various places where false ideas are producing lethal consequences. Until people stop believing that it is God's will for them to blow themselves up and kill hundreds of innocent people, suicide bombings will be with us.

Let's apply this more personally. Have you ever tried to convince a woman to end a relationship in which she is being physically abused? My local newspaper did a series on domestic violence in our city. They reported about a man named Gregory Hess.

> Gregory S. Hess beat his wife Kristi for years, broke her nose at least five times, struck her with an axe handle and then turned to stalking her when she freed herself from the abusive marriage. He has faced 20 domestic-violence related cases since 1995 and walked away from the charges, in most cases, with a lenient sentence. But Kristi's compassion for her abuser took hold. She started visiting with Hess, 40, in jail. They talked regularly on the telephone. She wrote letters asking for leniency. She said she wouldn't testify against him. Why does she do this? Because [she's convinced] that he loves her and wouldn't do it again.[4]

Twenty times she's been beaten—at least. Her nose has been broken five times. But she won't leave because she believes he loves her and she doesn't deserve any better. What we believe matters! As Weigel wrote, "Ideas have consequences and bad ideas can have lethal consequences!"

The notion that truth matters certainly applies to what is taught in churches. *The Atlantic* did a cover story several years ago in which journalist Hanna Rosin asked the question: "Did Christianity cause the economic crash?"[5] The article essentially suggested that for millions of Christian believers, the so-called prosperity gospel—the belief that if you have enough faith, God will bless you with wealth—has led to disastrous financial decisions.

Of course, Christianity is not solely responsible for causing the great global economic meltdown that occurred in the first decade of the twenty-first century. But the article does convincingly argue that churches in the United States bear some responsibility for the particular hardship suffered by millions of Christian believers. Although the article cited particular preachers, these quotations could be heard in thousands of churches around America. One preacher was quoted as yelling from the pulpit, "We declare financial blessings! Financial miracles this week. Now! Now! Now! More work! Better work! The best finances!" The pastor is reported to have held up the keys to his Mercedes-Benz and talked about how God had given him the car. He said that God is the owner of all the silver and gold in the world and anyone with enough faith could access God's wealth. Then his wife joined him on the stage and said, "Instead of saying, 'I'm poor,' say 'I'm rich!' The word of God will manifest itself in reality."[6]

As a result of this kind of prosperity teaching, many Christians overextended themselves by taking out loans they couldn't afford and buying houses they couldn't pay for, all the while believing that somehow God would miraculously give them the money to satisfy their desires and their greed. Rosin reported about the heartbreaking circumstances of many Christians, particularly the poor and immigrants, who believed the prosperity message taught to them by their pastors, and who, as a result, lost their homes and were forced onto the streets. What we believe matters.

THE BIBLE AND TRUTH

The Bible has a rich vocabulary concerning the word that we translate as *truth*. Truth may refer to something which is authentic, genuine or real. Thus, Jesus is the "true light," and he calls himself "the true bread" and the "true vine" (John 1:9; 6:32; 15:1). Truth may also refer to that which is reliable, firm or trustworthy. Thus, Jesus said, "Yes, you know me, and you know where I am from. I am not here on my own authority, but he who sent me is true" (John 7:28).

But truth in the Bible is also related to the concept of revelation. The apostle John writes in his prologue, "For the law was given through Moses; grace and truth came through Jesus Christ" (John 1:17). John is saying that the incarnation is the ultimate disclosure of the same Lord who revealed himself to Moses through the law at Sinai. Jesus reveals to us God *as he really is*. Thus, Jesus is the "truth." In the Bible, "truth is personal, not merely intellectual; truth is acquired through the revelation of God, not through mental applications; truth is not abstract, but has been individually revealed in history [supremely in Jesus Christ]."[7] When the Bible speaks about the truth, it is often referring to the truth of God and the truth of God's Word.

The triune God is true. First, God the Father is true (John 3:33). God the Father is the ultimate reality and is the source of all truth. Second, Jesus the Son is true. Jesus' message is true and the content of his message is himself, the truth. Thus, Jesus said, "I am the one who testifies for myself; my other witness is the Father, who sent me" (John 8:18). Thus, as both the messenger and the message, Jesus is the truth. Finally, the Holy Spirit is called "the Spirit of truth" for three reasons (John 14:17). First, because the Spirit is "the Spirit of God" and God is the truth, the Spirit is the "Spirit of truth." Second, the Spirit carries on the mission of Jesus by revealing to the world both the Father and the Son. Third, the Spirit leads followers of Christ into the truth by teaching us the knowledge of the Father and the Son (John 16:14).

So the triune God is the truth and God's Word, particularly God's Word about Jesus, is the truth. In other words, real, ultimate truth is to be found in God's Word. The content of this Word is Jesus.

Believing the truth. Because truth matters, and because ultimate reality makes a difference, our relationship to the truth matters. We are encouraged to buy the truth and not sell it (Proverbs 23:23), to think about truth (Philippians 4:8), to bind truth around our necks (Proverbs 3:3), to walk in the truth (2 John 1:4; 3 John 1:3), to obey the truth (1 Peter 1:22), to love the truth (2 Thessalonians 2:10) and to rejoice with the truth (1 Corinthians 13:6). Indeed, truth is so fundamental for the Christian that the apostle Paul describes the Christian life as "truthing" in love (Ephesians 4:15). While our English does not have a verb form for the word *truth*, the apostle Paul in Greek tells us that truth ought to be the quality of all of a Christian's actions.

According to the Bible, the results of embracing the truth in the ways described are powerful. If we embrace the truth, the truth will make us more like Jesus (John 17:17). A commitment to the truth will enable us to not care about the opinions of others (Matthew 22:16). Abiding in the truth will set us free—from sins, addictions and the traps of the devil (John 8:31-32). Truth will purify us (1 Peter 1:22). Truth will save us and protect us from the attacks of the enemy (2 Thessalonians 2:13; Ephesians 6:14).

Rejecting the truth. On the other hand, the apostle Paul speaks of sinners as suppressing the truth in unrighteousness (Romans 1:18), exchanging the truth about God for a lie (Romans 1:25), refusing to obey the truth (Romans 2:8), turning away from truth (2 Timothy 2:18), resisting the truth "just as Jannes and Jambres opposed Moses" (2 Timothy 3:8) and refusing to listen to the truth (Proverbs 1:24; 1 John 4:6). The consequence of rejecting truth is that we end up lying to others, lying to ourselves and ultimately trying to lie to God (1 John 1:6-10). As we progressively become more and more characterized by lies and lying, we become the subjects of God's ultimate condemnation (2 Thessalonians 2:9-12). Excluded from the kingdom of God is "everyone who loves and practices falsehood" (Revelation 22:15). If our embrace or our rejection of the truth is the ultimate determinant of whether or not we are to be saved, how do we know what's true?

HOW DO WE KNOW WHAT'S TRUE?

There are three sources of belief in almost any area, three foundations upon which people build their beliefs and ideas. One is *tradition*: what my family taught me, what the school system taught me, what my church teaches and what my culture teaches. The second source, which exercises disproportionate impact in the twenty-first century, is *personal authority*. This is illustrated with words like, "I believe this because this particular idea resonates inside of me."

I watched a two-hour PBS special on what makes people happy. This fascinating program featured a self-help guru who essentially preaches a message that what you think will determine your reality. She teaches people, for example, that if they have cancer, it is the result of "dis-ease" with their bodies. Cancer, according to this person, is merely the accumulation of negative thoughts—anxiety, anger, bitterness—that cause your body to attack itself.

The host of this PBS special challenged her, saying, "You don't have a shred of scientific evidence to back up your claim that all cancer is caused by having negative emotions."

The guru didn't even bat an eye. She said, "I don't believe in science. I listen to my inner ding."

The host said, "What's that?"

She said with a smile, "My inner ding. My ding—what it feels like to me, what resonates inside of me."

I read a story some years ago about a pilot who was flying a jet fighter. His instrument panel broke just as he was executing a series of very complex maneuvers. So at one point he thought that he was taking the plane into a steep ascent, but he discovered that because he was relying on a broken instrument panel, he was actually taking the plane into a steep descent and crashed into the ground. The Bible teaches that we are all born with broken instrument panels. We can't simply rely on our own discernment—or our inner ding—to gauge what we should do.

Imagine, for example, that you are a single woman and you've made terrible decisions about men. You've dated loser after loser. Now you've met another guy. Your friends are telling you, "This guy is a loser. We've watched the way he has treated you. This is not a good relationship for you." What do you do? You could say, "Well, I know I've made ten mistakes in the past, but I still trust my inner ding. I know that underneath that lump of coal there is a diamond in the rough, and I'm going to dig that diamond out." Or you could say, "My instrument panel is broken. I've learned from experience to call my own discernment into question. I'm humble enough to suspect myself. I don't know everything, but I do know that my inner ding won't rescue me! I need help!"

The third source of truth is *God*, especially as God has revealed himself in Christ and through the Scriptures. It is beyond the scope of this particular book to state all the reasons that I believe the Bible reliably communicates to us the truth about who Jesus is, what he said, his crucifixion and his resurrection. But let me state just a few reasons.

Eyewitness testimony. The first reason that I believe the Bible's reports about that first Easter Sunday is that these reports are based on eyewitness testimony. As a former attorney and business law professor, I understand and appreciate the power of eyewitness testimony. The very best book on the subject of the eyewitness testimony contained in the Gospels is *Jesus and the Eyewitnesses: The Gospels as Eyewitness Testimony*, written by one of the world's leading New Testament scholars, Richard Bauckham.[8] Bauckham points out that at the time the Gospels were written, many well-known eyewitnesses to Jesus' teaching and life were still living. Many of the people named in the Gospels were in the early churches and could serve as ongoing sources and guarantors of the truth of what was being reported by the Gospel writers.

For example, in Mark we read that Jesus had been so badly beaten by the Romans that he collapsed under the weight of the cross the Romans forced him to carry. So the Romans required another man, Simon from the city of Cyrene, to help carry the cross. Simon of Cyrene is mentioned in three of the Gospels: Matthew, Mark and Luke. But Mark adds one little detail about Simon of Cyrene that is easy to miss. Mark writes, "A certain man from Cyrene, Simon, *the father of Alexander and Rufus*, was passing by on his way in from the country, and they forced him to carry the cross" (Mark 15:21). Why did Mark add that detail? Mark includes this because he is writing his Gospel to the Christians living in Rome, and Alexander and Rufus are part of the church in Rome to whom he is writing. In essence, Mark is saying, "Alexander and Rufus, who are in your church, can vouch for the truth of what I'm writing in this Gospel. You can ask them, 'Is this what happened to your father? Was your father actually there carrying Jesus' cross?'" It's easy to forget that many of the people about whom the Gospel stories were written were present in the early church. Church members could ask them if the accounts written were actually true.

Improbable material. The second reason that I believe the Bible is because it contains a lot of material that should not have appeared if someone was just making up facts to support their religion. A lot of what is in the Gospels would have made the spread of Christianity more difficult for the early Christians, not easier. As pastor Tim Keller points out in *The Reason for God: Belief in an Age of Skepticism*, "Why would the leaders of the early Christian movement have made up the story of the crucifixion if it didn't happen? Any listener of the gospel either in the Jewish world, or in the Roman world, would have automatically suspected that Jesus could never have been the Jewish Messiah, or the King of the world, because he ended up crucified."[9] And we know who gets crucified: criminals!

Keller goes on to say, "Why make up the story of Jesus in the Garden of Gethsemane, begging God, if there was some other way for him to accomplish his mission?"[10] If you're going to make up a story, just have him walk courageously right to the cross. Keller argues, "Why have your leader not only crucified, but on the cross asking God, why did God abandon him?"[11] Again, if you are going to make something up, why not put into the mouth of Jesus words like, "I trust in you, Father, even while I'm hanging on the cross as I've always trusted in you. My faith remains unwavering." Why have him say, "My God, my God, why have you forsaken me?"

Keller also notes, "Why would you have the disciples, who were the early church leaders, the people spreading the message, look so—there is no kind way to put it—stupid, so utterly unreliable, so disloyal, if you are going to make something up?"[12] Since the apostles were trying to teach people to be loyal to Jesus in the face of pressure and persecution, why write this about the people spreading the message?

There is just too much unhelpful and embarrassing material in the Gospels for the whole story to be made up. Why do I believe the Bible is reliable? Because it reports what happened, not what a propagandist or a spin doctor or a marketer would claim happened when it really didn't happen.

As a Jewish believer in Jesus, I was personally moved by a discovery that the prophecies concerning Messiah in the Hebrew Bible were fulfilled by only one person in history: Jesus of Nazareth![13] And most importantly, the Bible has changed my life as I have studied it over the past four decades. It has done what it promised to do for me, as David Field writes, "It is a fire to warm and a hammer to break, water to cleanse, milk to nourish, meat to invigorate, light to guide, a sword for the fight, and a mirror to reveal."[14]

WHAT IS ORTHODOXY?

Orthodoxy is derived from the Greek *orthodoxia* (from *orthos*, meaning "straight" or "right," and *doxa*, meaning "opinion"). It means "right belief," as opposed to heresy or heterodoxy. The word *orthodoxy* is not a biblical word. Rather, it expresses the idea that certain statements accurately embody the truth as it is revealed in Christ and the Bible. Orthodoxy speaks about the common Christian faith that must be held by anyone, regardless of denomination, in order for that person to be called a Christian.

Roger Olson, in *The Mosaic of Christian Belief: Twenty Centuries of Unity & Diversity*, writes this:

> [By orthodoxy we are speaking about] being *thoroughly biblical and both faithful to the Great Tradition of Christianity as well as contemporary in its restatement of what Christians have always believed.* . . . [We are] valuing our common Christian heritage of belief—what will here be called the Great Tradition of Christian teaching. Other terms for the same stock of commonly held Christian beliefs include "consensual Christian tradition" and "mere Christianity." . . . [Thus] in spite of important differences of interpretation and opinion, for example, Christians in the Eastern Orthodox, Roman Catholic, Presbyterian, Methodist, Baptist and Pentecostal traditions share a common faith—insofar as they stand within their own *Christian* denominational heritages and have not succumbed to radical sectarianism or liberalized theology.[15]

Olson then goes on to helpfully distinguish between what he calls *dogmas, doctrines* and *opinions*.[16]

Dogma. Dogma, according to Olson, refers to those truths that are essential to Christianity: Christian orthodoxy. Denial of these would constitute rank heresy, if not outright apostasy. Christian identity is at stake with these.[17] Among those statements of dogma, almost all orthodox Christians would include the belief that the one true God is a Trinity (Father, Son and Holy Spirit); that Jesus Christ was one person with two natures (fully divine and fully human); and that Christ died for our sins, bodily rose from the dead, ascended into heaven and will return to judge the living and the dead. A fuller expression of orthodoxy is found in the Apostles', Nicene and Chalcedonian Creeds written in the first few centuries of the church. They contain the clearest expression of what some call the Great Tradition, what C. S. Lewis called mere Christianity and what Olson called dogma.

Doctrine. By doctrine, Olson refers to "a secondary category of beliefs that are important to a particular tradition-community of Christians (e.g., a denomination in the broad or narrow sense) but are not essential to Christianity itself."[18] For example, Olson states that Baptists agree with the dogma of Roman Catholicism and other Protestant Christians that Jesus is God incarnate, the second person of the Trinity. But Baptists also believe that Christians, to be baptized properly, ought to be baptized by immersion. While this doctrine is important to Baptists, it is not essential for Christian orthodoxy and ought not to be used to identify Christianity itself. Ordaining women would be a doctrine precious to our church, as would practicing all the gifts of the Holy Spirit. But neither of these—however precious—are part of dogma.

Opinions. With regard to opinions, Olson writes: "Almost all reasonable and reflective Christians recognize that some religious beliefs are mere opinions because there is no Christian consensus about them, they are not clearly taught in Scripture, and they do not touch on the gospel itself. Often they are of a speculative nature—mere guesswork without strong justification."[19]

What might an example of an opinion be? Olson mentions the belief that there might be intelligent life on other planets, the age of the earth itself and the identity of the antichrist. Distinguishing between dogma, doctrine and opinion is extremely helpful in being able to set the boundaries between orthodoxy and heresy. Only with respect to the narrow category of dogma should we ever use the term *heresy* when referring to another's beliefs.

But guess what most of us Christians spend our time fighting with each other about? Not dogma, not even doctrine, but opinions—our political opinions, our opinions about worship styles and opinions about small group practices. Then, most tragically, we judge and sometimes separate ourselves from people who hold different opinions. In our worst moments, we might even wonder whether someone who holds an opinion different from our own is even a Christian.

THE ORTHODOX LIFE

Recall from the early part of this chapter that truth is not merely something to be believed. According to the apostle Paul, truth is an activity. Again, although English does not have a verb "to truth," the apostle Paul uses such a verb when he urges the Ephesians that by "truthing" in love, they should grow up in Christ in all things (Ephesians 4:15). Truth, or orthodoxy, is a quality of life and action, not just a statement of belief and proposition.

In 1957 Carl Henry, who was then editor of *Christianity Today*, wrote a critique of fundamentalism in which he refers to fundamentalism's "perversion of the Biblical spirit." His words are worth repeating at length.

> The real bankruptcy of fundamentalism has resulted not so much from a reactionary spirit—lamentable as this was—as from a harsh temperament, a spirit of lovelessness and strife contributed by much of its leadership in the recent past. One of the ironies of contemporary church history is that the more fundamentalists stress separation from apostasy as a theme in their churches, the

more a spirit of lovelessness seems to prevail. The theological conflict with liberalism deteriorated into an attack upon organizations and personalities. This condemnation, in turn, grew to include conservative churchmen and churches not ready to align with separatist movements. It widens still further, to abuse evangelicals unhappy with the spirit of independency in such groups as the American Council of Churches and the International Council of Christian Churches. Then came internal debate and division among separatist fundamentalism within the American Council. More recently, the evangelistic ministry of Billy Graham and [the] efforts of other evangelical leaders, whose disapproval of liberalism and advocacy of conservative Christianity are beyond dispute, have become the target of bitter volubility. This character of fundamentalism as a temperament and not primarily fundamentalism as a theology, has brought the movement into contemporary discredit. . . . Historically, fundamentalism was a theological position; only gradually did the movement come to signify a mood and disposition as well. In its early [years] leadership reflected ballast, and less of bombast and battle. . . . If modernism stands discredited as a perversion of the scriptural theology, certainly fundamentalism in this contemporary expression stands discredited as a perversion of the Biblical spirit.[20]

In other words, heresy is not simply a matter of believing things that are contrary to the dogmas of Christianity. Heresy may also include living in a way that is contrary to the essential spirit of the Christian gospel. Belief and life came together in Scripture far more than we Westerners in the twenty-first century perceive. Indeed, the apostle Paul suggests that people "adorn the doctrine of God our Savior in every respect" by their lives and activities (Titus 2:9-10 NASB). And Jesus said, "You are the light of the world. A town built on a hill cannot be hidden. Neither do people light a lamp and put it under a bowl. Instead they put it on its stand, and it gives light to everyone in the house. In the same way, let your light shine before others, that they may see your good deeds and glorify your Father in heaven" (Matthew 5:14-16). According to Jesus and the apostle Paul, disciples of Jesus are to attract people to God not just by what we say we believe but by living in a way that is consistent with the gospel we proclaim. Both-And means holding together *orthopraxy* (right living) and *orthodoxy* (right belief).

RELEVANT HERESY AND IRRELEVANT ORTHODOXY

The great challenge for Christians today is to live out our Both-And existence in a world that is hostile to both Christian belief and Christian practice. We must be relevant so that the nonbelieving world can see and hear the gospel message in a language it understands. At the same time, the great challenge of mission is to try to *reach* the world without *becoming* the world. Or as Jesus put it, "You are the salt of the earth. But if the salt loses its saltiness, how can it be made salty again? It is no longer good for anything, except to be thrown out and trampled underfoot" (Matthew 5:13).

Relevant heresy. Failing to believe the essence of the gospel is what I would call *relevant heresy*. One may, for example, simply give up believing and teaching that the crucifixion of Christ is necessary for our salvation because it smacks of exclusivity and is unpopular in a postmodern context in which tolerance reigns supreme. Of even greater danger today in America is the reshaping of the gospel to fit our therapeutic society. God becomes the very best therapist you ever met: always available, always affirming and always supportive. God's goals for our lives become the goals of therapy: to increase our overall level of contentment and happiness while helping us to build healthy relationships with other human beings.

But the God of the Bible is not presented to us as an infinitely great therapist. He is our Father and our Judge, our Maker and our Savior. As infinite, holy God, he is not just affirming and accepting. In Scripture and in life, God is often confusing, confounding and downright disturbing. He is not just available. He often hides himself and allows us to feel alone. And he isn't primarily interested in building our kingdoms or helping us improve our lives. Rather, God is building the kingdom of God. And he invites us to work with him in this task. Orthodoxy must therefore be discerning and aware of the way in which God and the gospel are reshaped and repackaged by the culture in which we live.

Another way to think about the Both-And tension is to remember that the Christian God is both loving *and* righteous. John Stott, in my favorite of his books, *The Cross of Christ*, wrote this:

> Emil Brunner in *The Mediator* did not hesitate to write of God's "dual nature" as "the central mystery of the Christian revelation." For "God is not simply Love. The nature of God cannot be exhaustively stated in one single word." Indeed, modern opposition to forensic language in relation to the cross is mainly "due to the fact that the idea of the Divine Holiness has been swallowed up in that of the Divine love; this means that the biblical idea of God, in which the decisive element is this twofold nature of holiness and love, is being replaced by the modern, unilateral, monistic idea of God."[21]

I have found that the toughest decisions in ministry involve upholding the righteousness of God. Everyone supports me as a pastor when I uphold God's love. Everyone loves to be affirmed, welcomed, and supported in their views and behaviors. It is the rare person who likes to be challenged, corrected or disciplined. The loneliest times in Christian ministry are when we as Christian leaders are called to represent God's righteousness with a church member or in a situation that involves sin.

Irrelevant orthodoxy. Still, a church's teaching may be orthodox but its life may be contrary to the spirit of the gospel. I'd call that *irrelevant orthodoxy*. Consider, for example, the impact of the Roman Catholic Church's refusal to exercise discipline against thousands of Catholic priests who were known to be abusing children and teenagers. You can be orthodox and still not make a difference in this world.

In Ireland, which was the most Catholic nation on earth, the Irish government had a unique relationship with the Vatican. It used to be the case that the Vatican basically prescribed Irish legislation. But then the horrific child abuse by priests and the cover-up by the Roman Catholic hierarchy was exposed. During the 2000s, the number of Irish Catholics regularly attending mass dropped from 80 percent to less than 40 percent of Irish Catholics.

In America, the Roman Catholic Church is losing approximately five members for every one new convert. Certainly the reason for this mass exodus from the Roman Catholic Church is not due just to the growing secularism of our society. The child abuse scandal and its subsequent cover-up has had a profound impact on the Roman Catholic Church. Many Roman Catholics have said, "I don't want to be part of any institution that is capable of this. I certainly don't want to raise my children in an institution that tolerates and covers up the abuse of children."

A few decades ago, John Stott wrote, "The secular world is almost wholly unimpressed by the Church today. There is widespread departure from Christian moral standards. So long as the Church tolerates sin and does not judge itself . . . and fails to manifest visibly the power of Jesus Christ to save from sin, it will never attract the world to Christ."[22]

ASKING TOO MUCH OR TOO LITTLE?

I mentioned earlier that I was raised in a Jewish family in New York City. By the time I was a teenager, I had become an atheist. Then I went off to college in Cleveland, at Case Western Reserve University, and met Marlene, who began to talk to me about Jesus. After we became friends, what spoke most loudly to me about the reality of Marlene's faith was definitely not her words or her arguments but the extraordinary attractiveness of her life. Marlene was the first really decent human being that I had ever met. She told the truth. She went out of her way to apologize when she blew it. She maintained a really high moral standard concerning her dating and sex life. It was this distinctiveness of her life that drew me to Christ!

The Western world longs to believe, but no institution is credible enough to elicit faith. Can the Christian church rise to the challenge of eliciting faith again? Roger Finke and Rodney Stark examined church records from the founding of the United States in 1776 until 1990. Here is what these two sociologists of religion discovered about churchgoing in America throughout our history. "Many observers have discounted the rise in church membership on the grounds that it was accompanied by a decline in acceptance of traditional religious doctrines. But this simply isn't so. Not all denominations shared in this immense rise in membership rates [over the last 220 years], and to the degree that denominations rejected traditional doctrines and ceased to make serious demands on their followers, they ceased to prosper. The churching of America was accomplished by aggressive churches committed to vivid otherworldliness."[23]

Churches decline not because they ask too much of their members, but because they ask too little![24] Finke and Stark suggest that the only churches that have ever grown in America are deeply committed to the doctrines taught to us by Jesus and the apostles and to the distinctive life modeled by them. Often, attempts to be more inclusive and to lower the church's distinctiveness from the world end up shrinking the church instead. A few generations ago, Dietrich Bonhoeffer attempted to answer the question: how can we live the Christian life in the modern world? Here is part of his famous answer:

> The cross is laid on every Christian. The first Christ-suffering which every man must experience is the call to abandon the attachments of this world. It is that dying of the old man which is the result of his encounter with Christ. As we embark upon discipleship we surrender ourselves to Christ in union with his death—we give over our lives to death. Thus it begins; the cross is not the terrible end to an otherwise godfearing and happy life, but it meets us at the beginning of our communion with Christ. When Christ calls a man, he bids him come and die. It may be a

death like that of the first disciples who had to leave home and work to follow him, or it may be a death like Luther's, who had to leave the monastery and go out into the world. But it is the same death every time—death in Jesus Christ, the death of the old man at his call.[25]

It is the distinctiveness of relevant orthodoxy—the Both-And of right doctrine and right living—that makes the Christian church attractive.

Epilogue

FOLLOW ME!

Technology has brought the world closer together in ways that were never before possible. A boy in Kansas can use Skype to videoconference with his father, who is stationed in Kabul. A girl in Montreal can use Google Maps to see the house where her friend lives in Moscow. Rapid progress in technology has made the world smaller in great and wonderful ways. As the world gets smaller, however, we are even more painfully aware of the great fault lines that divide people in seven billion different ways. What we thought of as just a hairline fracture turned out to be the size of the Grand Canyon!

The culture war that has saturated our public discourse has hijacked every narrative, including the Christian narrative. Christians are finding it more and more difficult to live out the faith demonstrated by Jesus. The narrators of these culture wars are constantly challenging Christians to live an Either-Or faith and cut away the tension. But we believe Scripture calls us to live a Both-And faith that is radically Christ centered. Both-And does not involve advocating for the mean between two extremes or finding the average. Rather, it requires holding to both extremes at once and realizing the power that exists in this tension.

ORDINARY PEOPLE, EXTRAORDINARY LIVES

On the day of Pentecost, as the disciples of Jesus were gathered in the upper room, the Holy Spirit fell upon them in a mighty way. These disciples, now filled with the Holy Spirit, boldly proclaimed the good news of Jesus wherever they went, through rejection, humiliation, persecution and even unto death. Through the great trials and opposition, those filled and emboldened by the Spirit of God lived lives marked by selfless love, unending hope and incredible faith, even to their last breath.

This is the story of the birth of the church: a group of ordinary people who were filled with the Holy Spirit and began to live extraordinary lives. And this is our story! We have been invited into a life-changing relationship with Jesus. Our story does not end with our salvation! That's just the beginning. The rest of the story involves being a sent people. When God saves people, he doesn't just save them for heaven. He saves them for a purpose. Our purpose as "sent people" is to live lives shaped by the words of Jesus, who said, "Go and make disciples!" (Matthew 28:19).

But we too easily lose sight of this calling. We are like eager children reading a fairy tale book. We want to go immediately from "Once upon a time" to "Happily ever after." We forget that in between "Once upon a time" and "Happily ever after"—between the good beginning and the beautiful ending—is the meaningful middle. Are you living a meaningful middle?[1]

If we were honest, many of us would confess that we are not living a meaningful middle. Rather, we live moderate lives, make moderate sacrifices and have a moderate impact in this world. But as followers of Jesus, we are not called to live moderate lives. God is calling us to make an extraordinary impact on this world by taking up our crosses, following Jesus and making disciples of every nation. These tasks cannot be accomplished by making moderate sacrifices and moderate decisions. We are called to make extraordinary decisions and extraordinary sacrifices so that we can make an extraordinary impact for the sake of an extraordinary God!

There is no such a thing as Christianity in moderation. It is all or nothing! Frederick Buechner, an author and pastor, writes, "In terms of human wisdom, Jesus was a perfect fool. And if you think you can follow him without making something like the same kind of fool yourself, you are laboring not under the cross, but a delusion."[2]

In the eyes of the world, was it wise or foolish for Noah to obey God, who told him to build a boat on dry land? Was it wise or foolish for Abraham to obey God, who told him to offer up his only son as a sacrifice even though God had promised to bless him through his offspring? Was it wise or foolish for a brilliant and accomplished man named Paul to give up his reputation, his friends and his life to travel around the world to start new churches? Was it wise or foolish for Peter to heed the voice of Jesus to step out of a boat and walk on water? Was it wise or foolish for Mary to pour expensive perfume on the feet of Jesus and wipe them with her hair as an extravagant demonstration of her love? Was it wise or foolish for Jesus to not spend time with the religious leaders or powerful officials but to instead "waste his life" on prostitutes, tax collectors, the sick and the sinners? In the eyes of the world, was it wise or foolish for God—the eternal, everlasting, all-powerful, all-wise God—to enter into his very own creation, in the image of a frail human, and to die shamefully on a cross so that you and I can truly live?

Following Jesus is not just a one-time decision. Rather, it is an ongoing decision—right foot, left foot, right foot, left foot—of choosing again and again to say to Jesus, "Here I am! Send me, Lord!" Jesus beckons us to take up our cross and follow him. He calls us to forsake everything for the cause of the gospel. To the world, that is an utterly foolish way to live. To us who are being saved, it is the power of God and the wisdom of God.

We are called to be *both* evangelical *and* charismatic. We are called to celebrate *both* unity *and* diversity. We are called to do *both* mercy *and* justice. We must *both* proclaim *and* demonstrate the gospel. Our ethic must be *both* personal *and* social. We are called to live in between the already *and* the not yet, all the while striving for *both* relevant practice *and* orthodox doctrine! But none of this is done by moderate people who pursue a gospel of moderation. Taking up our cross to follow Jesus means to radically and passionately walk on the high wire of Both-And Christianity!

Notes

Introduction: The Both-And Christian
[1]Paul Krugman, "A Tale of Two Moralities," *New York Times*, January 13, 2011.
[2]Petit's amazing feat was documented in a movie called *Man on Wire*.
[3]Scripture passages exploring the triune nature of God include John 1:18; 10:30; 14:9, 16-17, 26; 15:26; and 2 Corinthians 3:17-18. Passages supporting the fully divine and fully human nature of Christ include John 1:14 and Philippians 2:5-7. Passages suggesting the good and fallen nature of creation include Romans 8:20-23. Passages supporting the already and not yet nature of the kingdom include Luke 17:20-37, and verses outlining the sinful and righteous nature of humanity include Ephesians 4:20-24.

Chapter 1: What Is Our Identity? Evangelical . . .
[1]*Empowered Evangelicals: Bringing Together the Best of the Evangelical and Charismatic Worlds* (Boise, ID: Ampelon Publishing, 1994).
[2]The vast majority of white evangelicals did vote Republican in 2012. But 71 percent of Hispanics, including the majority of Hispanic evangelicals, voted for Obama in 2012. Seventy-five percent of the Asian American vote, whose churchgoing population is largely evangelical, also went for Obama, as did 93 percent of the African American vote, whose churchgoing population overwhelming go to theologically conservative churches. When I use the term evangelical in these early sections, I'm using it in the media's sense: as referring to *white* evangelicals.
[3]"Columbus Mileposts March 6, 1946: Crowds Gather for Glimpse of Churchill," *Columbus Dispatch*, March 6, 2012.
[4]Virtually all evangelicals would support an abortion to save the life of the mother. Many would support (albeit with some unease) the use of a morning-after pill in cases of rape or incest. Most evangelicals would not oppose in-vitro fertilization as a means of treating infertility even if that meant that some fertilized eggs would not be used.
[5]The *Roe v. Wade* decision defined "viable" as being "potentially able to live outside the mother's womb, albeit with artificial aid," adding that viability "is

usually placed at about seven months (28 weeks) but may occur earlier, even at 24 weeks." Mary Wood and Lisa Hawkins, "State Regulation of Late Abortion and the Physician's Duty of Care to the Viable Fetus," 45 Mo. L. Rev. 394 (1980).

[6]The reasons that women give for having abortions underscore their understanding of the responsibilities of parenthood and family life. Three-fourths of women cite concern for or responsibility to other individuals; three-fourths say they cannot afford a child; three-fourths say that having a baby would interfere with work, school or the ability to care for dependents; and half say they do not want to be a single parent or are having problems with their husband or partner (L. B. Finer et al., "Reasons U.S. Women Have Abortions: Quantitative and Qualitative Perspective," *Perspectives on Sexual and Reproductive Health* 37, no. 3 [2005]: 110-18).

[7]David Kinnaman and Gabe Lyons, unChristian: What a New Generation Really Thinks About Christianity . . . and Why It Matters (Grand Rapids: Baker Books, 2007), pp. 153-80.

[8]James Davison Hunter, in *The Fundamentalist Phenomenon*, ed. Norman J. Cohen (Grand Rapids: Eerdmans, 1990), pp. 56-72. Emphasis in the original.

[9]Martin Marty, "What Is Fundamentalism? Theological Perspectives in H. P. Kung and J. Moltmann," *Fundamentalism as an Ecumenical Challenge*, Concilium 3 (London: SCM Press, 1992), pp. 3-13. Emphasis in the original.

[10]Many fundamentalists believe that the earth is not billions of years old, as geologists claim, but less than ten thousand years old. Fundamentalists generally reject evolution and the theory of the common ancestry of living things; they generally believe that God, as an act of "special creation," separately created each species without using evolution as a mechanism.

[11]Alister McGrath, *Evangelicalism and the Future of Christianity* (Downers Grove, IL: InterVarsity Press, 1995), p. 21.

[12]Benjamin Warfield, *Selected Shorter Writings* (Phillipsburg, NJ: P & R Publishing, 1970), pp. 463-65.

[13]Alister McGrath, *J. I. Packer: A Biography* (Grand Rapids: Baker Books, 1997), p. 200.

[14]*Dispensationalism* is an interpretive scheme of the Bible that is structured around a series of dispensations, or periods in history, in which God relates to human beings in different ways under different biblical covenants.

[15]As a direct result of the lack of support from the global Christian community, Palestinian Christians have found themselves squeezed between two hostile groups: the Israeli Jewish community and the Palestinian Muslim community. For many Palestinian Christians, the only viable option was to immigrate to America or to Europe. Whereas the Palestinian Christian community had lived in the Promised Land since earliest Christian times, Palestinian Christians now make up no more than a few percent of Palestinians in the twenty-first century. What is

the evangelical response to the diaspora of Palestinian Christians? For some, it is not a change of stance toward Israel or the Palestinians. Rather, we send American missionaries to bring Christianity to a land that formerly had Christians living in it: Christians who have been displaced by our foreign policy. How often do Christian political views undermine our primary Christian commitment to spread the gospel to all people?

[16]Eighty-four evangelical Christian leaders signed the "Evangelical Statement on Israel/Palestine," which calls for the Israelis and Palestinians to negotiate a fair, two-state solution.

[17]Genesis 15:18 says, "On that day the LORD made a covenant with Abram and said, 'To your descendants I give this land, from the Wadi of Egypt to the great river, the Euphrates.'"

[18]David Bebbington, *Evangelicalism in Modern Britain: A History from the 1730s to the 1980s* (London: Unwin Hyman, 1989), p. 3.

[19]Quoted in Tony Campolo, *Letters to a Young Evangelical* (New York: Basic Books, 2006), p. 11.

[20]These statistics are from the *2011 Yearbook of American & Canadian Churches*, published by the National Council of Churches. The yearbook can be ordered from their website at www.ncccusa.org/news/110210yearbook2011.html.

[21]McGrath, *Evangelicalism*, pp. 66-67.

[22]Donald G. Bloesch, *Essentials of Evangelical Theology* (San Francisco: Harper & Row, 1978), 1:ix.

[23]Martin Luther, *Commentary on the Epistle to the Galatians* (Grand Rapids: Zondervan, 1939), pp. 72-73.

[24]Martin Niemöller, quoted in Tony Campolo, *Letters to a Young Evangelical* (New York: Basic Books, 2006), pp. 42-43.

Chapter 2: What Is Our Identity? . . . and Charismatic

[1]Michael Bamberger, "Rolling Thunder," *Sports Illustrated*, March 1, 1999.

[2]Rick Warren, *The Purpose Driven Life: What on Earth Am I Here For?* (Grand Rapids: Zondervan, 2012).

[3]Billy Graham, Greater L.A. Crusade, 1949.

[4]Many observers of contemporary Christianity distinguish between the Pentecostal and charismatic movements. The term *Pentecostal* is often restricted to the historic Pentecostal movements that sprang from the Azusa Street Revival that began in 1906. These include Assemblies of God churches, the International Church of the Four Square Gospel, the Pentecostal Holiness Church and the Church of God in Christ. The *charismatic* movement, by way of distinction, is often seen as the spread of Pentecostal doctrine and experience to Protestant mainline churches such as Episcopal, Lutheran and Methodist churches, as well as the spread of

Pentecostal experience to the Roman Catholic Church. For the sake of simplicity in this chapter, I am combining both the Pentecostal and charismatic movements under the term *charismatic*.

[5]Quoted by Gary Tyra, *The Holy Spirit in Mission: Prophetic Speech and Action in Christian Witness* (Downers Grove, IL: InterVarsity Press, 2011), p. 11.

[6]Gordon D. Fee, *God's Empowering Presence: The Holy Spirit in the Letters of Paul* (London: Paternoster, 2001), p. xxi.

[7]Jaroslav Pelikan, quoted in Paul Thigpen, "Come, Holy Spirit! 2000 Years of Miracles," *Charisma*, September 1992, p. 25.

[8]Fawn Parish, quoted in Scot McKnight, "A Balanced Perspective of Images for Ministry," *Jesus Creed: Exploring the Significance of Jesus and the Orthodox Faith for the 21st Century* (blog), February 8, 2012, www.patheos.com/blogs/jesuscreed/2012/02/08/a-balanced-perspective-of-images-for-ministry/.

[9]The 10/40 Window refers to the region of the eastern hemisphere stretching between 10 and 40 degrees north of the equator. The 10/40 Window is home to some of the largest unreached people groups in the world.

[10]According to Cindy Bledsoe in "Evangelism in Sports and Recreation Ministry," www.csrm.org/article_bledsoe.html, "nearly half of all Americans who accept Jesus Christ as their savior do so before reaching the age of 13 (43%), and that two out of three born again Christians (64%) made that commitment to Christ before their 18th birthday. One out of eight born again people (13%) made their profession of faith while 18 to 21 years old. Less than one out of every four born again Christians (23%) embraced Christ after their twenty-first birthday." Barna noted that these figures are consistent with similar studies it has conducted during the past twenty years.

[11]Craig Keener, "Spirit at Work," *Discipleship Journal*, January/February 1996.

Chapter 3: What Is Our Community? Unity . . .

[1]Democratic, representative government has been ill equipped to deal with people who do not respect democratic society. For example, Dutch film director Theo van Gogh worked with Somali-born writer Ayaan Hirsi Ali to produce the film *Submission*, which criticized the treatment of women in Islam and aroused controversy among Muslims. On November 2, 2004, he was assassinated by Mohammed Bouyeri, a Dutch-Moroccan Muslim.

[2]As quoted in John Reed, *Ten Days That Shook the World* (London: Penguin Classics, 2007), p. 212.

[3]Klaus Wengst, *Pax Romana and the Peace of Jesus Christ* (Norwich, UK: SCM Press, 1987), pp. 1-2.

[4]Rick Love, "The Church as Reconciling Community: Reflections on the Comprehensive and Multidimensional Nature of Peacemaking" (paper, Society of Vineyard Scholars, Minneapolis, MN, April 26-28, 2012).

⁵John Stott, *The Message of Ephesians* (Downers Grove, IL: InterVarsity Press, 1984), p. 151.

⁶Ibid., p. 152.

⁷I borrowed and modified the terms found in "Conflict Management Strategies and Styles: Improving Group, Organizational or Team Dynamics When Conflict Occurs," Southern Nazarene University, http://home.snu.edu/~hculbert/conflict. htm.

⁸Timothy Keller, *The Reason for God: Belief in an Age of Skepticism* (New York: Dutton Publishing, 2008), pp. 20-21.

⁹This story is told by Jim Wallis in http://sojo.net/magazine/2004/11/power-recon ciliation.

Chapter 4: What Is Our Community? . . . and Diversity

¹For a fuller history of evangelicals and race relations, see Michael O. Emerson and Christian Smith, *Divided by Faith: Evangelical Religion and the Problem of Race in America* (New York: Oxford University Press, 2001), pp. 21-49. This section is largely dependent on Emerson and Smith's retelling of this history.

²Ibid., p. 27.

³Ibid., p. 41.

⁴Ibid., p. 46.

⁵Ibid., p. 47.

⁶Molly Worthen, "Southern Baptist Convergence," *New York Times*, June 18, 2012.

⁷Of course, racial diversity is not always possible in areas that are completely racially homogeneous. Some areas of the United States and other countries are still almost entirely monolithic. In such cases, I would encourage congregations to build partnerships with racially different congregations nearby (for example, a suburban white congregation may choose to build a relationship with an urban black congregation). Geographic proximity permits the building of friendships and personal relationships. Since domestic crosscultural missions tend to influence our racial views more than international short-term missions trips, I would encourage churches to build relationships with a church in another city and to send short-term teams to build friendships with people there.

⁸If you are interested in reading some books on this topic, I would recommend: Spencer Perkins and Chris Rice, *More Than Equals: Racial Healing for the Sake of the Gospel* (Downers Grove, IL: InterVarsity Press, 2000); Mark DeYmaz, *Building a Healthy Multi-Ethnic Church: Mandate, Commitments and Practices of a Diverse Congregation* (San Francisco: Jossey-Bass, 2007); and Emerson and Smith, *Divided by Faith*.

⁹Many churches today still don't grasp the implications of Jesus calling a child and placing that child "among them" (Matthew 18:2). My wife and I were once

ushered out of a megachurch service in Florida because we were there with our eight-year-old, who was very quiet and well behaved. We gently tried to explain that our eight-year-old was very accustomed to being well behaved at church and asked if she could stay with us, since she didn't know anyone at the church we were visiting. We were told that it would set a dangerous precedent if she were allowed to stay, since church policy prevented anyone under twelve from being in the public worship service. To top it off, the senior pastor handed us a paper explaining the church's exclusion of children under age twelve in terms of "families needing to not care about ourselves, but to put the interests of church above our own." Why the church was not asked to accommodate families with well-mannered children was left unexplained. Suffice it to say, adults' strong anti-child biases have not disappeared.

[10]Two extremely helpful books offer a Christian understanding of immigration: Matthew Soerens and Jenny Hwang, *Welcoming the Stranger: Justice, Compassion and Truth in the Immigration Debate* (Downers Grove, IL: InterVarsity Press, 2009); and M. Daniel Carroll, *Christians at the Border: Immigration, the Church, and the Bible* (Grand Rapids: Baker Academic, 2008).

Chapter 5: What Is Our Concern? Mercy . . .

[1]According to current American law, the family must wait for one of the children to reach age eighteen to apply for Jeanine's return. And then she cannot return to the United States for ten years after that.

[2]Karl Barth, *Church Dogmatics*, trans. A. T. Mackay adn T. H. L. Parker (Peabody, MA: Hendrickson Publishers, 2010), p. 370.

[3]Nowhere does the Bible teach salvation by works—the idea that we can receive eternal life because of what we do. Everywhere in Scripture, salvation is understood as being granted by grace alone through faith alone. Our activity toward the poor and the needy does not earn us our salvation, but our activity toward the poor is *evidence* of our salvation. Jesus teaches in Matthew 7 that you can't get good fruit from a bad tree. What we see on the outside of a person—feeding those who are hungry, caring for sick people, visiting folks in prison—is simply the evidence that God's Spirit has given the person a new heart. If your heart has been changed by grace, you will be converted from a life that is centered on your own needs and desires to a life that is centered on meeting the needs of others. So we are saved by faith alone; but how do we know that our faith is genuine? How do we know that we are not just fooling ourselves but that instead we have placed our faith in the real Christ? Jesus suggests in Matthew 25 that when we find ourselves helping the poor and caring about the needy—moving from a self-centered to an other-centered life and doing the things that God loves—we are proving that our hearts have been changed.

[4]While much has been written on this topic, numerous articles in the *Compendium of the Social Doctrine of the Church* (Washington, DC: USCCB Publishing, March 7, 2005) lay this out nicely.

[5]Mother Teresa, *In the Heart of the World: Thoughts, Stories, and Prayers* (Novato, CA: New World Library, 2010), pp. 57-58. Emphasis added.

[6]The Samaritan's act could be compared to that of an African American stopping on the road to help a victimized white person in the Jim Crow, pre–civil rights South.

[7]Comprehensive immigration reform favors giving an earned pathway to citizenship (including paying back taxes, learning English, having no criminal record and being gainfully employed) to the twelve million undocumented immigrants already here, while simultaneously putting policies into effect to discourage future undocumented immigration. These policies often include increased border security and employer sanctions for the hiring of undocumented immigrants.

Chapter 6: What Is Our Concern? . . . and Justice

[1]From a speech by Frederick Douglass, April 1886, in The Frederick Douglass Papers, 2 vols., ed. John Blassingame et al. (New Haven, CT: Yale University Press, 1979–1982).

[2]Gary Haugen, *Good News about Injustice: A Witness of Courage in a Hurting World*, 10th Anniversary ed. (Downers Grove, IL: InterVarsity Press, 2009), p. 86.

[3]Richard Stearns, *The Hole in Our Gospel: What Does God Require of Us? The Answer that Changed My Life and Might Just Change the World* (Nashville: Thomas Nelson, 2009), p. 2.

[4]Tobin Grant, "Glenn Beck: 'Leave Your Church,'" *Christianity Today*, March 12, 2010.

[5]Stan Jones, quoted in ibid.

[6]Nicholas Wolterstorff, quoted in Ronald J. Sider, *Toward an Evangelical Policy: Political Strategies for the Health of the Nation* (Grand Rapids: Baker Books, 2005), p. 164.

[7]*A Place at the Table*, A Pastoral Reflection of the U.S. Catholic Bishops, November 13, 2002.

[8]The Bible does not require equal *outcomes* for everyone. Nor does it require equal *access* for everyone. History teaches us that the attempt to provide equal outcomes or exactly equal access results in tyranny and the denial of natural differences in talent and industriousness. But while equality is not demanded by scriptural notions of justice, the Jubilee principle does demand access to the means of production so that a family's basic necessities are within reach.

[9]George Orwell, *1984* (New York: Plume, 1983).

[10]Harvie Conn, *A Clarified Vision for Urban Mission* (Grand Rapids: Zondervan, 1987), p. 147.

[11]*Rich Christians in an Age of Hunger: Moving from Affluence to Generosity* (Nashville: Thomas Nelson, 2005), pp. 219-20.

[12]An illustration of institutional sin in the Bible is the enslavement of the children of Israel in Egypt. The exodus story is the story of God's confrontation with a sinful structure, or spider web of sin. The notion of a spider web is that if you cut one strand of the web, it is still attached in so many other places that it remains fixed in place. A sinful system goes beyond the goodness or badness of any individual; the system distorts the whole society.

[13]Graham Nash, "Chicago/We Can Change the World," on *Songs for Beginners* (Los Angeles: Wally Heiders Studio III; San Francisco: Studio "C," 1971).

[14]See Charles Marsh, *The Beloved Community: How Faith Shapes Social Justice From the Civil Rights Movement to Today* (New York: Basic Books, 2006).

[15]Martin Luther King Jr., quoted in John R. W. Stott, *The Living Church: Convictions of a Lifelong Pastor* (Downers Grove, IL: InterVarsity Press, 2011), p. 137.

[16]Historic civil rights legislation, including a legislative response to racial discrimination in employment, housing, educational and voting rights, would be obvious examples of the necessity of political advocacy to work toward biblical justice.

[17]These principles were proposed by Cardinal Theodore McCarrick, who said, "The battles for human life and dignity and for the weak and vulnerable should be fought not at the communion rail but in the public square, in hearts and minds, in our pulpits and public advocacy, in our consciences and communities." From "Cardinal McCarrick: No Simple Answers on Bishop-Politician Relations" (Catholic News Service/USCCB), June 23, 2004. See McCarrick's writings for a fuller treatment of these principles.

[18]This quote is attributed to William Penn as well as Marcus Aurelius, Henry Drummond and Thomas à Kempis, among others.

Chapter 7: What Is Our Method? Proclamation . . .

[1]As quoted in Richard Stearns, *The Hole in Our Gospel: What Does God Expect of Us?* (Nashville: Thomas Nelson, 2010), p. 263.

[2]I have borrowed some of these terms from John Wimber and Kevin Springer, *Power Evangelism* (Ventura, CA: Regal, 2001) and Mark Stibbe, *Prophetic Evangelism: When God Speaks to Those Who Don't Know Him* (London: Authentic Lifestyle, 2004).

[3]Don Richardson, *Peace Child* (Ventura, CA: Regal, 1974).

[4]Don Richardson, *Eternity in Their Hearts: Startling Evidence of Belief in the One True God in Hundreds of Cultures Throughout the World* (Ventura, CA: Regal, 2006).

[5]These categories obviously total more than 100 percent. Many people mentioned more than one type of crisis in reporting the reason for coming to Christ. See

Stephen Van Dop, "Connecting to God: Exploring the Language, Motivation and Three Strategic Evidences in Conversion to Christ" (PhD diss., Asbury Theological Seminary, 2004).

[6]Ibid., p. 125.

[7]The Greek word that Luke uses, which is translated "proclaim good news," is *euangelisasthai*, which follows the Greek translation of Isaiah 61 (the Septuagint Version of the Hebrew Bible). From this Greek word we derive the English words *evangelize*, *evangelism*, *evangelist* and *evangelicals*. *Evangelicals* are people who proclaim good news.

[8]Rebecca Manley Pippert, *Out of the Saltshaker and into the World: Evangelism as a Way of Life* (Downers Grove, IL: InterVarsity Press, 1979).

[9]Billy Graham, quoted in William Martin, "Evangelicalism: Billy Graham," *Christianity History Magazine* 65 (2000).

Chapter 8: What Is Our Method? . . . and Demonstration

[1]William Temple, quoted in John R. W. Stott, *The Living Church: Convictions of a Lifelong Pastor* (Downers Grove, IL: InterVarsity Press, 2011), p. 51.

[2]Christopher J. H. Wright, *The Mission of God's People: A Biblical Theology of the Church's Mission* (Grand Rapids: Zondervan, 2010), p. 191.

[3]John R. W. Stott, *Christian Mission in the Modern World* (Downers Grove, IL: InterVarsity Press, 1975).

[4]Alpha is an opportunity to explore the meaning of life in a relaxed, friendly setting. The Alpha course usually meets once per week for ten weeks. During each session, people enjoy great food, laughter and learning in a fun and friendly atmosphere, where no question about life or God is seen as too simple or too hostile. You can find more information about Alpha at www.alpha.org.

[5]Charles H. Spurgeon, *The Autobiography of Charles H. Spurgeon* (Cincinnati: Curts & Jennings, 1899), 2:226-27.

[6]John Wimber and Keith Springer, *Power Evangelism* (Ventura, CA: Regal, 1986).

[7]John Poulton, *A Today Sort of Evangelism* (Cambridge: Lutterworth, 1972), pp. 60-61, 79.

[8]John R. W. Stott, *The Contemporary Christian: Applying God's Word to Today's World* (Downers Grove, IL: InterVarsity Press, 1995), pp. 254-55.

[9]Quoted by Rodney Stark in *The Rise of Christianity: How the Obscure, Marginal Jesus Movement Became the Dominant Religious Force in the Western World in a Few Centuries* (San Francisco: HarperSanFrancisco, 1997), pp. 82-83.

[10]Ibid., pp. 83-84.

[11]Ibid.

[12]Steve Sjogren, *Conspiracy of Kindness: A Unique Approach to Sharing the Love of Jesus*, rev. ed. (Ventura, CA: Regal, 2008), p. 18.

Chapter 9: What Is Our Ethic? Personal . . .

[1]Robert D. Putnam and David E. Campbell, *American Grace: How Religion Divides and Unites Us* (New York: Simon & Schuster, 2010).

[2]For an in-depth study of holiness, see Christopher J. H. Wright, *The Mission of God's People: A Biblical Theology of the Church's Mission* (Grand Rapids: Zondervan, 2010).

[3]C. S. Lewis, *Mere Christianity* (New York: HarperCollins, 2001), p. 95.

[4]Quoted in Tyler Charles, "(Almost) Everyone's Doing It," *Relevant Magazine*, September/October 2011.

[5]Wesley Hill, *Washed and Waiting: Reflections on Christian Faithfulness and Homosexuality* (Grand Rapids: Zondervan, 2010), p. 13.

[6]Ibid., p. 29.

[7]Dennis Hollinger, *Choosing the Good: Christian Ethics in a Complex World* (Grand Rapids: Baker Academic, 2002).

[8]William Byne and Bruce Parsons, "Human Sexual Orientation: The Biologic Theories Reappraised," *Archives of General Psychiatry* 50 (March 1993): 228-39.

[9]See Robert A. J. Gagnon, *The Bible and Homosexual Practice: Texts and Hermeneutics* (Nashville: Abingdon, 2001) for the most thorough and the best exegetical treatment on all the relevant passages in the Bible dealing with homosexuality. Unfortunately, his tone is, in my opinion, severe and at times off putting. Much better in tone and great in content is Richard Hays, *Moral Vision of the New Testament* (San Francisco: HarperOne, 1996), pp. 378-406.

[10]Quoted in Gabe Lyons and David Kinnaman, *UnChristian: What a New Generation Really Thinks About Christianity . . . and Why It Matters* (Grand Rapids: Baker Books, 2007), p. 198.

[11]Quoted in Charles, "(Almost) Everyone's Doing It."

[12]Hill, *Washed and Waiting*, pp. 72-73.

[13]The reason we cannot offer leadership to folks who are practicing sex outside of heterosexual marriage is because leadership in the Bible is primarily an issue of modeling behaviors Christ wants to see reproduced in his church. So the apostle Paul tells Timothy in 1 Timothy 4:12: "Don't let anyone look down on you because you are young, but *set an example* for the believers in speech, in conduct, in love, in faith and in purity." Sexual purity is a behavior leaders should model for the people of God.

[14]Roy P. Basler, *Abraham Lincoln: Great Speeches* (Mineola, NY: Dover, 1991), p. 25.

Chapter 10: What Is Our Ethic? . . . and Social

[1]The text in question is 1 Timothy 2:8-15. See Craig S. Keener, *Paul, Women, and Wives: Marriage and Women's Ministry in the Letters of Paul* (Peabody, MA: Hen-

drickson, 1992), p. 101. First Corinthians 14:34-35 does not speak directly to women in leadership. So what does Paul mean in 1 Corinthians 14:34-35 when he says, "Women should remain silent in the churches. They are not allowed to speak, but must be in submission, as the law says. If they want to inquire about something, they should ask their own husbands at home; for it is disgraceful for a woman to speak in the church"? Craig Keener and Stan Grenz argue that there is nothing in these verses that forbid women from interpreting prophecy, teaching or any other role. They suggest that women in the church were interrupting the scriptural exposition by asking questions. Women in that day would have been less educated and therefore would have asked questions due to their ignorance. But this is not a transcultural principle; similarly, the instruction that "they should eat at home" does not mean that one could never eat in a church building. Thus, "they should ask their husbands at home" does not mean that women can never speak in church. First Corinthians 14 offers no limitations on women's roles in the church.

[2]For a listing of major divergent views on twenty-five points of interpretation of 1 Timothy 2:8-15, see S. D. Hull "Exegetical Difficulties in the 'Hard Passages,'" in Gretchen Gaebelein Hull, *Equal to Serve: Women and Men in the Church and Home* (Old Tappan, NJ: Revell, 1987), pp. 259-60.

[3]See Keener, *Paul, Women, and Wives*; Stanley J. Grenz and Denise Muir Kjesbo, *Women in the Church: A Biblical Theology of Women in Ministry* (Downers Grove, IL: InterVarsity Press, 1995); William J. Webb, *Slaves, Women & Homosexuals: Exploring the Hermeneutics of Cultural Analysis* (Downers Grove, IL: InterVarsity Press, 2001).

[4]Wayne Grudem, *Evangelical Feminism and Biblical Truth* (Colorado Springs: Multnomah Publishing, 2004), pp. 89-97.

[5]See, for example, 1 Corinthians 12:7, 11; Romans 12:6-8.

[6]Ben Witherington, *Conflict and Community in Corinth: A Socio-Rhetorical Commentary on 1 and 2 Corinthians* (Grand Rapids: Eerdmans, 1995), p. 211. Emphasis added.

[7]David A. Carson, "Pauline Inconsistency: Reflections on 1 Corinthians 9:19-23 and Galatians 2:11-14," *Churchman* 100 (1986): 13.

[8]See, for example, 1 Corinthians 15:12; Galatians 1:6-9; 2:11-14.

[9]Webb, *Slaves, Women & Homosexuals*, p. 52.

[10]David deSilva, *An Introduction to the New Testament: Context, Methods and Ministry Formation* (Downers Grove, IL: InterVarsity Press, 2004), pp. 749-50.

[11]Ibid., p. 749.

[12]See "Priscilla" (Acts 18:2, 18-19, 26; Romans 16:3; 1 Corinthians 16:19; 2 Timothy 4:19); "Junia" (Romans 16:7); "Tryphena and Tryphosa" (Romans 16:12); and "Apphia" (Philemon 1:2) in *Dictionary of Paul and His Letters*, ed. Gerald F. Hawthorne et al. (Downers Grove, IL: InterVarsity Press, 1993).

[13]Quoted in Sir Edward Cook, *The Life of Florence Nightengale: 1820–1861* (London: Macmillan, 1914), p. 57.

[14]Dorothy L. Sayers, *Are Women Human? Penetrating, Sensible, and Witty Essays on the Role of Women in Society* (Grand Rapids: Eerdmans, 2005), p. 68.

[15]Robert D. Putnam and David E. Campbell, *American Grace: How Religion Divides and Unites Us* (New York: Simon & Schuster, 2010), p. 241.

Chapter 11: What Is Our Expectation? Already . . .

[1]For a scholarly treatment of miracles, both ancient and modern, see Craig S. Keener, *Miracles: The Credibility of the New Testament Accounts* (Grand Rapids: Baker Academic, 2011).

[2]"When I pray, coincidences happen!" is a quotation widely attributed to William Temple, a theologian and former archbishop of Canterbury.

[3]Member of Vineyard Columbus, letter to author, 1993. Reprinted with permission of writer.

Chapter 12: What Is Our Expectation? . . . and Not Yet

[1]Members of Vineyard Columbus, letter to author, 2003. Reprinted with permission of writers.

[2]See www.bread.org/hunger/global.

[3]See www.compassion.com/poverty/hunger.htm.

[4]See www.who.int/hdp/poverty/en.

[5]See www.unicef.org/sowc06/press/who.php.

[6]See www.govregistry.us/articles/crime_characteristics.html.

[7]See www.unicef.org/media/media_39201.html.

[8]See www.huffingtonpost.com/news/newtown-school-shooting.

[9]For an in-depth study of the kingdom of God, see George Eldon Ladd, *Gospel of the Kingdom: Scriptural Studies in the Kingdom of God* (Grand Rapids: Eerdmans, 1990).

[10]Hanna Rosin, "Did Christianity Cause the Crash?" *The Atlantic*, December 2009.

[11]See www.pewforum.org/uploadedfiles/Topics/hispanic-religion-07-final-mar08.pdf.

[12]For a more in-depth study of the prosperity gospel teaching, see Gordon D. Fee, *The Disease of the Health and Wealth Gospels* (Vancouver, BC: Regent College Publishing, 1985).

[13]Gordon D. Fee, "The Gospel of Prosperity—An Alien Gospel," *Reformation Today*, November/December 1984, p. 39.

[14]Joni Eareckson Tada, interview by Dan Wooding, February 24, 2012. See www.assistnews.net/stories/2012/s12020108.htm.

[15]"Exclusive Interview: Mark Galli of *Christianity Today* (pt. 1)," by Aaron G. Zimmerman, *Mockingbird*, November 20, 2009, http://blog.mbird.com/2009/11/

exclusive-interview-mark-galli-of/.

[16]Members of Vineyard Columbus, letter to author.

Chapter 13: What Is Our Calling? Relevant Practice . . .

[1]Allen Brummel, "William Cameron Townsend: Father of Wycliffe Bible Translators and Summer Institute of Linguistics," *The Standard Bearer*, March 2011.

[2]For more information about Wycliffe, see www.wycliffe.org.

[3]Arthur Glasser, *Announcing the Kingdom: The Story of God's Mission in the Bible* (Grand Rapids: Baker Academic, 2003), p. 330.

[4]G. B. Caird, quoted in Glasser, *Announcing the Kingdom*, p. 335.

[5]Glasser, *Announcing the Kingdom*, p. 335.

[6]Dwight D. Eisenhower, *Public Papers of the Presidents of the United States: Dwight D. Eisenhower, 1960* (Washington, DC: National Archives), pp. 1035-40.

[7]James K. A. Smith, *Desiring the Kingdom: Worship, Worldview, and Cultural Formation* (Grand Rapids: Baker Academic, 2009), p. 95.

[8]Ibid., p. 99.

[9]You can see these statistics and more in Robert D. Putnam, *Bowling Alone: The Collapse and Revival of American Community* (New York: Touchstone Books, 2001).

[10]For more information about Celebrate Recovery, go to www.celebraterecovery.com.

[11]Vineyard Columbus has a "Phase Three" ministry for post-career people who wish to contribute their time, talent and treasure to the advancement of the kingdom of God.

[12]Wade Horn, "Responsible Fatherhood and the Role of the Family" (plenary, Serious and Violent Offender Reentry Initiative Grantee Conference, Washington, DC, September 30, 2002).

[13]Robert D. Putnam and David E. Campbell, *American Grace: How Religion Divides and Unites Us* (New York: Simon & Schuster, 2010).

[14]Ibid., p 105.

[15]Armand M. Nicholi Jr., *The Question of God: C. S. Lewis and Sigmund Freud Debate God, Love, Sex, and the Meaning of Life* (New York: Free Press, 2003).

[16]Ibid., p. 115.

[17]Ibid., p. 109.

[18]Martin Luther, *Commentary on the Epistle to the Galatians* (Charleston: CreateSpace), pp. 5-6.

Chapter 14: What Is Our Calling? . . . and Orthodox Doctrine

[1]Duncan Gardham, "Detroit Bomber: Internet Forum Traces Journey from Lonely Schoolboy to Islamic Fundamentalist," *The Telegraph*, December 30, 2009.

[2]George Weigel, "Europe's Problem—and Ours," *First Things*, February 2004, www.firstthings.com/article/.../europersquos-problemmdashand-ours-9.

[3]George Weigel, "Two Ideas of Freedom" (the Inaugural William E. Simon Lecture, Ethics and Public Policy Center, Washington, DC, December 1, 2001).

[4]Jill Riepenhoff, "Repeat Abuser Gets Six Months," *The Columbus Dispatch*, December 19, 2009.

[5]Hanna Rosin, "Did Christianity Cause the Crash?" *The Atlantic*, December 2009.

[6]Ibid.

[7]D. M. Crump, "Truth," in *The Dictionary of Jesus and the Gospels*, ed. Joel B. Green, Scot McKnight and I. Howard Marshall (Downers Grove, IL: InterVarsity Press, 1992), p. 861.

[8]Richard Bauckham, *Jesus and the Eyewitnesses: The Gospels as Eyewitness Testimony* (Grand Rapids: Eerdmans, 2008).

[9]Timothy Keller, *The Reason for God: Belief in an Age of Skepticism* (New York: Dutton, 2008), p. 104.

[10]Ibid., p. 105.

[11]Ibid.

[12]Ibid., p. 104.

[13]Michael Brown's four-volume work *Answering Jewish Objections to Jesus: General and Historical Objections* (Grand Rapids: Baker Books, 2000) does a remarkable job of sifting through the messianic prophecies in the Hebrew Bible and demonstrating why these prophecies were fulfilled only by Jesus of Nazareth.

[14]David Field, *Eerdmans' Handbook to the Bible* (Grand Rapids: Eerdmans, 1973) p. 48.

[15]Roger E. Olson, *The Mosaic of Christian Belief: Twenty Centuries of Unity & Diversity* (Downers Grove, IL: InterVarsity Press, 2002), pp. 11-12. Emphasis in original.

[16]Ibid., pp. 44-45.

[17]Ibid., p. 44.

[18]Ibid.

[19]Ibid., pp. 44-45.

[20]Carl Henry, "Dare We Renew The Controversy?" *Christianity Today*, June 24, 1957.

[21]John Stott, *The Cross of Christ*, 20th Anniversary ed. (Downers Grove, IL: InterVarsity Press, 2006), pp. 130-31.

[22]John Stott, quoted in John White and Ken Blue, *Healing the Wounded: The Costly Love of Church Discipline* (Downers Grove, IL: InterVarsity Press, 1985), p. 20.

[23]Roger Finke and Rodney Stark, *The Churching of America 1776-1990: Winners and Losers in Our Religious Economy* (New Brunswick, NJ: Rutgers University Press, 1993), p. 275.

[24]Ibid., p. 249.

[25]Dietrich Bonhoeffer, *The Cost of Discipleship* (London: SCM Press, 1948), p. 44.

Epilogue: Follow Me!

[1]This illustration concept is borrowed from Erwin Raphael McManus, *Seizing Your Divine Moment: Dare to Live a Life of Adventure* (Nashville: Thomas Nelson, 2002), p. 142.

[2]Frederick Buechner, quoted in Joe Roos, "The Foolishness of the Cross," *Sojourners*, August 2007.